PHONOPOETICS

PHONO· POETICS

The Making of Early Literary Recordings

JASON CAMLOT

STANFORD UNIVERSITY PRESS

Stanford, California

STANFORD UNIVERSITY PRESS
Stanford, California

Printed in the United States of America on acid-free, archival-quality paper

Library of Congress Cataloging-in-Publication Data

Names: Camlot, Jason, 1967– author.
Title: Phonopoetics : the making of early literary recordings / Jason Camlot.
Description: Stanford, California : Stanford University Press, 2019. | Includes
    bibliographical references and index.
Identifiers: LCCN 2018042110 (print) | LCCN 2018058290 (ebook) | ISBN
    9781503609716 | ISBN 9781503605213 (cloth : alk. paper)
Subjects: LCSH: English literature—Audio adaptations—History and criticism.
    | Literature and technology—History. | Sound recordings—History. | Oral
    interpretation—History. | Phonograph—History.
Classification: LCC PR149.A93 (ebook) | LCC PR149.A93 C36 2019 (print) | DDC
    820.9/008—dc23
LC record available at https://lccn.loc.gov/2018042110

Cover Design: Kevin Barrett Kane
Cover Image: Phonograph horn from the Musée des Ondes Emile Berliner collection.
Photograph by Heather Pepper.

CONTENTS

Acknowledgments vii

List of Figures and Table xi

List of Recordings xiii

Introduction: Audiotextual Criticism 1

1 The Voice of the Phonograph 27

2 Charles Dickens in Three Minutes or Less:
Early Phonographic Fiction 71

3 Alfred, Lord Tennyson's Spectral Energy:
Historical Intonation in Dramatic Recitation 100

4 T. S. Eliot's Recorded Experiments
in Modernist Verse Speaking 137

Conclusion: Analog, Digital, Conceptual 169

Notes 185

Index 219

ACKNOWLEDGMENTS

THIS BOOK HAS been produced with the support of a great number of organizations and institutions and many great colleagues and friends. Research on sound and recorded literary performance is perhaps best delivered in a live conference or symposium setting where recordings can be played, visualized, mimicked by the speaker, and discussed in situ. I have benefitted enormously over the past two decades from opportunities to present my research on early spoken recordings and methods of digital engagement with such recordings at numerous scholarly conferences. I gratefully acknowledge the following associations and conferences that have provided platforms for sharing, testing, and recalibrating my approach to phonopoetics: the North American Victorian Studies Association (NAVSA) (2017, 2013, 2011, 2008, 2007, 2006, 2004), Modern Language Association (2017), Society for the History of Authorship, Research and Publishing (SHARP) (2016, 2004, 2000), Humanities Online Research and Education Symposium, Purdue University (2016), Canadian Society of Digital Humanities (2015), Victorian Studies Association of Western Canada (2012), American Culture Association (ACA) (2012, 2007), Popular Culture Association (PCA) (2011, 2006), Click on Knowledge Conference, University of Copenhagen (2011); Forms of Science in 19c Britain Conference, McGill University (2008), Modernist Studies Association (2004), International Gothic Association / Association of Canadian College and University Teachers of English (2004), Victorian Soundings conference, University of California, Santa Cruz (2003), American Studies Association (2001), and the Northeastern Victorian Studies Association (1999).

I have also benefitted significantly from invitations to present my work in plenary and workshopping situations. For these opportunities I am most grateful to Tina Choi and her many great colleagues of the Victorian Studies

Association of Ontario for an invitation to serve as a plenary at the VSAO annual conference in Toronto, April 29, 2017; Justin Tackett and colleagues involved in the Stanford Humanities Center's Material Imagination Series at which I presented a seminar, March 10, 2017; Christopher Keep and Organizers of the 2014 NAVSA conference in Western Ontario at which I delivered a seminar; Karis Shearer for the invitation to present a keynote address on phonopoetical methods at the Poetry Off the Page, Editing Modernism in Canada (EMiCs) conference, University of British Columbia, Okanagan, August 2, 2013; Matthew Rubery and his colleagues and graduate students at Queen Mary University, London, for hosting me as a visiting scholar in residence and engaging with several workshops and lectures I delivered there in May 2013; Regenia Gagnier, Paul Young, and colleagues at the University of Exeter for hosting a talk on digital approaches to early spoken recordings in May 2013; James Emmott and colleagues associated with the London Nineteenth-Century Studies Seminar for hosting a presentation at the Institute of English Studies, London, May 25, 2013; Al Filreis and Steve Evans for inviting me to share the stage with them for a panel on literary sound archives as part of the Beyond the Text: Literary Archives in the 21st Century gathering at the Beinecke Library and Whitman Humanities Center, Yale University, April 26, 2013; Jessica Riddell and Linda Morra for inviting me to present my research in a plenary talk before a great crowd of emerging undergraduate scholars at the Quebec Universities English Undergraduate Conference (QUEUC) conference, Bishop's University, Lennoxville, QC, March 26, 2010; Audrey Jaffe, and my many wonderful colleagues at the University of Toronto for inviting me to present work in progress at their regular WINCS seminar, March 24, 2010; Alessandro Porco for hosting me as a plenary speaker at the Pop Goes the Poem graduate student conference, SUNY, Buffalo, March 23, 2007; and John Picker and Leah Price for hosting me as an invited lecturer at the Harvard University Humanities Center, April 27, 2006.

It is clear from the lists above that for the past decade, NAVSA events have served as a near annual venue for the development of this research on early spoken recordings. This association and its members represent the best interdisciplinary community of scholars I could have hoped for to test out my ideas since this project began. I wish to acknowledge my many

NAVSA-associated colleagues and friends, and my wider circle of research collaborators, for the inspiring research they have shared, and in many cases for the great feedback, conversations, and support they have provided to this project over the years. In particular I thank: Emily Allen, Laurel Brake, James Buzard, Mary Wilson Carpenter, Tanya Clement, Alison Chapman, Bassam Chiblack, Tina Choi, Jay Clayton, Eleanor Courtemanche, Dennis Dennisoff, Michael Eberle-Sinatra, Andrew Elfenbein, Jennifer Esmail, Patrick Feaster, Dino Felluga, Renee Fox, Regenia Gagnier, Barbara Gelpi, Lisa Gitelman, Daniel Hack, Steven High, Jayne Hildebrand, Natalie Houston, Priti Joshi, Lorraine Janzen Kooistra, Ivan Kreilkamp, Christopher Keep, Barbara Leckie, Mary-Elizabeth Leighton, Margaret Linley, Diana Maltz, Jill Matus, Richard Menke, Helena Michie, Monique Morgan, Linda Morra, Annie Murray, Chris Mustazza, Daniel Novak, Marjorie Perloff, John Picker, Charles Reiss, Catherine Robson, Matthew Rubery, Jonathan Rose, Jonathan Sterne, Simon Reader, David Seubert, Lisa Surridge, Joanna Swafford, Jennifer Terni, Marlene Tromp, Chip Tucker, Jeremy Valentine, Sharon Aranofsky Weltman, and Jared Wiercinski.

Research in the form of archival visits and conference travel that led to this book could not have been accomplished without the generous support I have received from the Social Science and Humanities Research Council of Canada, Le Fonds de recherche du Québec—Société et culture, and from both the vice-president of Research and Graduate Studies, and the Faculty of Arts and Science, at Concordia University. My colleagues and students, past and present, in the Department of English at Concordia University have provided an ongoing environment of collegiality and intelligence that has made my research and teaching stronger and more enjoyable. I am grateful for the intellectual and moral support I have received for this research project from Sally Brooke Cameron, Jill Didur, Mary Esteve, Meredith Evans, Deanna Fong, Marcie Frank, Andre Furlani, Judith Herz, Patrick Leroux, Katherine McLeod, John Miller, Omri Moses, Nicola Nixon, Kevin Pask, Jonathan Sachs, Manish Sharma, and Darren Wershler, among many others. Other colleagues at Concordia have provided support and inspiration even at the seemingly least-inspiring times (as when serving on administrative committees). For their support of my research "by other means" I would like to acknowledge Richard Bernier, Bonnie-Jean Campbell, John Capobianco,

Emilie Champagne, Miranda D'Amico, Nadia D'Arienzo, Sharon Frank, Paul Joyce, Bradley Nelson, Andre Roy, Kim Sawchuck, Rae Staseson, Esther Ste-Croix, and Soheyla Salari.

Earlier versions of portions of this work have appeared in the following venues under the following titles: "Early Talking Books: Spoken Recordings and Recitation Anthologies, 1880–1920," *Book History* 6 (2003): 147–73; "Alfred, Lord Tennyson, 'The Charge of the Light Brigade' (1854)," *Victorian Review: An Interdisciplinary Journal of Victorian Studies* 35 (2009): 27–32; "The Three Minute Victorian Novel: Early Adaptations of Books to Sound," *Audiobooks, Sound Studies and Literature*, ed. Matthew Rubery (New York: Routledge, 2011), 24–43; and "Historicist Audio Forensics: The Archive of Voices as Repository of Material and Conceptual Artifacts," *19: Interdisciplinary Studies in the Long Nineteenth Century* 21 (2015): n.p. (21 pages), http://doi.org/10.16995/ntn.744.

I am grateful to the readers of the manuscript I submitted to the Press for their invaluable comments and recommendations. Their insights challenged and inspired me as I revised the book for final submission. James Taylor and Deanna Fong were of great assistance in preparing and formatting images for the book, and Faith Wilson Stein of Stanford University Press provided expert guidance throughout the production process. I am most grateful to Emily-Jane Cohen who has been unwavering in her support of this project, and who has seen it through the entire editorial process with great insight, humor, and generosity. Thank you EJC.

Nothing would be written, or worth writing, without my extended family and friends. Thank you Matt, Arj, and Heather (who took photos at the Musée des Ondes, Emile Berliner in Montréal for the cover), and our beloved friend Adam, who would have been so proud of this book, and to whose memory it is dedicated. Cory, Oscar, and Nava, my loves and my life.

FIGURES AND TABLE

Figures

1.   Advertisement for "The Reginaphone"   40

2.   Advertisement from 1898, in which The Gramophone
     speaks a riddle   41

3.   Robert J. Wildhack cartoon illustrating "Snores"
     and "Sneezes"   49

4.   Photograph of Victrola used in classroom teaching   95

5.   Catalogue pages depicting William Sterling Battis
     "Dickens Man" recordings   96

6.   Record catalogue description of "A Dramatic Recitation
     by Rose Coghlan"   121

7.   Praat interval annotation showing tremor and prolongation
     pitch contours in Lewis Waller's recitation of "The Charge
     of the Light Brigade"   128

8.   Praat interval annotation showing tremor and prolongation
     pitch contours in Canon Fleming's recitation of
     "The Charge of the Light Brigade"   129

9.   Praat interval annotation showing tremor and
     prolongation pitch contours in Henry Ainley's
     recitation of "The Charge of the Light Brigade"   130

10. Detail depicting "degrees of force" in vocal expression   132

11. Chart depicting vocal force, form, and quality   133

12.   Praat interval annotation showing pitch contours
       in Henry Ainley's delivery of the words "he said"   134

13.   Multitrack comparison of wave forms, T. S. Eliot
       reading "The Burial of the Dead"   145

14.   Praat annotated visualization of Robert Speaight
       reading "Death by Water"   163

15.   Praat annotated visualization of T. S. Eliot reading
       "Death by Water"   164

16.   Praat annotated visualization of T. S. Eliot reading
       "Burial of the Dead" depicting "excessive intonation curves"   165

17.   Praat annotated visualization of T. S. Eliot reading "Burial
       of the Dead" depicting "truncated intonation curves"   166

Table

T. S. Eliot's multiple 1933 instantaneous disc recordings
of *The Waste Land*   143

RECORDINGS

RECORDINGS AVAILABLE FOR listening at the Stanford University Press *Phonopoetics* website, {ADD URL HERE>}, are distinguished in boldface throughout the text.

Introduction

Alfred Tennyson, "The Charge of the Light Brigade." Alfred Tennyson, performer. Pre-commercial cylinder, 1890.

George Bernard Shaw, "Spoken English and Broken English." Linguaphone, SH 1E, 12" record, 1927.

Chapter 1

Florence Nightingale, "When I am no longer a memory . . . " Introduced by Mary Helen Ferguson. Florence Nightingale, speaker. Non-commercial brown wax cylinder, July 30, 1890.

Horatio Nelson Powers, "The Phonograph's Salutation." Horatio Nelson Powers, performer. Wax cylinder, 1888.

"I am The Edison Phonograph." Len Spencer, performer. Advertising Record. Edison black wax cylinder, 1906.

Sally Stembler, and Edward Meeker, "Laughing Record (Henry's Music Lesson)." Sally Stembler and Edward Meeker, performers. Edison 51063-R, 1923.

Robert J. Wildhack, "Sneezes." Robert J. Wildhack, performer. Victor 35590-B, shellac 12" disc, 78 rpm, January 1917.

Robert J. Wildhack, "Snores." Robert J. Wildhack, performer. Victor 35590-A, shellac 12" disc, 78 rpm, January 1917.

"Cohen on His Honeymoon." Monroe Silver, performer. Edison Diamond Disc Record 7154, 1920.

"Cohen on the Telephone." Joe Hayman, performer. Columbia, A1516, 1913.

"What I Heard at the Vaudeville." Len Spencer, performer. Edison Gold molded record 8693, 1904/5.

"Drama in One Act." George Graham, performer. Berliner 627Z, 1896.

"A Study in Mimicry—Vaudeville." Introduced by Len Spencer. John Orren and Lillian Drew, performers. Edison 50485-R, 1918.

Chapter 2

"Uncle Tom's Cabin (Flogging Scene)." Len Spencer, performer. Edison Standard 8656, 1904.

"The Transformation Scene from Dr. Jekyll and Mr. Hyde." Len Spencer, performer. Columbia matrix, [1904] 1908.

"Svengali Mesmerizes Trilby." Herbert Beerbohm Tree, performer. Gramophone concert record, 10" Black Label disc, GC 1313, 1906.

"The Late Sir Henry Irving in The Dream Scene From 'The Bells' (Leopold Lewis): Dramatic Recital by Bransby Williams." Bransby Williams, performer. Columbia 408, 12" disc, 1913.

"A Christmas Carol in Prose (Charles Dickens): Scrooge's awakening (w Carol Singers [male quartet])." Bransby Williams, performer. Edison 13353, 1905.

"The Awakening of Scrooge." Bransby Williams, performer. Edison Amberol 12378, 1911.

"A Christmas Carol—Scrooge—After the Dream." Bransby Williams, performer. Columbia 6277, 1912/1924.

"A Christmas Carol—Bob Cratchit Telling of Scrooge (Dickens)." Bransby Williams, Performer. HMV 2632f 01012, 1912.

"David Copperfield (Charles Dickens)—Wilkins Micawber's Advice." Bransby Williams, performer. Edison cylinder 13508, 1906.

"Micawber (from 'David Copperfield')." William Sterling Battis, performer. Victor 35556 B, 12" disc, 1916.

Chapter 3

Alfred Tennyson, "The Charge of the Light Brigade." Alfred Tennyson, performer. Non-commercial cylinder, 1890.

Alfred Tennyson, "The Charge of the Light Brigade." Rose Coghlan, performer. Victor 31728, 12" shellac disc, 1909.

Alfred Tennyson, "The Charge of the Light Brigade." Edgar L. Davenport, performer. United Talking Machine Co. A1371, 10" shellac disc, 1913.

Alfred Tennyson, "The Charge of the Light Brigade." Performer unknown. Emerson Phonograph Co. 755, 7" disc, ca. 1917.

Alfred Tennyson, "The Charge of the Light Brigade." Lewis Waller, performer. HMVE164, ca. 1907.

Alfred Tennyson, "The Charge of the Light Brigade." Canon Fleming, performer. HMV E-160, 10" shellac disc, 1910.

Alfred Tennyson, "The Charge of the Light Brigade." Henry Ainley, performer. The Gramophone Co., B393, 10" disc, 1912.

Chapter 4

T. S. Eliot, *The Waste Land*. Robert Speaight, performer. New Rochelle, N.Y.: Spoken Arts, LP Record, 1956.

T. S. Eliot, *The Waste Land*. T. S. Eliot, performer. Instantaneous discs / audio tape. Brander Matthews Dramatic Museum Collection, Library of Congress, ca. 1933.

T. S. Eliot, *T. S. Eliot Reading His Own Poems*. 78 rpm mono 12" records, 1946. Washington, D.C.: Library of Congress Recording Laboratory, 1949.

Conclusion

"Au clair de la lune." Phonotogram, April 9, 1860, Digital sonification, March 2008. www.firstsounds.org/sounds/earlier-playback.php#auclair.

PHONOPOETICS

INTRODUCTION

Audiotextual Criticism

THE EXPERIENCE OF listening to an old, spoken recording is nothing less than strange. Listen to the voice of **Alfred Tennyson reading his poem "The Charge of the Light Brigade"** recorded on an Edison phonograph cylinder in 1890. The sound recording of Tennyson's voice is strange for many reasons:

(1) It does something strange. It's weird to have sound emanating from someone thought dead and gone forever (except for the immortality of Tennyson's poetry, of course) resonate, vibrate through the air, and trigger our ears with physical pressure, creating the "disembodiment" and "teleportation" phenomena that Jeffrey Sconce associates with "electronic presence" in what he calls "haunted media."[1]

(2) It sounds strange. Aside from the strangeness of hearing the voice of a dead person, the recording itself does not sound normal to us. The audio signal we are getting is not clear or intelligible, according to our present standards of fidelity for audio playback, because we are listening to a digitized version of sound recorded on a late Victorian brown wax cylinder. The particular cylinder used in this recording was not preserved according to best archival practices either. It was stored at the back of a South African barn from 1890 until the 1960s, losing some of its shape over time and adding an additional curve to the sound, distorting the voice of the poet

eerily.[2] Some of the sound distortions include collateral noise, crackle, and a muffled hum. This noise of the wax cylinder is the voice of the medium itself, audible "media-archeological information (about the physically real event)."[3] It communicates a past temporal presence, and the substances used to capture and preserve it. The strangeness of this effect is compounded because the actual material at the source of these sounds (the curved voice, the noise of wax) is communicated in the absence of the cylinder itself. That sound has long since migrated from the cylinder "into" a laptop computer. Without the material artifact before our eyes, without a metal stylus navigating the hills and dales of the wax surface of the cylinder's body, we are not in a position to attribute what we are hearing to its material source, and there is a certain dissonance between the crackling signal, which suggests a tangible source for the sound, and the digital software and hardware by which we reproduce it in the present. This recording's status as an "aural object"—a phrase reflecting our inclination to attribute the aural profile of a sound to a corresponding material object—is unclear, estranging (us from) the sound we hear.[4]

(3) It contains strange sounds. There are unidentifiable sounds on the recording, not attributable to voice, that make the audio artifact even weirder. Starting from about 1:33 into the recording, we hear a loud banging sound. Is this a defect in the cylinder evoking human action (a knock on the door?) from the time when the recording was made? Is it Tennyson getting carried away with his recitation, banging on the table as he performs (as one scholar proposes in his interpretation of the recording)?[5] Or is it (more likely) the amplification of a crack in the cylinder that we have integrated into our listening narrative of the recording, just as listeners at early phonograph exhibitions are reported to have interpreted thumps and roars arising from flaws in a cylinder to foot-tapping or mechanical sound effects?[6] We can't tell what we hear. Our inability to attribute aspects of the signal to a material source and our natural inclination to integrate such aspects of the signal into our narrative of listening reveals our inherent desire, our need, for a legitimate source.

(4) It is strangely disconnected or fugitive. In fact, we cannot tell much at all from listening to this sound recording about the context in which the recording was made. The knocking sound may make us ask what

Tennyson was doing while he was making this recording, but the sound recording as a whole prompts a broader version of this question: What was he doing, making this recording? The voice stripped of its social and material contexts estranges the signal for us when we hear it again in our own immediate space. So many early sound recordings are strange because they come to us as "fugitive" signals from another place, increasingly via digital media, stripped of their own informing spaces, situations, and reasons, and ripped from their original media formats.[7] The idea of the status of the fugitive, ephemeral entity preoccupied the inventors of early sound-recording technologies as they worked to develop a means of capturing previously fugitive sounds, voices, and events for the long term. As James Lastra has argued, those who first experimented with sound recording and preservation through phonographic methods were engaged in a process of inverting the frameworks that informed our attention to substances: "By preserving the purely contingent, these phonographic systems effectively reversed the rational hierarchy between the essential and inessential, between substance and accident."[8] As historically postliminary listeners and as researchers, we are presented with the challenge of restoring some of the most basic information that is needed to understand the meaning of a sound after the fact of its occurrence. The repeatable sound signal does not always explain itself.

(5) It is strangely real. For all this missing information, when we hear a historical voice recording, when we listen to Tennyson read "The Charge of The Light Brigade" again, over a century and a quarter after he recited it into a phonograph, there is something very real about it. The real-time quality of recorded sound, that it puts us *into* time that has already passed and opens a tunnel connection with the past, triggers what the philosopher Wolfgang Ernst has called "the drama of time-critical media."[9] An encounter with recorded sound develops as an experience of real-time processing. The listener gets the sense that the overheard time frame is somehow alive in the present, replicating the *live* sonic event of which it is apparently a real-time reproduction. Sound recording works on human perception itself, and on our perception of time, in particular. Ernst's argument about the strange drama of sound recording is based on his idea that we are not cognitively equipped to process events from two temporal dimensions simultaneously.

When we immerse ourselves in real-time sound, we perceive it as "live" and this jars our awareness of time.

The strange distortions in the signal I have been describing are offshoots of the fact that sound recording is a time-based medium, and we, as humans, are time-sensitive listening creatures. If the timing of a voice is off, we are pretty quick to notice. If your friend's voice sharing a story with you at a café began to accelerate and rise in pitch in a manner that emulates an LP record (meant to be played at 33⅓ revolutions per minute [rpm]) being played at 45 or 78 rpm, you would begin to question your perception of reality. There were variable standards for recording and playback speeds from 1890, when Tennyson made his early literary recordings, to the 1920s. The speed at which a recording was made had an impact on the sound quality, volume, and, of course, the potential duration of a record.[10] As sound recording became increasingly commercialized as a technology, with set record formats, firmer standards were developed, but as late as the 1920s, the playback device that controlled the speed of replay (sometimes referred to as "the governor") might require regular adjustment. In an amusing recording entitled **"Spoken English and Broken English" (1927),** George Bernard Shaw illustrates the sensitivity that informs our perception of time in relation to the sound recorded voice, noting that attention to "the screw, which regulates the speed" may be necessary to realize the true vocal presence of the speaker whose voice has been recorded.[11] Technical knowledge and adjustments in the present are required to calibrate the signal for it to be perceived as a plausibly real emanation from the past.

The present book is about how to engage critically with early sound recordings as literary works. The audible strangeness of such sound recordings, which I have begun to identify and explain, represents a safeguard against such critical analysis. I sympathize with the recordings. I want to keep them weird, to preserve their status as objects of wonder. But at the same time, I am interested in learning more about them, how and why they were made, circulated, categorized, used, preserved, written about, discarded, rediscovered, copied, then circulated, used and categorized again. To think critically about sound recordings as literary works, we need to explore the historically specific convergences between audio-recording technologies, media formats, and the institutions and practices of the literary context.

Phonopoetics as a concept refers to the emergence and making (poesis) of literary speech sounds (phono) as they can be heard in early spoken recordings. That such sounds were apprehended (captured) on replayable records allows us to apprehend (understand) their literary historical significance. It is one of my working assumptions that temporal specificity—the location of a sound recording within a specific historical context—is key to understanding the meaning of any literary sound recording. In order to make sense of particular sound recordings produced during the acoustic and electrical periods, many different kinds of them must be considered. My own area of interest in historical audiotexts relates especially to the meaning of "the literary" as an informing framework and ideology of audiotextual production and use. Considering the concept of the literary in relation to early spoken recordings demands a sociological approach, since the project necessarily challenges the sequence of restrictive criteria that have been placed on the concept of literature since the nineteenth century. As Raymond Williams pointed out long ago, literature as a professional concept was governed first by "a restriction to printed texts, then a narrowing to what are called 'imaginative' works, and then finally [by] a circumscription to a critically established minority of 'canonical' texts."[12] Early literary recordings in the sense in which I propose we use the term, on the other hand, are not printed, only occasionally imaginative in the high literary sense, and often would not have qualified as canonical when they first appeared, or have done so at any time since. The literary recording in the widest sense helped mobilize an ideology and practical engagement with sounds that were associated with ideas of literary performance, experience, and enculturation. These sounds might be of an elocutionist reciting Tennyson or an actor declaiming Shakespeare, but they might also be of a preacher reading a passage from the King James Bible, or a professional recording artist performing a sketch in dialect. The early literary recording is the result of the social and cultural forces that produced it and informed its meaning for the people who used it, and, as D. F. McKenzie has argued, the diverse "forms of record and communication" that we study are "not disparate but interdependent, whether at any one time or successively down through the years."[13]

My approach to the literary historical study of the audiotext does not identify the literary nature of a sound recording exclusively with particular, extrinsically identifiable qualities of the sound signal under examination, and even less so with the imagined intentions of the performative reader whose voice and performance we may now study in the form of an audiotext, but rather with a diverse range of psychological, ideological, institutional, aesthetic, and social associations that informed that recorded signal's production and subsequent use. Research concerning the informing theories and techniques of performance heard in a literary recording are indeed of significant interest to audiotextual criticism. However, these elements discerned in an audiotextual signal should not be approached wholly from the perspective of the performer's authority over those informing techniques (i.e., his or her mastery of elocution). Rather, they are potentially important factors at work within a wider range of contextualizing elements, forces, and associations. This aligns the method of audiotextual criticism I am proposing here with the mode of textual criticism proposed by Jerome McGann and Donald McKenzie in the 1980s.[14] Audiotextual criticism is an expansion of the sociology of texts, introduced by textual critics and book historians, into the realms of media history, sound studies, performance studies, format theory, and other related approaches to the production and circulation of audible literary works.

Speaking of the technology of the book, but really in reference to all artifacts of communication, McKenzie articulated an idea of a sociology of texts that is useful for imagining a sociology of the audiotext, asserting that "a book is never simply a remarkable *object*. Like every other technology it is invariably the product of human agency in complex and highly volatile contexts which a responsible scholarship must seek to recover if we are to understand better the creation and communication of meaning as the defining characteristic of human societies." A sociology of the audiotext certainly attends to the formal structure of the signal under consideration, but only as one facet of the broader consideration of the social realities and functions of the media in which it has appeared, and, again in the words of McKenzie, of "the human motives and interactions which texts involve at every stage of their production, transmission and consumption," including "the roles of institutions, and their own complex structures, in affecting the forms of social discourse, past and present."[15]

To proceed with a critical project of this nature, it is necessary to understand the generic, formal, material, and ideological classifications that were used to categorize spoken records in the early periods of sustainable sound recording (1888–1925). To this end, I will briefly outline some key concepts and points of method useful for approaching these fascinating artifacts, critically, in the context of literary studies. These concepts include that of the sound signal as an object of critical analysis, the idea of a "literary" recording as a discernible category of recorded sound, definitions of audiotextual forms and genres, and the material history that has mediated and continues to mediate our engagement with these cultural artifacts. The chapters that follow offer classificatory analysis in a descriptive sense (what were the different classes of spoken recordings in the early era of sound recording); in a metacritical sense (what are the most useful categories of historical analysis available to us for interpreting early spoken recordings); and, finally, in an applied analytical and interpretive sense (what happens when we attempt to unpack the significance of the descriptive categories by applying our suggested methods of historical analysis).

By focusing on examples from the early period of sound recording, this book presents a historically located iteration of a phonopoetics, a poetics of the sound-recorded performances of the literary. This early period encompasses what are often referred to as the acoustic and electrical eras of audio-recording technology. These broad descriptive categories of technological history span the period that included Edison's tinfoil cylinder phonograph (ca. 1877, although no recordings exist from this period), Edison's "Perfected" cylinder phonograph (ca. 1888), Berliner's flat disc gramophone (ca. 1894), the Columbia Records and Victor Talking Machine Co. experiments with "electrical" recording techniques that used electromagnetic microphones, amplifiers, and disc-cutting machines (ca. 1925), including Cecil Watts's instantaneous disc recorder (ca. 1934), and the many technological variations and improvements on each of these devices that emerged prior to the introduction of analogue tape recording technology for widespread use in the 1960s. My historical narratives based on case-studies from these early periods of recorded sound illustrate a range of methods that we may employ to better understand the significance of how sound recording was deployed for literary purposes before the advent of tape (which marked the beginning of the "analogue" or "magnetic" era of recording, ca. 1950) and, more recently, of digital recording technologies (ca. 1992). Technological and media specifications do not determine the story of literary recordings but are part of larger networks of ideas, discourses, ideologies, institutions, and practices that must inform our interpretation of such artifacts from the perspective of the present. Audiotextual criticism begins with the conceptual conversion of a sound into a signal of interpretive significance.

Sound and Signal

A *sound* is produced when a source object vibrates in a manner that causes the surrounding air to move, and when those vibrations are of such a quality that they can be heard by a perceiving entity (for our purposes, a human being with the capacity to hear). The source object will, for example, pulsate in a manner that works to compress and rarefy the surrounding air molecules in a pattern that will in turn travel to an ear to be heard. The form in which the compressions and rarefactions travel are often described as a wave with particular characteristics that have implications for the nature of the sound that has been produced. The oscillation rate of the source determines what is called the frequency of the sound wave and is characterized in hearing as the pitch of the sound. If the vibrations are less frequent, the sound will be lower (more bassy) than if they are more frequent, when the sound will be higher (more trebly). The degree of compression and rarefaction created by the source's motion determines what is called the amplitude of the sound wave and refers to the loudness of the sound when it is perceived.[16] The ear hears these vibratory waves as sounds due to its capacity as a tympanic mechanism for transducing vibrations.[17]

In this simple attempt to provide a description of the physics of sound and hearing, I have necessarily lapsed from the topic of sound into that of signal, from vibrational and auditory entity into representation. The physical characteristics of sound and hearing have an extensive and complex set of linguistic, numerical, and visual resources and methods for their representation. Audiotextual criticism necessarily draws on these representational resources. We measure the frequency of sounds according to their rate of oscillation in hertz (Hz) and kilohertz (kHz) or cycles per second. (Most humans can hear frequencies within the range of 20 Hz to 20,000

Hz [20 kHz], and are especially receptive to sounds ranging between 1 and 4 kHz).[18] We measure the amplitude of sounds in decibels (dB), a method of representing the ratio of one sound in relation to another, of metering the sound as a signal. The understanding of hearing as tympanic transduction evolved in the nineteenth century and offers a rich and far-reaching story of cultural and technological representation. Jonathan Sterne devotes a whole chapter to the topic in his book *The Audible Past* (2003). All this to say that at times these terms function as useful shorthand for explaining how a media technology works or how the results of its functioning are heard, but they are always also historically rich and resonant metaphors, to which we should attend both for their interesting historicity and for the breadth of their explicative powers.

The term "phonography" (sound writing) held multiple historical meanings in the nineteenth and twentieth centuries, referring both to written systems of phonetic transcription (shorthand scripts) and to applications of the phonograph for the recording of sound. Lisa Gitelman's *Scripts, Grooves and Writing Machines* (1999) is one compelling telling among many possible accounts of the meaning of this historical (and ongoing) metaphorical continuum between writing and sound, inscription and aurality.[19] As Stefan Helmreich has observed, a historically resonant and metaphorically powerful term such as "transduction"—used to describe what happens to sound as it traverses media while traveling from source to ear, turning from one kind of energy into another[20]—has been "an appealing concept because it narrows the distance between cultural analysis and technical description, offering a conceptual language partially shared between scholars in the humanities and in engineering and science circles."[21] Many of the keywords deployed in discussing sound-oriented practices and sound media technologies possess meanings that are shared, or partially shared, across disciplines in the humanities, social sciences, sciences, and engineering. Furthermore, many of these keywords resonated historically in multiple frequencies simultaneously, and part of our work as critics of literary recordings and historical sounds of all kinds is to parse the conceptual overtones and undertones from the historically situated fundamental frequency.

When we refer to the sound in our critical accounts, we are often speaking metaphorically, in the terms of *the signal*. An audio signal is a representation of a sound. Engineers can refer to the "bumps and pits on a wax cylinder" as "the raw audio signal," but in doing so they are splitting hairs between degrees of separation between sound and representation. Proceeding with a theory that separates sound from signal clarifies the status of the recorded audio signal as a representational and manipulable artifact of a sound event that once occurred, sometime, somewhere. The audio signal as a figurative entity that is conceptualized as variation over time may be approached as measurable for the purposes of analysis and transformation. The figurative nature of the signal may be qualified depending on the medium—an analogue signal represented as a continuous flow of fluctuating electrical voltage will differ from a digital signal understood as a dense series of discrete values—but its status as representation remains.

The idea of the wave as a metaphor that is useful for describing the formal characteristics of sound, introduced as an explanatory analogy by Hermann von Helmholtz in 1863, was the first step toward his goal of identifying the distinguishing characteristics of different musical tones. "The waves of air proceeding from a sounding body," he writes, "transport the tremor to the human ear exactly in the same way as the water transports the tremor produced by the stone to the floating chip."[22] From this first analogy he could proceed to unpack far more granular metaphors concerning the characteristics of force, pitch, quality, and so forth, of musical sound. The signal moved from descriptive analogy to observable phenomenon when systems designed specifically for the analysis of signal content were developed. The psychologist Frank Seashore reported on his development of the voice tonoscope in 1902, "a device constructed on the principle of the stroboscope; that is, the vibrations of the voice are made visible upon a moving surface by the action of intermittent light."[23] The tonoscope—an early mechanical realization of the metaphor of the signal—was "intended to be a general measuring instrument" to be deployed "in a number of ways,"[24] and, indeed, scores of studies analyzing musical and speech performance from the disciplinary perspectives of psychology, music, and speech education were published based on information gathered using Seashore's device through the 1930s.[25]

The signal, in such historical examples, was still a specialized source of information generated by equipment that required regular calibration and improvement. Even the more familiar widespread examples of signal visualization, such as the analog Vu meters standardized in the early 1940s—those illuminated needle gauges with peak or overload areas marked with red on the right part of the numbered arc—while providing measured information about the audio signal, were mostly applied to the practical concerns of setting the levels of broadcast voice properly.[26] In effect, it is the development of digital signal processing combined with a growing corpus of digital audio data and speedy processers that has made the audio signal such a potentially important *working* metaphor for the critical analysis of sound. As Alexander Lerch has observed, the combination of factors just mentioned "has significantly increased both the need and the possibilities of automatic systems for analyzing audio content, resulting in a lively and growing research field."[27] The implications for audiotextual criticism of this lively activity in the development of automatic techniques for the analysis and visualization of sound may be compelling, because the tools that are emerging on a regular basis suggest new questions we can ask our signals about historical media, social relations, prosodic performance, affect, and any number of other points of interest. Over time, digital audio signal processing can lead us to expect increasingly articulate answers from the signals we study. It will certainly continue to impact our understanding of the qualities of literary sounds, or audiotexts, and move us further down the path of Roland Barthes's understanding of "The Text" as "a methodological field" (as opposed to "the work," which is "a fragment of substance"),[28] and most likely toward increasingly elaborate "rationales of audio text" realized in relation to information systems for the purposes of software analysis, content modeling, and cataloguing.[29] The audiotext is an interpretive concept by which sound is conceptualized as a signal with ideational, aesthetic, social, cultural, and formal qualities of historical significance. The identification of an audiotextual signal with literature as an expressive art form entails explanation of how and why its sonic features can be understood to signify meaningfully in the context of the literary.

What Is a Literary Recording?

Poetry and the literary in general, when historically defined beneath the broader umbrella of belles lettres, and even to some extent in its narrower definitions that still fell within certain late eighteenth- and early nine-teenth-century theories of rhetoric, did not exclude the oral performance of a work of literature. While these definitions predate sound recording, the idea of a "literary" sound recording is not an oxymoron if imagined coun-terfactually through the broader sensorium of eighteenth-century theories of rhetoric. Raymond Williams's assertion in *Keywords* that nineteenth-century notions of literature tended to exclude "speaking" helps identify some of the historical and definitional complexity of a sound-recorded performance of a literary work when the technology finally arrived at the end of the nineteenth century to realize and deliver such a thing.[30] By the end of the nineteenth century, literature was mostly identified with printed material artifacts: periodicals, pamphlets, and books. This identification of literature with print media explains why Thomas Edison, as early as 1878, imagined literary recordings as "phonographic books" and put forward a series of claims for "the advantages of such books over those printed."[31] The emergence of the possibility of a "literary" recording represents a challenge to this accrued assumption that the literary is constitutionally embedded in the visual and silent media of paper and ink. In challenging such a basic assumption about the material media formats in which "literature" can be found, the idea of a "literary" recording raises questions about the method-ologies that have been developed over the past century for the purpose of literary analysis, and, indeed, about the institutions (educational and other) that have supported the literary as a theoretical concept.

Spoken recordings of different kinds may be discerned as literary in rela-tion to a host of contextualizing circumstances that need to be unpacked, often on a case-by-case basis. Jonathan Sterne has noted that terms such as "mediality" and "literariness" are "mundane" for their lack of concrete definitional purpose and demand significant work in explicating "the gen-eral web of practice and reference" that informs their use if they are to function as meaningful, eventful, and remarkable terms.[32] The discern-ibility of a spoken recording as "literary" may depend as much on when it is approached as such as on the context in which it first appeared as an artifact in the world. This is why it is important to proceed with a critical awareness of our present circumstances of interpretation when embarking on a historical account of the literary recording as an artifact of interest, and why it is equally important to qualify the significance of what might have been understood as "literary" about a recording in specific historical eras.

One of the most significant attempts to articulate the import of the literary reading as an object of critical engagement remains Charles Bernstein's introduction to a volume of essays he edited, *Close Listening: Poetry and the Performed Word* (1998). The primary aims of Bernstein's critical intervention (with its focus on poetry reading, in particular) are to ensure that the sounded work be approached as a primary source for critical consideration rather than as an auxiliary extension of the printed text, and to suggest the possibilities of a new kind of "aural" prosody that takes into account the sonic elements of the acoustic performance of a literary text.[33] To this end he introduces the term "audiotext" to describe the artifact in question, that is, "the audible acoustic text of the poem."[34] The audiotext as an object of study demands our consideration of multifoliate (including multiphonic) versions as different performances of a text.

Bernstein defines the poetry reading "as its own medium" characterized by its "anti-performative" or "anti-rhetorical" qualities.[35] He focuses on the mono-valence of certain methods of poetry reading as definitive of the poetry reading as a medium. In doing so he is working to achieve a powerfully formalist approach to the aesthetic effect of mono-valence, as opposed to dramatic or theatrical modes of reading, which interpret and perform literary works differently. The designation of anti-performative monovalence to the poetry reading associates one historical method of delivering poetry out loud—a method typically used to read and interpret poetry since the 1950s—with poetry reading in general. This generic association of the poetry reading with an implicit lack of spectacle or drama, while relevant primarily to some modern and contemporary reading styles, raises important questions about how we should go about historicizing methods of poetry reading from a longer historical timeline, and how to explain why particular anti-expressivist methods of verse speaking are now so prevalent. One of the purposes of the present study is to provide a prehistory of the perceived anti-theatricality of modern and contemporary literary performance. The poetry readings we hear on early spoken recordings do not sound anti-theatrical.

When we listen to an early sound recording of a Victorian actor or elocutionist performing a poem, our first affective response will often be one of embarrassment or amusement. We are embarrassed by the seeming grandiosity of the vocal tactics deployed by the performer to communicate the meaning of the poem as dramatic scenario; we are amused by the excessive amplitude, the crushing pronunciation of consonants, and the stylized vibrato. These are historically conditioned responses resulting in a kind of affective immunity to, or culturally determined predilection against, certain conventions and styles of oral performance and, in some cases, the conditions of recording that demanded such oral features. We are trained to listen to reading and speech for particular kinds of affective cues that communicate qualities we are supposed to expect and appreciate according to our socio-historical location. Thus, in approaching early literary recordings, as critics, we are necessarily engaged in negotiating our historical neglect of certain styles of literary performance, and in attempting to reconstruct an understanding of the affective importance these reading styles may have had, despite such neglect.[36]

The sound of early literary recordings is informed by alternate conceptions and methods of how to vocalize the literary, but it was also informed by the media context in which those vocalizations were produced and captured. While no sound recording offers a transparent or unmediated record of a performance event, early sound recordings demanded greater accommodation of the affordances of the recording technology and preservation media than those made after the widespread use of tape recording. Even for an amateur home recordist working with an Edison phonograph at the turn of the century, there were many technical and performance considerations to take into account to achieve an audible sounding recording. In a chapter entitled "The Secret of Making Phonograph Records" from the *Openeer Papers* (1900),[37] the author provides a litany of considerations, ranging from the adjustment and adaptation of the recorder, the thickness of the diaphragm to be used, the state of the rubber washers that support the diaphragm, the tightness of the diaphragm clamp, the shape and material qualities of the horn, the condition of the recording cylinder, the functioning of the phonograph motor works, the acoustical effects of the furniture and draperies in the room, and, of course, the techniques of speaking into the recording tube or horn. To make even a basic speech recording demanded significant technical experimentation and artistry from the recordist and performer.[38]

The story of the professional recording studio during the era of acoustic recording tells of a space that gradually transformed itself from inventor's experimental laboratory to one designed for the implementation of acoustical expertise by professional "recordists" (the predecessors of latter-day sound engineers) who understood how best to place musicians and vocal performers, and how to select from a vast assortment of diaphragms and speaking horns "depending on the type of performance, the humidity of the air, or any of a host of other factors."[39] It also tells of the emergence of a new class of performers from whom the industry demanded recurrent perfectionism in vocal delivery as they faced the technically limited capabilities of the acoustical recording apparatus and spoke or sang. These studio recording artists were required to adjust their vocal style, physical posture, and movements in relation to such limitations. As Susan Schmidt Horning has noted, this necessary consideration of the phonograph's technological affordances may have "inhibited spontaneity by forcing the performer to divide his or her concentration between artistic interpretation and recall of the 'staging' required before the recording horn."[40] The recording artist was performing for the machine at the same time as he or she was singing or declaiming to an unseen human audience, thus enacting a new and sophisticated form of acoustical staging in recorded performance. The emergence of the professional recording artist during the early period of recorded sound has been identified as primarily an American phenomenon,[41] with stage performers doing most of the commercial recording in England and the rest of the world. In all cases, the early spoken recording offers itself as an audible representation of the spatial location of a speaker in several senses. There is the speaker before the acoustic recording horn or later (in the 1920s) a carbon or condenser microphone for electrical recording, in the first instance, and there is the speaker of the text whose speaking location and situation are depicted through performance in the recording, sometimes explicitly, as in recordings that present descriptive sketches, dramatic scenes, or character speeches set in imagined locations, and sometimes more subtly, as in recordings of lyric poems. Sound recordings are best understood not as reproductions but as representations of three-dimensional events, and consequently the role of the critic is to attend to and analyze "the representational capabilities of sound recording."[42] Early spoken recordings are immanently engaged in an artful representation of the temporally located scenarios they envoice.

Audiotextual Genres: Micro and Macro

The generic features of early audiotexts are largely discernible in their located sound, often as part of a process of excerption (or entextualization), recontextualization, and generic consolidation in performance. Richard Bauman usefully defines "entextualization" as a process of "bounding off a stretch of discourse" and "endowing it with cohesive formal properties" so that it becomes objectified and "extractable from its context of production." Recontextualization, he continues, "amounts to a rekeying of the text, a shift in its illocutionary force and perlocutionary effect—what it counts as and what it does." In the case of early spoken recordings, recontextualized speech is generically instantiated in recorded performances, acts of expression "framed as display" and open to "interpretive and evaluative scrutiny by an audience both in terms of its intrinsic qualities and its associational resonances."[43] The generic features of an audiotext thus become discernible in the located, contextualized sound displayed in a recorded speech performance.

There are two dominant, mutually informing scales by which we can effectively conceptualize genre for audiotexts. There is the granular scale of the elocutionary microgenres that informed particular moments and performative motifs *within* recorded readings; and there is the macro scale that encompasses broader generic categories of literary recordings as they were developed and organized for commercial markets and in cultural communities of use.[44]

To focus on the more granular scale first, audiotexts as artifacts of interpretation invite the development of a theory of elocutionary microgenres that focus less on the print-based generic categorization of the originating literary work (i.e., whether it is a poem, a play, or a novel, etc.) than on the affective forms developed as discernible speech genres for the purpose of communicating meaningful forms of character, thought, and emotion with the human voice. These audiotextual microgenres entail audibly discernible, affective forms that are untethered from the printed generic forms that may have been used to categorize and describe the performance text as it appeared on the page. For example, in elocution manuals that presented techniques for vocalizing Tennyson's "The Charge of the Light Brigade," the lineated poem and its metrical characteristics that might have been used to define the printed text generically, as, say, an example of dactylic occasional verse or a commemorative battle poem in a martial meter, were dissolved into prose paragraphs with instructions to consider it as a collection of expressive parts, affective enunciations defined by "contrasts, oppositions and changes in movement" that "have a certain relation to the spirit of the whole."[45] While the spirit of the whole is acknowledged, it is not always the primary point of formal focus in the context of oral interpretation. Audiotextual elocutionary microgenres disrupt the idea of literary genre as entities in a hierarchical structure of transcendent forms. The conception of prosody that informs their study is sonic rather than visual, and their generic forms can be excerpted as utterances and effusions without losing a coherent generic status in their own right. We can discuss oratorical microgeneric categories of emphasis, amplitude, force, and pitch as occurring in a particular recorded performance or across a range of recorded performances. Audiotextual microgenres are always located in a speaking context and are implicitly loquacious.

When thinking about speech in such microgeneric terms, it is useful to remember that even everyday speech acts can be said to have identifiable formal, generic features, and that these forms arise from formulaic scripts and the forces that inform contexts of utterance. Mikhail Bakhtin argues that the expression of an utterance "always *responds* to a greater or lesser degree, that is, it expresses the speakers' attitude toward others' utterances and not just his attitude toward the object of his utterance."[46] This granular conception of the genres of speech focuses as much on the situational positioning of the speaker as on the relationship between intonation and the thematic content of the speech itself. The numerous attitudinal changes that occur within a longer speech have been described by Erving Goffman as shifts in a speaker's "footing," wherein the speaker's vocal stance or alignment can be discerned through analysis of "sound markers" such as "pitch, volume, rhythm, stress, tonal quality" and other features, which are often shorter than a grammatical sentence and so entail generic units that are "[p] rosodic, not syntactic." Goffman suggests using the term "phonemic clause" to describe such microgeneric units of speech, observing that a change in "footing is another way of talking about a change in our frame for events" and such changes are a "persistent feature of natural talk."[47]

Early spoken recordings are not, of course, spontaneously situated, responsive expressions of speech, but, on the contrary, were often heavily planned and highly formulaic in their structure and delivery. The formulaic and sometimes overdetermined nature of speech recordings can be understood as compensatory for the absence of an immediately identifiable situation justifying the speech heard, or, as Patrick Feaster has put it, "phonography [speech writing/recording] . . . implies the existence of techniques for overcoming that disorientation to render radically decontextualized sounds intelligible."[48] In the absence of quotation marks and other conventions of depicting speech and dialogue that had been developed as print conventions in the novel, without the visual aid of elocutionary gesture, and without the cues of costume, stage set and a cast of characters to situate a particular three-minute speech within a much broader dramatic context, new generic tactics and formulae were required to help the listener situate speeches heard emanating from machines in meaningful ways. Marjorie Garber has discussed how speaking a quotation before a live audience reminds us that "writing is *displacement*," and that quoting in speech represents a kind of performance of the inherent displacement and ensuing anxieties about the relative authenticity, authority, attribution, and opacity of all speech acts.[49] Discussion of the reading format or the genre of the early spoken recording entails consideration of the tactics deployed to efface displacement, compose anxiety, and defray the costs of phonographic speech.

While traditional literary methods of generic designation, whether based on fixed outer forms (e.g., the metrical and rhyming characteristics of the sonnet), subject matter (e.g., a funeral elegy or epithalamion), intended effect (e.g., horror) or inner tonal elements such as the piece's attitude or valence (e.g., satire, irony),[50] will certainly inform our discussion of the generic format of an early literary sound recording, such aspects of the critical idiom surrounding literary genre will always be supplemented, and sometimes drowned out by, the audiotextual codes and restrictions that work to inform the framing of a recorded speech with the aim of shaping the overarching expectations of a listener. Feaster usefully identifies a few clear examples of such tactics of broad or macrogeneric audiotextual formatting, ranging from explicit introductory announcements that introduce, name, or describe the sounds to follow to the regularization of formats informing more complex audiotexts that combined multiple sonic elements, such as "descriptive" and "minstrel" records, audiotextual formats that quickly developed holistic generic meaning in the early culture of sound recording.[51]

Early record catalogues can be informative for understanding this broader, macrogeneric scale by which early spoken recordings were delineated. An Edison-Bell Consolidated Phonograph Company record list from 1898 reveals that numerous phonographic genres—dialect pieces, comic monologues and dialogues, descriptive sketches, historical accounts, nursery rhymes, burlesques, political and topical speeches, memorial statements, dramatic scenes, prayers, talks, and many others—were all organized under the broad rubric "Recitations, Speeches and Dialogues."[52] This two-and-a-half-page list extracted from a twenty-one-page catalogue provides a fairly comprehensive sense of the range of genres of voice recordings that were being made and sold in Britain at the end of the nineteenth century, even though we will not likely hear many or any of these specific recordings, do not know whose voices were heard on the records, nor always what a title on the list might have referred to when realized as an actual sound recording.[53] This 1898 record list shows an interesting combination of either duplicated or imitated American dialect character recordings (a "Negro Dialogue," six Uncle Josh the rube, eight Casey the Irishman, and seven Schultz the German recordings in series that were originally popularized by the American recording artists Cal Stewart, Russell Hunting, and Frank Kennedy, respectively), and records aimed more specifically at an English audience, including a set of seven Prime Minister William Gladstone–themed cylinders, a "Hyde Park Socialist (Burlesque)," and a few records based on the work of the English music hall or *Punch* magazine humorists H. G. Snazelle, R. G. Knowles, and Douglas William Jerrold.

All the recordings mentioned thus far fall into the categories of "Speeches" and "Dialogues," but "In Memoriam—Tennyson," also on the list, would most likely have been seen as a "Recitation." We have no information about the reader of the poem, or what sections comprised this recording, but the nature of the printed text, and its identification with a past poet laureate—it is the only item on the list that provides both a title and author's name—suggest recorded performance of literary, elocutionary culture. Other records on the list that would have been identified with literary recitation are a set of six Shakespeare pieces, including "Marc Anthony (Julius Caesar)," "Hamlet's Soliloquy," and "The Seven Ages of Man" from *As You Like It*; a "Selection from 'The School for Scandal'" by Sheridan; "The Lord's Prayer and 23rd Psalm"; and "The Sermon on the Mount."[54]

One important sense of the word "recitation" at the end of the nineteenth century was that of an elevated and artistic performance of a text recognized as a source of serious expressive value. There were many different kinds of recitation and recitation records in 1898, but what I am identifying here as literary recitation implied a certain combination of aesthetic authority, gravity, and elocutionary prowess that, together, would have an important cultivating effect on the listening subject, or, better, citizen. The qualities Raymond Williams identifies with an eighteenth-century conception of poetry—namely, "the high skills of writing and speaking in the special context of high imagination"—persisted in a nineteenth-century conception of literature and the literary in early literary recordings.[55] Recitation as a broad audiotextual generic category might have covered a thematically diverse range of texts, but from an elocutionary perspective they would have been perceived as generically related.

Elocutionary records and literary recordings were not necessarily the same thing, but these terms often converged to define a particular generic category of early spoken recording. A slightly earlier example of record cataloguing illustrates this point. Emile Berliner's United States Gramophone Co.'s earliest known American "List of Plates in Stock" (November 1, 1894), offering forty-nine recordings, identifies thirteen record categories: Band Music, Instrumental Quartette, Barytone, Clarionet (*sic*), Cornet, Drum and Fife, Trombone, Piano, Children's Songs, Indian Songs, Soprano, Recitation, and Vocal Quartette.[56] Two of the categories are generically specific, identifying the genre of song—"Children's" and "Indian"—offered on the record. The one title listed under the category of "Recitation" is "Marc Anthony's Curse: A Lesson in Elocution."[57] Speeches and selections from Shakespeare provided much material for the recitation category of early record catalogues (as the Edison-Bell Consolidated Phonograph Company list shows). Our focus at the moment is on the significance of the subtitle "A Lesson in

Elocution" in relation to the recording of a speech from Shakespeare's *Julius Caesar*, act 3, scene 1. What was a lesson in elocutionary performance, and what did it have to do with the performance of a speech from Shakespeare? In an expanded list of Berliner plates from about a year later (January 1895), another title was added to the Recitation category, with this note:

RECITATION.
We have for this important department
secured the co-operation of the eminent versatile elocutionist, Mr. David C. Bangs.
602 Mark Anthony's Curse
A Lesson in Elocution
600 The Village Blacksmith
(Many others in preparation.)[58]

The addition of Henry Wadsworth Longfellow's poem "The Village Blacksmith" to the list, the identification by name of the eminent elocutionist employed—the only name to appear on the expanded list of some eighty-five recordings—and the suggestion that this was a growing department of the company's inventory suggest that The United States Gramophone Co. was beginning to discover the potential of the gramophone as a literary and pedagogical medium. As Catherine Robson has shown, in both America and Britain at the end of the nineteenth century, "recitation" meant a studied, refined literary performance. The end-of-term public "Examination" or "Exhibition Day" at many American schools was also referred to as a "Recitation" featuring different forms of scholarly performance—grammar, spelling, arithmetic, and penmanship—and culminating in "the individual recitation of poetic and oratorical selections."[59] A recorded recitation of a selection from Shakespeare or Longfellow by an "eminent, versatile elocutionist" was an artifact that captured a standard of excellence in oratory and literary interpretation, two areas that were still a significant part of the curriculum at the turn of the century.

The way the elocutionist, David C. Bangs, is described is worthy of note. The alleged eminence of Bangs echoes the power of that descriptor when used to define the significance of recordings by eminent figures, such as the eminent statesman Gladstone, and suggests that Bangs's performances will function as models worth preserving in one's personal library of voices. His advertised versatility also suggested that he was capable of delivering exemplary performances of spoken pieces of all genres and elevations, and not just those of the lofty, literary and elocutionary variety. Indeed, between 1894 and 1895, Bangs made the two recordings already mentioned, as well as recordings of a comic monologue, a children's record, and a monologue in high elocutionary mode from the gramophone's own personified first-person perspective,[60] and in 1896, he recorded "The Lord's Prayer and Psalm 100."[61] This is a repertoire of modest range compared to other recording artists of the period and indicates that Bangs focused on elocutionary eminence rather than versatility.

The distance between a recorded selection from Shakespeare, a poem by Longfellow, and a prayer or psalm was not great if understood within the context of elocutionary delivery and the moral and cultural purpose of generic literary recitation at this time. As Joan Shelly Rubin has shown, there was a strong "congruence of the form of the recitation in both church and public schools," which rested on a "liberalized theology" that identified the moral power of poetry with that of prayer.[62] This congruence can be heard in the techniques used by recording artists to perform poems and prayers and would explain why early recordings of poetry and biblical passages often share the grave sounds of prolonged vowels, recurrent, slow-falling intonation, occasional vibrato or trilling, and ubiquitous rolled r's.[63] That these same grave elocutionary techniques were parodied in comic records underscores the degree to which the "literary" recordings and elocutionary recitations were in constant play with numerous other genres of spoken performance that mimicked, challenged, reinforced, and defined the emerging sound of the literary. As we listen to the wide range of speech recordings discussed in this book, and consider how they inflected their mutual significance on the historically located continuum of speech sounds, the sound of the literary in early spoken recordings will become increasingly audible and critically discernible to us.

Phonopoetics tells the story of the early period of spoken recordings with the aim of explaining the emergence of what I have been calling the literary recording as a differential cultural artifact, that is, an artifact that represents one recognizable, material manifestation of literary expression, meaning, and practice among other related artifacts, ideologies and practices. In doing so, this book necessarily challenges certain textual and visual assumptions that inform contemporary literary criticism by taking the recorded text—the heard audiotext and the sounded "phonotext"—as a primary object of analysis. To explain what early literary recordings meant as aesthetic and cultural entities, I interpret such things as the early promotional fantasies about the phonograph as a new kind of speaker; early sound adaptations of novels, poems, and plays by a variety of actors, elocutionists and recordings artists; initiatives to use the phonograph for teaching elocution and as a means of achieving a heightened literary experience; and the voice archive as a new form of cultural memory. Throughout the book I engage in audiotextual "interpretations" of spoken records representative of a range of genres, and especially of recordings that illustrate historical performances of literary interpretation, refined speech, and cultural fluency. Even as it maps and enacts methods of phonopoetic critical practice through the synchronic historical location of particular case studies, this book will also present a diachronic account of the changing techniques and styles of reading literature out loud as audible in literary recordings, from Tennyson to T. S. Eliot, and the great variety of voices that were recorded and heard in between.

Chapter 1 unpacks the early promotional discourse surrounding the phonograph as a medium of natural fidelity and then situates this idea of the phonograph as a medium without corrupting accent in the context of popular recitation anthologies in order to identify some of the elocutionary preconceptions that informed the vocal performances heard in early spoken recordings. In explaining the formal and cultural affinities between late Victorian short spoken recordings (testimonials, dialect monologues, and literary recitations) and the brief texts meant for speaking aloud that were collected in nineteenth-century recitation compilations, I provide an account of the preconceived notions surrounding the meaning of this new recording medium, in general, and the significance of sound-recording technology for the performance of literary texts, in particular.

Continuing the previous chapter's discussion of the generic categories informing early spoken recordings, chapter 2 focuses on the development and production of some of the earliest sound recordings based on the novels of Charles Dickens. The Dickens recordings of Bransby Williams and William Sterling Battis stand as the earliest fiction-based audio adaptations produced specifically for pedagogical application, and thus represent an interesting bridge between earlier conceptions of the talking record as a novel form of popular entertainment, and the later, pedagogically motivated category of the literary recording. One key element of this historical transition from "talking record" to "literary recording" is the identification of the sound-recording material with the print book. The recordings examined in this chapter also serve as a useful focus for speculation about the particular kinds of literary adaptation, condensation, entextualization, and recital that resulted from the earliest recordings that were produced specifically for such pedagogical application. While the story of Battis's recordings must, significantly, begin with Dickens himself, both as a novelist and as an adaptor, public reader, and performer of his own work, the overarching trajectory of the plot pursued in this chapter moves from the Lyceum Stage upon which Battis made his reputation as a Dickens impersonator, to a discussion of the context in which a certain kind of public, popular entertainment (with pedagogical motives) was redirected and condensed into a new argument for literary encounter in the classroom, and into an early form of what we now call educational technology.

My discussion of literary recordings in the context of pedagogy continues in chapter 3 with analysis and historical location of recordings made between 1890 and 1920 of Alfred Tennyson's "The Charge of The Light Brigade." While considering the methods of performance that would have informed the production of these acoustic records, including discussion of the audiotextual genre of the dramatic recitation with orchestral accompaniment, this chapter locates the modes of recitation heard in these recordings—ranging from my return to Tennyson's own recording of 1890 to early twentieth-century recordings of the poem made by specific elocutionists and actors—within debates surrounding methods of elocution and verse speaking from the period. My discussion of late Victorian methods of "dramatic" interpretation, as elaborated by Samuel Silas Curry in his 1896 book *Imagination and Dramatic Instinct: Some Practical Steps for Their*

Development, opens into a longer genealogy of such methods of oral interpretation as a legitimate approach to literary study in the 1940s and 1960s
and considers the import of New Criticism as a method of literary interpretation that worked to silence oral performance and the study of literary
recordings in the classroom. With this genealogy of oral interpretation and
the impact that New Criticism had on it explained, the chapter then considers what might be lost in our understanding of Tennyson's occasional poem
when the voice is omitted from the process of interpretation, and explores
the potential of digital speech-analysis tools to help us to fix and visualize
specific elocutionary, prosodic features of these recordings of "The Charge."

Chapter 4 offers a series of interpretive takes on T. S. Eliot's 1930s electri-
cally recorded voice experiments in rendering his poem *The Waste Land.*
These discussions provide a means of comparing what Victorian elocutionary delivery looks like in relation to Eliot's attempts to invent a manner of
reading that is appropriate for the delivery of modernist poetry. I first provide the context in which the 1933 recordings were produced and consider
the significance of that context of production, and the media format he
recorded with, for the nature of his experiments in reading. I then situate Eliot's audible reading experiments within contemporary debates surrounding
the English verse-speaking movement, and Eliot's own report, written for
the BBC, on how poetry should be read out loud for the purpose of recording. In its third and final interpretive take, the chapter moves into a formal
analysis of Eliot's reading experiments by focusing on Eliot's attempts to
discover a way to read *The Waste Land* through recorded experimentation
with duration and amplitude, as well as a series of techniques of nonsemantic phrasing and intonation, the use of monotone, and the cultivation of a
harmonically rich drone in speech. In my analysis of the sonic elements of
Eliot's early recording experiments in the context of historical theories of
performance and literary interpretation, I argue that the abstract conception of "voice" that functions as an organizing principle in New Critical
discourse is performed in Eliot's recorded readings as a subtle alternating
use of authoritative epic speech, lyrical modulation, and localized dramatic
scenario, within an organizing method of incantation that evokes the possibility of an overarching oracular or otherworldly voice.

Segueing from this final chapter's discussion of a poet's experiments in performing and capturing the sound of the oracular voice, I conclude *Phonopoetics* with an exploration of conceptions of voice preservation and models of the voice archive, arguing that the stress placed in early ideas of the voice archive upon the materiality of the audible artifact, and the event-oriented scenario of its use, represent useful points of departure for a historically motivated theorization of the voice recording and voice archive at the present time, specifically in relation to the impact of digital media technologies on the status of the record and its archive. I conclude by thinking about how the analogue artifact of the sound archive has shaped our ideas and expectations about what a digital repository should be, reflecting on the status of our artifact of study as we move increasingly from the study of material media artifacts to virtual instantiations of the signals those media may once have held.

1 THE VOICE OF THE PHONOGRAPH

IN 1878, WHEN Thomas Edison first speculated in print on the practical significance of his invention of a sound-recording device, or talking machine, in his essay "The Phonograph and Its Future," and then in 1888, when he reported on "The Perfected Phonograph," the phonographic cylinder suggested itself as a material artifact that would bear the voices of a culture into the distant future, not to be read, but simply to be experienced as they had been heard when they were first captured. In the first of these essays, Edison grandly and optimistically predicted the ascendancy of sound over print resulting from a technology that could replicate speech without the "mediating" practice of reading.[1] In the second, he likened the markings of a phonographic recording to those found on ancient Assyrian and Babylonian clay cylinders, only to move from the inscriptive analogy to an argument about the phonograph's ultimate eclipse of writing, so that "wax cylinders speak for themselves" without having "to wait dumbly for centuries to be deciphered."[2]

Edison was not alone in identifying his invention as an apparent transcendence of the "technology" of reading (as decipherment), leading to an experience that was even more immediate and intimate than that of the reader with his book. Late Victorian fantasies about a book that talks often focused on the author's immediate, individualized presence for the "reader" as a result of the preservation of his voice. According to one journalist in the 1880s, the phonographic book represented the fantasy of "a spoken literature, not a written one" that would allow writers to communicate "with all the living reality of the present moment."[3] Similarly, the first article in the inaugural issue of *The Phonoscope: A Monthly Journal Devoted to Scientific and Amusement Inventions Appertaining to Sound and Sight* (1896) explained: "It is by the voice that men communicate with each other in all the fullness of their individuality. The voice, formerly invisible and irretrievably lost as soon as uttered, can now be caught in its passage and preserved practically forever."[4] And yet another enthusiast of the period stated that the phonograph was remarkable, not only because it preserved literature (after all, print had already accomplished that), but because it preserved the voices of the authors, "which are the indices of the characters of those originating them."[5]

Such claims suggest that even before the phonograph became ubiquitous, there was already a well-developed yearning for a technology that would make the reading experience more immediate—that would, in a sense, capture the character and subjectivity of an author without the mediation of the printed page. Much of the literature published in the field of practical elocution since the mid eighteenth century was concerned with the development of a means of capturing in symbolic or alphabetical script the detailed elements of speech prosody (as well as gesture and facial expression). Musing in his book *Prosodia Rationalis* (1779) about the "very great advantages" that might arise from a reformed alphabet able to "contain distinct elementary sounds" or by a method of "reducing common speech to regular notes,"[6] Sir Joshua Steele sounds much like Edison prognosticating on the benefits that will arise from the phonograph's status as an "elocutionary teacher" and as a way to secure a comparative record of modern speech in relation to oratory of the past.[7] "Had some of the celebrated speeches from Shakespeare been noted and accented as they spoke them, we should be able now to judge whether the oratory of our stage is improved or debased," Steele asserts.[8]

Closer to Edison's time, one can point to a variety of practices that involve the manipulation or interpretation of written scripts or printed texts and identify them with this desire to move beyond the text to an indexical tracing of character. Interpretive techniques like graphology (the analysis of handwriting) studied signatures for "selfhood epitomized."[9] The new "science" of stylistics emerging in the 1880s sought to determine each individual author's identifiable "characteristic curve," "sentence-sense," or "instinct of sentence thought" by counting the number of words in his or her sentences to show patterns.[10] Suggestions at this time that the human voice was the locus of character can be understood as attempts to capture this characterological essence by the development of new ways of inscribing the shape and patterns of voice. From the development of detailed voice scripts like Melville Bell's "visible speech," which "emphasized the mouth, inscribing its movements onto paper,"[11] to devices such as Édouard-Léon Scott de Martinville's phonautograph, which etched a graphic image of vocal wave forms on smoked glass, the nineteenth century produced an array of inventive attempts to preserve the particularities of the individual voice.[12] One might add to this list the proliferation in the nineteenth century of systems of phonography or "shorthand" as developed by the likes of Sir Isaac Pitman and Henry Sweet, on whom Henry Higgins of Shaw's *Pygmalion* was modeled. Practitioners of shorthand in the nineteenth century promoted their systems "as reformations of writing through vocalization," suggesting a transcription medium by which speech could be recorded in squiggly lines exactly as it had been uttered.[13] The logical consummation of this inscriptive work—and the apparent transcendence of writing as the medium for the communication of identity (here equated with voice)—arguably was realized in Edison's invention of the phonograph, after which writing ceased to be synonymous with the serial storage of human experience. As the late media theorist Friedrich Kittler put it rather dramatically: with Edison's invention, "[t]he dream of a real . . . audible world arising from words has come to an end," and a new "reality" medium had emerged in its place.[14]

During the initial period of this technology's promotion, we find an enthusiastic willingness in some quarters to embrace the phonograph as something of a transparent medium, and to imagine a collection of voice recordings as a kind of archive of authentic characters, present to be revived with the turn of a crank for eternity. As Kittler's observation suggests, recent scholarship on this period of the medium has sometimes concurred with this version of what the phonograph meant to late Victorians, namely, that the earliest spoken recordings were received as a kind of oral reality. Roland Gelatt notes how those first writings about the phonograph "prated of the 'absolutely perfect reproduction of the voice,' just as they were to continue to do regularly for the next eight decades."[15] However, as we have already noted, the concepts of fidelity and naturalness as they pertained to the phonograph entailed an enactment of rehearsed technical practices for recording production and an equally rehearsed set of protocols by which recorded sound could be received as natural and true. As Jonathan Sterne puts it, "[s]pontaneity"—and by extension, naturalness—was spontaneous only through artifice."[16] Further, as Lisa Gitelman has shown, contemporaries who attempted to understand what the early phonograph was, and what it meant, often demonstrated "a willingness to unify oral and inscriptive action and a desire to produce legibility from orality."[17] Not only did the inscriptive experiments and inventions mentioned above represent a desire to move beyond the visual medium of print, but once the phonograph seemed to have accomplished that, people tried to understand its success by describing its accomplishment in terms of the writing technologies they already knew. Print technologies had themselves become sufficiently naturalized to be a powerful frame for the reception and understanding of this new medium of information storage and reproduction. Donald McKenzie makes this point in relation to our ongoing historical bias to associate texts with printed materials, arguing that "we are now having to re-learn . . . that print is only a phase in the history of textual transmission, and that we may be at risk of over-stating its importance."[18] The late Victorians' tendency to draw on the written and printed models familiar to them and call the phonograph cylinder a talking book or talking letter (a phonogram) is an early instance of such overstatement. Gitelman's historical examples reveal much about the process by which the mechanical storage and reproduction of orality was originally understood, and such analogies to scripts and writing machines are invaluable for correcting the assumption that the early phonograph was transparently and naturally integrated into the Victorian understanding, shedding light on the "preconceptions" that helped "determine [its] early identity as a product."[19] My own approach in this chapter to the meaning of early spoken recordings in relation to reading and print media focuses, however, on articulative and elocutionary preconceptions in thinking about the phonograph rather than on inscriptive or writerly ones.

Edison's image of the phonographic cylinder as an inscribed tablet that no longer needs to be deciphered because it "speaks for itself" is further complicated because speaking, too, was a mediating factor involving practice and skill. The neutrality and immediacy associated with the phonograph—among other associations—was actually informed by an array of speech practices, including the elocutionary art of concealing the speaker's artfulness. To say that a cylinder "speaks for itself" bypasses the matter of what is spoken. This interesting trope for the phonograph record, suggesting a voice identity devoid of imposed vocal content, was much used in early promotions of the technology, and suggests a representation of the sound-recording medium as no medium at all, but rather as a repository of the pure voice of nature. It is a trope borrowed from romantic rhetoric, and from romantic poetry in particular. Exploring the rhetorical underpinnings of this common, early trope of the phonograph as a vehicle of natural, unmediated expression, and approaching early spoken recordings in relation to preexisting recitation anthologies and the social practices of recitation and elocution they assert, infuses this sense of the neutrality of the medium with more complicated conceptions of media and reading.

Pure Voice

Looking at the phonograph cylinder or disc as a material artifact, what does one see? An illegible graph of a person's vocal identity? The true voice (of nature) inscribed upon a tabula rasa? Theodor Adorno remarked that the phonograph record disc "is covered with curves, a delicately scribbled, utterly illegible writing."[20] He focused on the importance of the illegibility of this inscription,[21] finding the likeness of the phonographic disc or cylinder to a tablet bearing the marks of an unreadable language liberating, because it suggested the future possibility of recording sound "without it ever having sounded."[22] Or, to put it another way, it allows us to imagine the writing of a sound event that is *not* subject to temporality, is not the trace and preservation of a sound source that existed in an earlier span of time, and thus is not necessarily to be understood as indexical of a passage of time, or inscriptive of reality. In the context of my present discussion of the recorded voice, this suggests a technology allowing for the creation of a unique vocal identity that has never been associated with an actual, living character, a technological language that speaks on its own and is not the trace of a speaking body. Adorno was thinking of the possibility in the 1930s of composing for mechanical pianos by making perforations directly on scrolls that could function as data for pianolas to decipher as music. We might think of the contemporary possibility of the digital synthesis of a previously nonexistent audible voice, and of the virtuality that seems to come with a digital interface. Both ideas lead us to the *inverse* of the late Victorian correlation between sound recording and personal identity.

In the 1890s, the phonographic cylinder was often promoted as something superior to any written record. It was deemed superior, not only to the spontaneous overflow of powerful feeling (of being) captured in verse by romantic poets, to the realistic characters and heroes described by novelists and historians, and to the characteristic scrawls of self preserved in facsimile autographs—each of which, after all, required literacy, relative proficiencies in reading and interpretation for their import to be grasped—but superior even to the imprinting technology of the photograph, because it captured a longer moment than a single photo could. Due to this sense of the medium as a time-capture device, Edison suggested from the beginning that his invention could be used to archive the living voices of the dead, their utterances "transmitted to posterity, centuries afterwards, as freshly and forcibly as if those later generations heard his living accents."[23] He proposed the use of recordings to celebrate great voices and historical events of national importance "in every town and hamlet in the country upon our holidays."[24] If the continuity of a powerful identity depended on a significant collective memory, replaying the speech of a person whose voice and character were captured on cylinder would guarantee that continuity, as against the forgetting or rewriting of history. The past would not so much be remembered as relived on memorial occasions by each subsequent generation.[25]

One early example of this kind of occasion, a promotional idea that took its cue from Edison's grand vision, was an event scheduled in 1890 by "The Light Brigade Relief Fund" to raise money for those soldiers who had survived the ill-advised charge "into the valley of death" led by Lord Cardigan at Balaclava in 1854. Again, Edison's marketing agent in London, George Gouraud, was involved in the organization of the event and the fantasy it worked to promote. A military man sympathetic to this cause arranged to have recordings made of Florence Nightingale (who established her name during the Crimean War) and the trumpeter Martin Lanfried (who had sounded the bugle call at the original battle), both of which were played at the event, along with a recording of Tennyson reciting his poem "The Charge of the Light Brigade" made by Charles Steytler for Gouraud, also in 1890.[26] While the main purpose of this particular "voice demonstration" was supposedly to raise funds for the British soldiers who had survived the battle, the ulterior motive was, as always, to display the wonderful potential of this new technology, to demonstrate its ability to deliver a variety of sounds and capture time and character.

The most important genre of speech highlighted in this particular phonograph demonstration was that of the testimonial, praising Edison for his great invention and the technology for its powers of granting immortality to the speaker. For example, the scripted short speech that **Florence Nightingale** recorded for the sake of the Light Brigade Relief Fund, which included the statement, "When I am no longer even a memory, just a name, I hope my voice may perpetuate the great work of my life," promoted the idea of the sound recording as a synecdoche for the entire person, and of the voice as an alternative to bodily presence.[27] To advertise the first promotional lectures on (and about) the perfected phonograph, Gouraud sent out invitations to an "at home," "To meet Prof. Edison" / Non presentem, sed alloquentem! (Not present but in voice)."[28] Gouraud provided Edison with strict instructions for the script of the recording that would be played before his guests. He told Edison to identify himself clearly by stating his name and home address, to remark, "what a happy escape . . . from the drudgery of the pen" the phonograph represents, and especially to start with a line from Wordsworth's poem "To the Cuckoo" that he had already registered for promotional use: "Shall I call thee bird, or but a wandering voice?"[29] Bird or wandering voice?—this alternative posed as a question provokes a response by the phonograph that rejects any such dichotomy. Albeit a "wandering" artifact speaking without its bodily context, the voice recording is still meant to be understood as an artifact of presence.

Quoting Wordsworth's 1804 poem retrospectively to the invention of the phonograph not only conveyed nostalgia and the hope that the new technology seemed to promise for the preservation of self but made romantic rhetorical assumptions about it. The phonograph, like Wordsworth's cuckoo, promised a natural yet mysterious recurrence of time heard but not seen, the promise of a "blithe newcomer" bringing a happy tale from the past, not merely sounding "the same" as it did in our youth, but being "[t]he same whom in my school-boy days / I listened to" (ll. 17–18). Like Keats's nightingale whose "voice" he hears was heard "in ancient days" (ll. 63–64)[30] and is singing "[p]erhaps the self-same song" (l.65) as was heard by the biblical Ruth, Wordsworth's cuckoo is imagined as a creature that preserves a changeless song and voice simply by its survival as a species. When the bird begets a new generation, it performs an act of natural and perfect vocal replication, without having to learn the art of song. But the voice of the bird is not merely immediately present in Wordsworth's scenario, it is also mysteriously invisible, "twofold" (l. 6), as Wordsworth puts it, because "From hill to hill it seems to pass / At once far off and near" (ll. 7–8). Wordsworth evokes two kinds of aural replication in this poem, one figured as nature's replication of its own voice (the bird's self-replication and the bird's voice echoing in the hills), the second suggesting the replication of sound as an act of human memory reconstructing an experience of a voice heard "far off":

> And I can listen to thee yet;
> Can lie upon the plain
> And listen, till I do beget
> That golden time again.[31]

Here it is not the bird that begets itself "the same" but the poet who begets a memory of past encounters with that same voice, through an act of imaginative memory. I raise the distinction to point out that in its initial promotion, the phonograph is identified first of all with the voice and begetting of the bird in all its immediate self-sameness. The power of the romantic poem is drawn from the natural sounds and voices it represents, even as it sets these natural voices in opposition to the poet's act of imaginative begetting, which for all its attentive listening, its seeking and its longing, stands as a mediated, unnatural procedure. The "oral fallacy" that nature speaks more profoundly than books is staged repeatedly in romantic poetry as a struggle between written poetry as artifice, on the one hand, and poetry as the unmediated expression of nature's sounds and of natural feeling, on the other.[32]

In the early conception of the phonograph this binary between nature and artifice is refigured as different kinds of reading. A specific narrative about transduction is told. In this narrative, the phonograph is portrayed as a most natural reader of the sounds of nature and not as a mediating, bookish imitator. It is perceived as a naturalized medium because it does not "read" or "perform" or "mimic" but simply delivers the voices inscribed on itself. Insofar as it can be understood as reciting a text aloud (the needle and not the reader interpreting those illegible grooves alluded to by Edison and Adorno), it does so only as a means of "speaking itself" and not as an act of elocutionary interpretation. Because it is not performing another's voice, but always being a self (if not *itself*), the phonograph—according to this version of the phonographic imaginary—occupies the position of a natural medium for conveying presence through voice.

In the Michigan poet Will Carleton's 1881 poem "The Festival of Praise; or, Thanksgiving Day," God's all-forgiving, all-hearing (high-fidelity, we might say) soul is likened to a phonograph. Dejected by the inherent futility of an attempt to thank a God so benevolent, Carleton is consoled by the fact

That when our voice in kind behalf
Of any grief is heard,
Heaven's wondrous gold-foiled phonograph
Is taking every word[33]

The boundary between the living voice and its celestial recording dissolves, and thanksgiving is recorded for eternity on the celestial phonograph.

In early promotions of the idea of the phonograph, the loss of "aura" or the failure of a sound recording to convey authentic presence is rarely identified with the degrading effects of mechanical reproduction. Even in accounts of early tin-foil phonograph demonstrations, we find claims for the "exasperating fidelity" of the phonograph,[34] claims reinforced in advertisements from 1878 and 1879 that describe it as a "simple mechanism . . . that reproduces with wonderful exactness the human voice in all its possible variations," and as a mechanism that will "talk, laugh, cry, sing, whistle, etc., reproducing with great fidelity the character of the original words."[35] In such claims, phonographic purity as a mechanism of human reproduction is reinforced by its ability to render all sounds that emanate from the human body equally well, without prejudice.

This idea of an unbiased capacity for replication safeguards the phonograph's pure "intentions." If corruption figures into the scenario and *is* attributed to the mechanical medium, the infidelity of replication is interestingly described using terms more commonly applied to vocal rendition: a recording is said to have "an amusing tendency to burlesque," or "something irresistibly comic in its absurd imitation."[36] Distinctions between mechanical fidelity (as natural, "reality" capture) and human imitation, or mimicry, arise in these accounts as examples of nascent attempts to comprehend the implications of mechanical versus human productions of speech sounds.

In fact, claims to the perceived fidelity of early sound recordings were helped along by invisible cultural conventions, idiomatic structures, and practiced performative techniques. The repeated use of widely known, memorized scripts, such as "Mary Had a Little Lamb," as samples for recording during the earliest demonstrations of Edison's tinfoil phonograph underscores the degree to which the perceived fidelity of a recording played back depended on the familiarity of the listener with what had been recorded.[37] Trained speakers and the conventionalization of "photophonic as opposed to 'everyday' conversation," also played a significant part in "help[ing] the machine reproduce speech" so that it would be received as exact replication.[38] The accommodation of this need for familiarity and conventions to achieve the perception and attestation of fidelity was fulfilled, not only by the use of familiar scripts, but by the demonstration scenario itself, in which the recording was made in public, thus allowing the audience to hear the speech they were intended to recognize prior to playback. As the technology developed and perceived fidelity improved following the release of Edison's "Perfected Phonograph" in 1888, attention to the manner in which a speech was delivered, the grain, pitch, timbre, and other distinguishable qualities of an individual's voice grew more prevalent, and the analogy between sound recording and vocal performance as forms of sonic mimicry acquired new implications.

The problem of mimicry (as opposed to that of unwarranted mechanical duplication or copying) was addressed by J. Lewis Young in an editorial for his promotional magazine the *Phonogram*, in which he suggests that, "[w]hen the Phonograph comes into general use in this country, a new law will be wanted. We cannot find in any work on the criminal code a punishment for the forgery of voices. There are some excellent mimics, who might do great mischief by imitating one's voice in the Phonograph."[39] Such a statement demonstrates an awareness of mimicry as a popular form of entertainment on the music hall and vaudeville stage, and of the possible implications of transferring that expertise in sounding like another to a medium that separates the sound of the speaking voice from its producer's body. Phonograph companies went about marketing their products with this idea of imitation as fraudulent mimicry in mind. For example, a Frank Seaman Advertisement (1898) claims that his newly renamed machine, The Zon-o-phone, "does not distort or caricature the Voice," and "has never brought discredit on itself by amateur or fraudulent records," because Zon-o-phone only hires "the most celebrated artists" and "public speakers . . . each of whom has signed his or her name, which appears on the record as proof of its authenticity."[40] A National Gram-o-phone advertisement from the same year, pitches the authenticity of their "signed" records according to a similar understanding of this distinction between reproduction and imitation: "Gram-o-phone records reproduce the actual sounds and tone qualities of the original while all other records only imitate."[41]

There is a telling slippage between reproduction and imitation where the phonograph's perceived capacities of reproduction are identified as a superlative or transcendent form of sonic replication. The authentic talking machine was marketed, not exactly as a technology that has perfected the art of mimicry, but as a kind of perfectly pure mimic, an innocent replicator, written on by nature and preserving the natural moment eternally. Compared to the phonograph's purported natural means of capturing and replicating sound, the human ability to mimic voices and sound comes off as an act of artfulness (or artifice). Despite my assertion of this distinction between reproduction and imitation as one conceptual framework by which the reproductive capacities of the phonograph were understood, the purity of the talking machine's voice as I have been explaining it can also be understood to have had its equivalent in certain prescriptive models of human reading.

I Am the Phonograph

The conflation of the human elocutionary model of "natural" voice with that of the "natural and pure" voice of the phonograph is especially apparent in poems written to be recited from the perspective of the phonograph, the talking machine speaking on behalf, not just of any self, in this case, but *it*self, and in its own voice. This genre of recited piece harkens back to that most archaic form of poetry, the artifact riddle (like those in the Anglo-Saxon *Exeter Book*) in which an object articulates its inherent characteristics. In the case of the phonograph poem, the voice in which it speaks (the voice of the phonograph as performed by an actor playing the character of the phonograph) underscores the content of the self-representation, and the rhetorical assumptions informing the literary significance of this technology. Such play with assumptions concerning the presence of the speaker enacted in first-person phonograph recordings "demands the impossible," because "to understand its discourse, one must fulfill the absent self-referential subject of the 'I' with a mechanical presence that confounds the very notion of the subject."[42] The scenario of phonographic recitation demands that the listener play along with the possibility of the phonograph as a special and peculiar kind of speaker. First-person phonograph recitation recordings are especially suggestive for their representation of the phonograph as the supreme kind of virtuoso elocutionist that functions as a medium of perfect neutrality.

We can hear the logic of this fantasy of the pure voice of the phonograph in Horatio Nelson Powers's recording of his poem **"The Phonograph's Salutation."** The text that frames the reading states that "the phonograph will speak for itself. Now listen to its voice."[43] In the first verse of the poem, Powers has Edison's machine say:

> I seize the palpitating air. I hoard
> Music and speech. All lips that breathe air are mine.
> I speak, and the inviolable word
> Authenticates its origin and sign.[44]

The poem first of all suggests that the phonograph can voice itself in any imaginable mode of human speech, possessing as it does "[a]ll lips that breathe air," and further that the words it speaks are "inviolable"—that is, they are kept sacredly free from profanation or corruption because they are authenticated by their incarnate origins. Unlike a mimic who may successfully capture the *manner* of another's speech (or distort it in mimicking it), the phonograph tells us that it captures both the manner of the speech and the essence of the speaker to whom it is inextricably connected: "In me are souls embalmed. I am an ear / Flawless as truth: and truth's own tongue am I." The phonograph captures both the speech *and* the souls of its speakers, and in doing so claims its identity as "truth's own tongue"—a tongue that cannot be forked or speak a lie because it repeats exactly what its perfectly innocent ear has heard. Everything in this description of the phonograph asserts that its identity depends on its special ability to speak *other* voices. But the conceit of Powers's poem, sent as a phonogram (phonographic letter) across the Atlantic Ocean, is that the phonograph is *presently* speaking in its own voice.[45]

What are the qualities of the phonograph's voice? In print advertisements that represented the talking machine speaking for itself (in cartoon-like bubbles emanating from the amplifying horn), the voice of the phonograph was usually a simple first-person ventriloquization of the salesman or jobber's voice: "I am the Reginaphone . . . I am sold for cash or on the easy payment plan, as you prefer," the phonograph says in a 1904 Regina Music Box Company ad (fig. 1).[46] In other instances, the voice of the machine would articulate its technological genealogy, suggesting an almost genetic relationship to previous versions and models of itself. For example, when Charles Sumner Tainter and his team deposited the wax-cylinder Graphophone, their early improvement on Edison's tinfoil phonograph, at the Smithsonian Institution, their deposit included a cylinder with a card indicating that it would say, if played, "I am a graphophone and my mother was the phonograph."[47]

Based on Powers's recording of "The Phonograph's Salutation," it seems that the talking machine possesses no inherent vocal qualities at all. The voice of the phonograph is free of any preexisting cultural accent and is, by reason of this neutrality, the perfect medium by which the voices of others can be captured and conveyed. Powers's phonograph seems also paradoxically to be voicing its own voicelessness in the opening lines of a poem titled "A Riddle—Read" shown as emanating from a gramophone horn in an 1898 record catalogue (fig. 2):

Figure 1. Advertisement for "The Reginaphone" record player. *The Cosmopolitan,* April 1904, back matter.

No tongue I have, no hands, nor yet a voice,
Yet talk, or sing, or play, which is your choice?
There is no instrument that you can name
I am not mistress of: 'tis all the same
With song, I sing untiring with the purest tone,
Soprano, Alto, Bass or Baritone.
All languages are mine, with wondrous skill
I talk, weep, laugh, and will your senses thrill
With stirring scenes, from playwrights, comic, tragic

RECORD CATALOGUE.

A RIDDLE—READ

No tongue I have, no hands, nor yet a voice,
  Yet talk, or sing, or play, which is your choice?
There is no instrument that you can name,
  I am not mistress of; 'tis all the same
With song, I sing untiring with the purest tone,
  Soprano, Alto, Bass or Baritone.
All languages are mine, with wondrous skill
  I talk, weep, laugh, and will your senses thrill
With stirring scenes, from playwrights, comic, tragic
  All bow in turn to my resistless magic.
Music and song my captives, sound my throne,
  I reign supreme, their Queen,

THE GRAMOPHONE.

IN ORDERING please select a considerably larger proportion than you require, or make a double selection, so that we may substitute where we cannot execute from our Stock. Do not judge the record by its appearance, but by its SOUND. No record is sent out unless the sound production is perfect.

Figure 2. Advertisement from 1898, in which The Gramophone speaks a riddle. Record catalogue stock list, November 16, 1898. Catalogue Collection of the Music Division, Library and Archives Canada, R13984 183.

> All bow in turn to my restless magic.
>
> Music and song my captives, sound my throne,
>
> I reign supreme, their Queen, THE GRAMOPHONE.[48]

Lacking the human apparatus of speech and voice, the gramophone seems to benefit from this, since it can "talk" without ever getting tongue-tied. Its emanations (if not, strictly speaking, articulations) are of limitless variety, delivered "with the purest tone," indiscriminately, which is to say, without bias or intention, aside from pure replication. The machine's infinitely versatile capacity for reproduction is conflated with the "wondrous skill" of the virtuoso performer, since the logic of the poem collapses the concepts of technique and technology into one imaginary self-promotional utterance. The gramophone's repertoire ranges from inarticulate weeping and laughter to eloquence and song.

Another answer to this question posed by the Powers recording—what are the qualities of the voice of the phonograph?—might reasonably claim that when the phonograph speaks itself, it sounds like Horatio Nelson

Powers, both author and speaker of the poem. Powers was commissioned to have been overwhelmed in his "contemplation" of the "wonderful character and performances" of the phonograph, like Wordsworth by nature, and "naturally" to have sought to vent his feelings in verse. His poem, already framed as a natural romantic effusion, is then further naturalized by his decision to assign his own lyric voice to the phonograph, and then to perform that lyric voice in his recitation of the poem for the purpose of making the recording. A trained preacher, described in an American newspaper as "one of the most brilliant pulpit orators in the West," with a "voice melodious and powerful,"[49] Powers delivers his poem with a calm and fluid declamation that refrains from any marked or exaggerated use of expulsive or explosive aspirational force. His delivery is restrained in its occasional prolongation of sounded vowels and subtle in its very occasional use of vocal tremor. The performance as a whole suggests a tranquil confidence in being heard, no matter the audience or venue of delivery. The punctuation of the sentences rather than the poem's lineation is honored in performance with pauses, with an effect that underplays the ABAB rhyme scheme, a generic feature of the printed poem, and gives a sense of gravity in caesura as it moves from one assertion to another concerning the phonograph's actions, iterative incarnations, and significance for humanity. With the rare exception, Powers maintains a rhotic pronunciation of words containing the letter *r*, although sometimes without rounding out the sound of the *o* that precedes it (as in his pronunciation of "word" (/'wɜːd/) and "record" (/'rekɔːd/) as *wurd* (/wɜːrd/) and *recurd* (/'rekərd/). Still though, even as the reading works to stress an elocutionary and pronunciational mode that evokes a kind of globally received or standard (read: mildly southwestern UK English-sounding) English, one can also hear the American bleed through in certain vowels of his delivery (as in the examples just mentioned) and particularly in the disproportionately loud, non-rhotic pronunciation of "New York" in the sign-off "New *Yawk*." These elements of Powers's performance may be read as enacting (in the character of the Phonograph) a developing fusion between "English" and "American" speech—a phonetic vision that is especially relevant to the final stanza of the poem, where an Arnoldian "sweetness and light" and brotherhood are associated with the commercial trophies won by American entrepreneurial ingenuity. This speaking phonograph is envoicing the future global ascendency of a transatlantically infused English speech.

A similar mode of delivery can be heard in another early advertising record, **"I am the Edison Phonograph"** (ca. 1906), in which Len Spencer, an experienced recording artist who performs on a great range of talking records, speaks from the point of view of the phonograph and (as in the other advertisements) claims he can perform all levels of entertainment, all voices, all languages with absolute naturalness.[50] "My voice is the clearest, smoothest and most natural of any talking machine" he says, again in an elevated, slightly "English"-sounding, but not overly dramatic style and pronunciation. The style of delivery suggests not only that the Edison phonograph is the superior mechanical elocutionist among all talking machines, but that the high elocutionary style he uses to perform the true voice of the phonograph can serve as the transparent medium for the performance of other (say less pure) voices and characters without losing its own identification with a clear and natural sound. In Spencer's recording the voice of the phonograph is both represented and performed in mutually reinforcing ways, suggesting an unbounded capacity to affect its listener, "no matter what may be your mood," to sing "tender songs of love," to tell "merry tales" evoking "joyous laughter," to call the hearer "to join in the rhythmic dance," "to lull the babe to sweet repose / Or waken in the aged hear soft memories of youthful days."[51] The scenario of use for this recording, like that of the Powers recording, was one of display. Where the Powers recording would be played and reported on by journalists in London, Spencer's advertising record was used at the opening of touring phonograph exhibitions in the northeastern United States, and in the display rooms of phonograph merchants, the phonograph's address inviting the listeners to get to know the phonograph and its remarkable capacities well enough to want to take it home with them:[52] "The more you become acquainted with me, the better you will like me. Ask the dealer."[53] The explicitly clever, commercial purpose of such a recording delivered in the voice of the phonograph does not undermine the cultural significance of the way that voice was made to speak.

In both these audiotexts, the voice of the phonograph is imagined and performed as an elevated, natural mode of speech that aims to make its hearers "forget the messenger."⁵⁴ If the phonograph captures time and character for eternity, then it is only logical that its voice should be imagined as equally transcendent and, according to the paradoxical logic by which new media aimed to become indispensable to the point of invisibility, unmediated. Things get interesting when we consider what this voice might have sounded like to early phonograph listeners. For in fact the pure voice of the phonograph is saturated in rhetorical assumptions, audible in early spoken recordings, which evoke a continuum of vocal sounds that range from the grunts of animals to the whispers of angels.

Early Novelty Records and (Dis)articulation

David Appelbaum argues that the human voice is concealed somewhere behind speech. The acquired practice of speech functions as "a technology of concealment," or as he puts it more precisely, "[t]he technology that hides through speaking the loss of one's own voice is that of phonemic sound production." Appelbaum's attempt to free the voice from the protective mask of speech—a mask that assigns to it the limited function of spoken recitation, and consequently traps it in a (Derridean) opposition with writing—leads him to investigate the possibility of "freeing the voice's body from the place of concealment" by highlighting its non-speech or speech-interrupting productions, such as coughs, laughs, and breathing. Coughing, laughing, breathing, snorting, hacking, sneezing make their appearance "as an interruption of the voicing process" and distort "the text and texture of voice with the unexpectancy of the body." Appelbaum's useful framework for thinking about voice associates what I have been referring to as the "naturalization" of speech with a process of assigning voice to a "mental space" that is "pristine, angelic, soulful, and unperturbed by bodily upheavals."⁵⁵ The imaginary status of the phonograph's voice as natural and pure is attributable to the speaker's lack of corporeality (the possibility of record skipping and other mechanical breakdowns aside).

If we consider a dramatic instantiation of this idea, for a moment: The recurrent paroxysm of "Ah-ah-ow-oo!" that emanates from Eliza Doolittle's mouth through the first two acts of Shaw's *Pygmalion* functions as an involuntary, corporeal response that interrupts the mentalizing technology of speech that Liza will eventually acquire through great and painful, repetitive practice. Liza's "unengineered voice" is replete with disruptive bodily noise, and in the end that noise persists as a core element of her identity.[56] When Liza is taking her leave from Professor Henry Higgins, who says that he'll miss her "voice and appearance," the following exchange ensues:

> LIZA. Well, you have both of them on your gramophone and in your book of photographs. When you feel lonely without me, you can turn the machine on. It's got no feelings to hurt.
>
> HIGGINS. I cant turn your soul on. Leave me those feelings; and you can take away the voice and the face. They are not you.[57]

Soul is identified here, in what is in effect a discussion of sound reproduction, with the effusions, outbursts, accents, flaws, and disruptions that interrupt phonemic perfection, revealing a feeling body and, counterintuitively, a pure, soulful self. According to Higgins, aberrant and disruptive articulations in speech provide true access to the individual.[58] Only speakers with bodies can disrupt the technology of speech. Machines can't cough.

The association of articulatory disruption sourced in the human body with a notion of phonetic authenticity may furnish one explanation for the early interest among phonograph listeners in hearing the new medium reproduce disruptive sounds. One of the prominent capacities of the phonograph for pleasure and wonder was its ability to reproduce sounds of all kinds and not only sounds intended to function rhetorically or meaningfully. Mouth-made bell sounds, snoring, sneezing, and laughing are all examples of the unencumbered voice sounds the phonograph offered to early listeners. At the earliest phonograph demonstrations, in the late 1870s, Edison "coughed, sneezed, and laughed at the mouthpiece" to demonstrate the machine's ability to reproduce even the most inarticulate sounds, and newspaper accounts attempted to convey in print what the phonograph could capture to perfection—"Ahem! Heck! heck! heck! (coughing) . . . Whoa-a-a!"—as evidence that "laughter and whistling, singing and sighing and groans—in fact, every utterance of which the human voice is capable— was stored in that wondrous wheel and emitted when it was turned."[59]

Jacob Smith has read the significance of such records of disruptive articulation (and of "laughing records," in particular) as having revealed the phonograph's capacity to deliver a "powerful index of presence" by sounding the body behind coherent talk and speech, "establishing the credibility and authenticity of early recordings, [and] alleviating the anxiety of hearing a disembodied, recorded voice."[60] Smith notes that the uninhibited laughter heard in early laughing records was enacted by speakers "typically considered to be culturally 'other': women, African Americans, . . . the country rube."[61] Recorded laughter framed in the songs and sketches presented in early recordings was disruptive, not only of articulate speech in the abstract sense, but of the linear narratives and social scenarios of fluid performance within which it erupted. For example, the **"Laughing Record (Henry's Music Lesson)"**[62] recorded in 1923 by Sally Stembler and Edward Meeker for the Edison label, presents an American music student, Henry, pursuing his cornet lesson with a European (i.e., Jewish)-accented professor, and the professor's daughter, Lina providing piano accompaniment. During the first two minutes of the recording, Lina erupts in "unrestrained" laughter at each false note from Henry's cornet, to the point where her laughter overwhelms Henry's attempt to play a fluid melody on his instrument. As the lesson proceeds, the professor does not admonish his daughter for laughing but instead criticizes his student's playing, until, for the final minute of the short recording, the only sounds we hear are Lina and the professor's relentless and extravagant laughter, punctuated by the occasional squeak or squawk of Henry's horn. Fluid cornet melody peppered with interruptive laughter evolves into fluid laughter peppered with interruptive horn squeals.

Appelbaum asserts that laughter, something that disrupts expressive fluency, can itself become a form of such fluency because it "does not embody a pure interruption" but "is an intermediate joint between the cough and verbosity," an eloquent and loquacious combination of "pitch, modulation, tonality, tempo and amplitude" that can, like speech, be "musically scored" with the "symbols of a grammar."[63] The laugh, a nonsemantic phonetic disarticulation popular in early spoken recordings, "diverts us from itself" toward the imaginative dramatic or emotional frames that might explain it. The explanatory scene that justifies the extended fugue of laughter in the last third of "Laughing Record (Henry's Music Lesson)" is the music lesson itself, and Henry's weak cornet playing. And yet, as the laughing persists, we also hear an inversion of the roles of Henry (a fluent English speaker) and the professor and Lina (immigrants with accents) as the revenge of the other against phonetic normalcy. As the laughter persists, it evolves into an increasingly mannered form of disarticulation that is less spontaneous outburst than deliberate vocal performance. If not quite operatic, it sounds increasingly like a controlled exploration of the nonmusical vocal utterances that laughter as a mode of social expression affords. The laughter in this recording escapes its explanatory frame (the lesson) and transmogrifies from explicable spontaneity (Lina can't help laughing at Henry) into a more forced, formal (and even creepy) performance. The last minute of the recording can be read back into the framing social scenario of the sketch, not as a socially inappropriate outburst, but as a joint musical performance of vocal otherness by Lina and her father. In both cases, the laugh vibrates semiotically, but the second scenario is replete with riotous social meaning.

We would be deaf to much if we analyzed early spoken recordings for their content and subject matter alone, and yet it is hard not to. The performance of disarticulate sounds—sounds that disrupt meaningful speech—invites us to listen for the relative presence (in a vocal sound) of "shared intention." As Appelbaum puts it, "[t]he laugh (voice) is not free until it is free from the germ of intention which continually revises history in order to unburden it of interruptions." This "germ of intention" refers to our predisposition to hear meaning in the phonetic sounds that humans make. We can't help it, it seems; we hear meaningful communication in phonetic combinations whenever we can. We will sooner believe the veracity of our mishearings, mondegreens and malapropisms than admit that we could not catch a sound's meaning. Freedom from the germ of intention is a challenging goal that must be pursued against the grain of our inclination to seek meaning even to the point of self-deceit. Appelbaum offers the example of tongue twisters as one form of vocal play that aims to make intentional signification fall by the wayside, working "to bring forth a voice not encumbered by conventions of sound production" that we have such difficulty hearing and conceptualizing.[64] Other examples of early novelty speech recordings that performed disarticulations can be read along similar lines as performances that offer binaural signification, semantically intended meaningful sounds in one ear and semiotically resonant, disarticulate ones in the other.

I will pursue a few examples of the first track (let's call it the right headphone reading), to begin with, since the overarching intention of early spoken recordings was to sound on a continuum of differentiating signals of meaning—from the dialectically corrupt and inarticulate to the elocutionary or pure—with the ultimate goal of establishing hierarchies and shared intentions of normativity. Like laughing records, snoring and sneezing records and dialect performances often prompted the listener to judge unwieldy sound emanating from an other, whose alterity they worked (or at least aimed) to control by simplifying it into abnormality or lack of developmental capacity (in the case of dialect), motive (in the case of laughter), or character traits (in the case of snores and sneezes).

Snores and sneezes as performed in early comedic novelty recordings are excellent examples of this objectification of involuntary articulations. Robert J. Wildhack, a professional illustrator, and poster artist who designed numerous covers for major American magazines during the first three decades of the twentieth century[65] also had some success as a vaudeville comedian, and based on his vaudeville acts, he recorded a two-sided, twelve-inch comic record, **"Sneezes"** and **"Snores,"** for the Victor label in 1917.[66] The Victor catalogue entry for the "Wildhack Records" included cartoon sketches drawn by Wildhack to illustrate the nature of his records, and the following promotional blurb:

> Do you snore? Of course not; but if so, is your snore a blond or a brunette? Or if it is neither of these, perhaps it is type 3B, the "conversational, or troubled conscience" variety. This weighty question can only be finally solved by consultation with Mr. Wildhack who has it "all figure[d] out" here. The same thoroughness of research has also been given to "sneezes," so that you may now, says Mr. Wildhack, "learn to recognize a friend by his sneeze." "Snores" and "Sneezes" are not "talking records" in the ordinary sense, but are illustrated entertainments, veritable humorous sound classics, dealing with some of the funniest sounds in nature, and have no competition in the entire talking machine field. The humor of the sounds is obvious enough to delight any child, and the humor of the description is subtle enough to satisfy the most sophisticated listener.[67]

Capitalizing on Wildhack's reputation as an illustrator, the blurb underscores the distinction between a speech description of a sonic event and an illustration of a sonic event by the actual production of sounds. The Wildhack cartoons integrated into the catalogue present this distinction graphically

Figure 3. Robert J. Wildhack cartoon illustrating his own talking records "Snores" and "Sneezes." *Victor Records 1917 Catalogue, with biographical sketches, opera plots, new portraits and special Red Seal section* (Camden, NJ: Victor Talking Machine Co., November 1917), Wi.

through the contrast of typographical captions ("Do you snore?") with a visual representation of snoring sounds as five zigzagging lines emanating from the nose and mouth of a man depicted sleeping on his back (fig. 3). The word "snore" names the sound illustrated with sharp-twisting lines, a cartoon depiction of the sound signal of snoring. The next two panels in the cartoon present two scenes from the drama of a sneeze in two acts, "A sneeze–Act I" showing the figure of a man holding a handkerchief and about to sneeze, with a bare, illuminated light bulb hanging from a wire in front of him, followed by "A sneeze–Act 2" which shows a blackened panel with white-lined, typographical (uh-CHUH!) and linear graphic depictions of the sneeze that has been powerful enough to extinguish (or shatter) the light bulb. These last two panels play with the relationship between the producing body (visible in Act I) and the bodily sound now visible, in the absence of the producing body, only as onomatopoeic letters and illustrative lines. The recordings, the catalogue tells us, "are not 'talking records' in the ordinary sense, but are illustrated entertainments." They dramatize and rationalize the sounds of disarticulation by integrating those sounds into the category of illustrations of "sounds in nature."[68]

The generic conceit of these two Wildhack recordings is that of the illustrative lecture or talk. The talk, as we have already noted, was a common genre of talking record, allowing a speaker the opportunity to present a three-minute essay with arguments and examples on a specific topic of either comic superfluity or serious import. In this case, the lecturer has

performed his research and is now in a position to present an anatomy of
two kinds of involuntary articulation. The speaker chooses to discuss the
kinds of phonemic disruptions and unwanted articulations that professional
recording artists were normally expected to banish from their performances,
but he frames these sounds in such a way that they function as the central
feature and interest of the recording. The genre of lecture functions as the
first "germ of intention," in this case the intention to frame the sounds
of sneezes and snores as forms of meaningful human expression. This is
accomplished by numerically and alphabetically cataloguing the sounds
of snores and sneezes into characteristic types, and in many cases by at-
tributing expressive or affective motivation to sounds that we had previously thought to be inarticulate and devoid of expressive motivation. In the
"Snores" record, the lecturer identifies eight overarching types of snoring,
some of which have subcategories. In "Sneezes" the lecturer explains: "We're
all so familiar with sneezes that it may be well to name them, list them, and
become acquainted with the different forms and types so that we may learn
to recognize our friend by his sneeze." In the examples he enumerates, the
attribution of expressive motivation to accidental expulsions from the mouth
and nose integrates disarticulate sounds back into the sphere of meaningful
communication. The anatomizing is presented as a method of character
recognition, identification, and stereotyping. The other dominant means by
which the disarticulate is rendered articulate is by the speaker's consistent
focus on the productive techniques that lie behind the different varieties of
(in)articulate sounds categorized. Snoring is described by the lecturer "in
scientific terms" as "soft palate calisthenics," and in the categorization of
both sneezing and snoring sounds we hear the deployment of the kind of
technical vocabulary familiar from elocution manuals, with discussion of
varieties of expirational and inspirational movement and forms, descending,
ascending, and double "diapason."[69]

In these comic techniques of framing snores and sneezes as expressive
and technically sophisticated modes of articulation, the vocabulary and
motivations of elocutionary thinking work to identify and align the contours of disarticulate sounds with those of more obviously expressive texts.
Elocutionary frames are widened to accommodate even the most explosive
expulsions of breath and to neutralize the disruptive effect of the sounds

that fall within Appelbaum's "rogue gallery" of bodily phonation breakers.[70] Involuntary articulations (even unconscious ones, in the case of snoring) are framed and explained in a manner that imposes a form of control on them that is usually reserved for the sounds of intelligible speech. It is an audible form of rationalizing the sounds of human speech for the purpose of analytic control that we more commonly associate with the typographical transcript of heard speech.[71]

Speech transcription, the practice of converting spoken sounds into written text, often works to protect the intentionality of speech. By rendering intelligible speech in printed text and giving names to the inarticulate sounds that will not reproduce well, orthographically, in square brackets (i.e. [*clearing throat, sneeze*]) we separate the two kinds of articulation—speech versus other voice sounds—and impose a force of typographical control over both. Primitive textual renderings of sneezes ("Aaah-CHOO!") aside, the status of the speech disruptors are safely barracked by typographical means, and reside, along with instances of auditory unintelligibility [*unintelligible*] as benign specimens of acknowledged difficulty, unwieldy, but not unrenderable. In the case of the novelty "disarticulation" recordings I have been discussing, a typographical separation of speech from speech disruptor both enables the process of critical discussion I wish to pursue, and forces a return to the sounds presented in the recording itself. The abstraction of the bracketed indicators—too general to be critically satisfying—demands the granular subtlety of the sound source one attempts to transcribe.

The controlling motivation of transcription as I have been describing it is reproduced in Wildhack's performance, which, one might say, sonically transcribes inherently disruptive articulations into sound shapes that match the descriptive categories he uses to bring them to order, whether by grounding them in affective motivation, or harnessing their opaque, acousmatic qualities in identifiable, material sources of sound (the pussycat, the trombone, the seltzer siphon, the clockworks, the carburetor). Unlike the symphonic howls and cachinnations (convulsive laughter) that shape the finale of the Stembler and Meeker laughing record, Wildehack's novelty records do not devolve into formal studies or musical études of sternutation and stertoration (sneezing and snoring), but maintain their comical explanatory frames and scripts to the end.

Humanly produced phonation-breaking sounds may reside at one end of the elocutionary continuum, with some idealized notion of fluent, unaccented speech residing at the other. Between such markers, in the context of the corpus of early spoken recordings, we find a wide range of speech performance that includes dramatic or elocutionary renderings of poems and (in a different register) scenes and sketches delivered in dialect. The range of the continuum in dialect recordings moves along another gauge of cultural meaning from foreign to normative, corrupt to pure, black to white. Jennifer Stoever's concept of "the sonic color line" represents one useful way of explaining the sociological meaning of this continuum of ethnicized and "racialized sound," and "how and why certain bodies are expected to produce, desire, and live amongst particular sounds."[72] The range of early recorded speech-sounds from this perspective evokes a contrasting version to the "pure" voice of the phonograph as corporeal absence ("No tongue I have, no hands, nor yet a voice, / Yet talk") by stressing the "historical connections between black voices and the 'inhuman' voice of the phonograph."[73] The machine's inhumanity in this case is heard as a voice that is "corporeal, inarticulate, prelinguistic, and pushed to the extremes of embodiment,"[74] placing the phonograph at the opposite end of the voice continuum from where I have placed it so far.

Gustavus Stadler has explored this embodied version of the phonograph as voice in his account of early acoustically recorded reenactments of the torture and lynching of black men (recordings of which we have print documentation but no extant audible examples.) Stadler proposes that such recordings reveal fantasies "about perfect fidelity, with the implication that the sounds of a lynching align neatly with the authentic 'phonograph voice.'"[75] In such an example, it is not the involuntary sneeze or unconscious snore— trifling examples of disruptive speech, by comparison—but "the moans and screams" of the tortured black man that "cannot be described" by a listener who reported hearing such a recording.[76] The scream is a phonetic disruptor of the greatest ethical magnitude, and, within the context of human-made sounds, may exist in a unique category of both sonic and social destruction and reversion. As Elaine Scarry explains: "Physical pain does not simply resist language but actively destroys it, bringing about an immediate reversion to a state anterior to language, to the sounds and cries a human being makes before language is learned."[77] The scream precedes speech like no other form of human utterance, and resists transcription and analysis (although, as we shall see, the scream can also figure prominently in certain early dramatic recordings). As a sonic metaphor, the scream occupies both poles of the sonic continuum at once: as a sound "anterior to language" signaling the destruction of the speaker's body, and as a sound expressing the obliteration of the speaker's consciousness. It is an acute example that informs other less extreme examples of phonographic performance with its metaphor of positionality. Our relationship to the human sound signal, and the historical listener's relationship to that signal are informed by a sense of the degree of humanity it signifies on a continuum from primitive prelinguistic corporeal scream to postlingual ethereal utterance. To identify where, historically, the voice of a recorded speaker is positioned in relation to the phonetic sounds of acculturation, normativity, purity, affectivity and authenticity, is one of the challenges of audiotextual criticism.

In all cases, the problematics of transcription, metaphorically and practically, help us conceptualize how our acts of audiotextual criticism seize and hold fast, for the distance of a page or two, the sonic and cultural complexity of human speech sounds. Charles Bernstein summarizes the difficulty I am using as a broader metaphor for the object at the center of audiotextual criticism in his account of second-wave modernist poets' practices of scoring speech in their poetic works:

> [T]he closer we get to transcribing the actual sound of speech, the odder the transcription may appear. The dialect spelling looks strained if not condescending: if it gestures at a spoken language that is unself-conscious and fluid, it presents at the same time an ethnographic distortion or slur in the very method of its means of reproduction. In performance, however, much of this strangeness, though by no means all, disappears.[78]

Any attempt to spell a sneeze or snore, or to transcribe the tonal texture of a scream in words accurately will illustrate Bernstein's point. More important is his observation that transcription as a method of speech reproduction necessarily functions as a form of "ethnographic distortion," awkwardly abstracting the social and cultural nuance that might inform a signal of recorded speech. This brief metacritical point about the challenges that speech sounds pose to any alphabetically inclined critical approach (including my own) is especially relevant to the next section of this chapter, which focuses on the relationship between early spoken recordings (dialect and otherwise) and the print-based recitation genres that preceded them.

The Recitation Anthology as Early Talking Book

Early spoken recordings employed generic models that already existed in nineteenth-century recitation book anthologies, and functioned as a logical extension of a substantial Victorian reading and elocutionary culture.[79] There were many hundreds of such books published between 1800 and 1920. Early Victorian recitation books functioned as manuals and public-speaking primers for educated upper- and upper-middle-class males pursuing careers that might involve public speaking. Recitation anthologies of the last two decades of the nineteenth century were aimed at a far broader audience. The majority of these later anthologies contained specimens of both high elocutionary texts (like passages from Shakespeare, and short poems of Tennyson and Poe) *and* comic dialect sketches between the same covers.[80] In addition to these anthologies, individuals would sometimes compile their own personal scrapbooks of favorite recitation pieces from a diverse range of print publications. Mass-market versions of such home-made scrapbooks emerged at the end of the nineteenth century, drawing on submissions from their own readers, and disseminating the model of the parochial reading circle on a national scale. H. M. Soper's *Scrap-Book Recitation Series* (which ran from 1879 to –1919) combined pieces from various periodicals and other published recitation books, excerpts from published stories, texts adapted for recitation by professional public readers, and portions from actual private recitation scrapbooks sent in from all parts of the United States and Britain.[81] The mass-market recitation scrapbook was produced cheaply, with paper covers, and offered, at first glance, no obvious prescriptive order or arrangement of the pieces, not even an alphabetical one. Only a cursory editorial voice indicated the sources of some of the selections and stated the purpose of the collection, which was to provide materials with "the greatest possible range of style" for use "on all occasions" by speakers who included "the ten year old school boy" and "the would-be congressman"—in short, a democratic conception of pleasure and improvement of "everyone."[82]

The title pages of these books tell us that the texts have been "carefully chosen, as being peculiarly well adapted for reciting before select audiences, in refined domestic circles," as the subtitle of *Prescott's Drawing Room Recitations* has it. These same "carefully chosen" selections are organized haphazardly, are intermixed—if not miscegenated, at least desegregated—and appear thus, without the anxiety about "corruption" that one might expect, all in the name of providing "fine opportunities to Elocutionists of every style." While there is no obvious prescriptive arrangement to the selections, there is an informing logic behind the apparent disorder of such anthologies in their recognition that all forms of speech can be approached for their elocutionary potential. As with the dialect sound recordings, we are led to ask whether these comic dialect recitation texts did not simply function as the elocutionary rubes to the serious texts that demanded a more "lofty impassioned declamation."[83] In light of remarks made by Henry James in his 1905 lecture to the young ladies of Bryn Mawr College, "On the Question of Our Speech," one would certainly think that they did play a role of negative example. James argued that there was a direct, reflective correlation between "the degree in which a society is civilized" and "the vocal form, the vocal tone, the personal, social accent and sound of its intercourse."[84] He warned against the negative impact on the *vox Americana* of the common school, the newspaper, and especially, of "the vast contingent of aliens whom we make welcome, and whose main contention . . . is that, from the moment of their arrival, they have just as much property in our speech as we have, and just as good a right to do what they choose with it." He imagined anxiously that "all the while we sleep" these "innumerable aliens are sitting up" at night "to work their will on our inheritance." Such anxiety is not explicitly present in the general or common-school approach to the development of voice culture. Popular recitation books accommodated difference on the surface, but engaged in linguistic accommodation on its own terms, with the ultimate aim of erasure by assimilation of dialect into a linguistic standard.[85] Unlike the dialect recordings and dialect-speech transcripts that were collected and studied by organizations like the English Dialect Society (1873–96) and the American Dialect Society (1889–) with the aim of considering empirically reliable examples of regional dialects in relation to the study of global trends in the development of the English language, commercial "dialect" recordings and recitation pieces were more like popular renditions of dialectical speech, some relatively subtle and others based on the stereotyped sounds of regional or "alien" versions of English.

Recitation anthologies presented both high literary works and dialect pieces as necessary for the expansion of one's range as a cultured elocutionist. The goal of recitation was figured in these books (as in James's lecture) as the act of removing "bad, artificial habits, and supplanting them by better,"[86] but contrary to James's anxiety about the "alien" influence on "our speech," the average recitation book sees an ethnic or racial corruption of standard speech (in the form of a comical or challenging dialect recitation) as a useful means by which to "render the vocal organs flexible," and thus, to accomplish this goal of vocalized speech development. Specimens were chosen for these anthologies because they provided "elocutionary possibilities" for the reader to demonstrate his vocal range and virtuoso skills in reading.

Alliterative poems such as those of Edgar Allan Poe were especially common in recitation books. "The Bells" in particular was heavily anthologized because, as one periodical recitation series explains, "no other poem of the language affords so wide and varied a scope for vocal culture, as it sounds the whole gamut of pitch, covers every shade of force, and admits of every variety of time."[87] A masterful control over the vocal effects of sonic frequency (pitch) understood as tone and intonation, loudness of sound (force) understood as volume and energy, and duration (time) understood as prolongation, tempo, and similar gradations, was the sine qua non of a refined vocal culture. Poe's poem, in its repetition of words across entire lines, seems to offer itself up as an empty bell jar whose pitch, shade of force, and tempo are wholly dependent on how the poem is sounded by its reader, especially in those sections where the same word scans most of a line (as in "tinkle" and "time" below), and sometimes even more than a single line (as with "bells"):

> Hear the sledges with the bells-
> Silver bells!
> What a world of merriment their melody foretells!
> How they tinkle, tinkle, tinkle,
> In the icy air of night!

While the stars that oversprinkle
All the heavens, seem to twinkle
With a crystalline delight;
Keeping time, time, time,
In a sort of Runic rhyme,
To the tintinnabulation that so musically wells
From the bells, bells, bells, bells,
Bells, bells, bells-
From the jingling and the tinkling of the bells.[88]

In addition to poetry heavy in alliteration, assonance and consonance, dialect pieces with their uncommon syllable and vowel combinations also were approached as usefully challenging in their varied demands of pitch, force, and time.

The actual content of the material collected in recitation anthologies seems to have been less important than the opportunity they afforded to a reader to expand his vocal scope and range of tonal registers from the dramatic to the comic. For example, the elocutionist and recitation anthologist J. E. Frobisher took "the tintinnabulation that so musically wells" from Poe's silver sledge bells and transformed them into the comical (yet orally challenging) "clanging, / Whanging, / Clang-ee-tee-bang, tee-bang[ing]" of a hotel's morning bells. Such a parody shows that the tone of the "high" culture elocutionist can be treated as a mode of dialect reading in its own right.[89] A medley of dialect versions of "Mary Had a Little Lamb" is presented in the first number of Soper's *Scrap-Book Recitation Series* (1879), the Chinese version describing Mary's fleece as "all samee white snow," the Irish version saying that "the wool was white intoirly."[90] Given the status of this nursery rhyme as the Ur speech-text for early phonograph demonstrations, and as a "synecdoche for the 'stereotyped sentence' in general," dialectical parodies of well-known texts such as this were a means of accenting and, in a sense, deforming the most familiar recitation pieces to new ends.[91] Ethnic dialect performances were deemed justified in the introductions of recitation anthologies not only for their drollery but as a means of exercising the voice in new and challenging ways. Consequently, a "humorous Dutch dialect" piece entitled "Main Katrine's Brudder Hans" could be advertised as "suitable for gentlemen."[92]

In the instructions that accompany the more expensive editions of these recitation books, we find that the primary lesson to learn in one's development as a reciter is that of naturalization. "The best orators are the most natural," J. E. Frobisher asserts in the appendix to his recitation anthology. To read naturally meant to deliver text in a manner that concealed the fact of reading with a practice of deep immersion in the character whose voice was enacted, no matter how inane or scripted it might seem.[93] The call for naturalization in recitation was a call for what seems to have been assumed about the earliest noncommercial spoken recordings, that the voice functions as a natural index of character. But here the artfulness of naturalization comes into play, complicating the identification of voice with character and suggesting instead that character is created by the trained voice.[94]

The idea of performance as an art of naturalization was not necessarily antithetical to the concept of performance as an imitative art. As Susan Glenn has argued, turn-of-the-century debates about acting and interpretive reading negotiated a constellation of values concerning mimetic performance that included romantic ideals of imaginative creation, a "nineteenth-century bourgeois fascination with imitation and the early twentieth-century 'modernist' intellectual glorification of 'authenticity.'"[95] Comedic character imitation, so popular on the variety stage in the forms of parody, burlesque, ethnic caricature, blackface minstrelsy, and celebrity mimicry, came to be theorized and defended as equivalent to "new methods of 'realistic' acting" that "emphasized 'natural' speech, subtle physical gestures and the 'inner' psychology of the character being played."[96] The first principles of "true" imitation and mimicry, according to the celebrated music hall performer J. Arthur Bleackley, entailed the cultivation of the performer's "acuteness of observation," "great retention of what is observed," and "great pliancy of organs to represent what is observed"—suggesting that naturalization in mimetic performance demanded extensive practice.[97] The practice of these technical skills, while crucial, had to be supplemented with the development of the performer's imagination (a category to which Bleackley devotes an entire chapter in his book *The Art of Mimicry*). Without imaginative capacity, mimicry remained "false, counterfeit," "mechanical," and subject to "phonographic convention." This last phrase (borrowed by Bleackley from Max Beerbohm) interestingly positions the authenticity of human mimetic performance against soulless forms of mechanical re-production.[98] True mimicry (and remember we are talking about comedic impersonation, parody, burlesque, and ethnic character performance, here) demanded a combination of technique and imagination.[99] While the mimic's "imagination" is required to make his imitations "original"[100] (as Bleackley puts it in one of his paradoxical formulations), it is the cultivation of those principal skills of observation, retention, and pliancy that represent the foundation of imitative performance, and that can be said to underscore the purpose of Victorian recitation anthologies as a platform for the cultivation of mimetic reading.[101]

A long passage (quoted from Philip Gibbs's *Knowledge Is Power* [1903]) that closes the introduction to Bleackley's *The Art of Mimicry*, illustrating the first action item of his treatise—"Look at nature and notice everything"— strongly echoes the sonorously rich and diverse texts (with their clanging, whanging, and tee-banging) that populated recitation anthologies as raw materials for the cultivation of inspired mimetic performances:

> Nature—so full of noises that suggest words, harsh noises of clanging and bang-ing and jingling and jangling, dull noises of rumbling and grumbling, drowsy noises of humming and murmuring, watery noises of dripping and dropping and whirling and swirling and gurgling and rippling, and dashing and splashing; noises through the air; whizzing and whistling and whirring; metallic noises of clinging and ringing; quarrelsome noises of slapping and whacking, knocking and thumping; peculiar noises of sneezing and wheezing; hissing and spitting; plaintive noises of sighing and sobbing, and so on all the day long.[102]

Noticing the sounds of nature, including the equally diverse plethora of human speech sounds, and then practicing the articulation of those sounds, were key motives in the development of recitation culture. When consid-ered in relation to the performance of identity, this seemingly benign or leisure-oriented activity suddenly becomes the site of significant social and ideological challenge. Bleackley's argument "that the distinction of mimetic originality can be conferred upon *anyone*" asserts the mass cultivation of distinctive mimetic capacities.[103] It is precisely this idea of recitation practice as an art of wide-reaching social performance and possibility that makes these odd little recitation pieces and talking records interesting artifacts. The practice of mimetic performance evoked possibilities of self-transformation by the conscious application of careful observation, empathetic imagination, and technical performance.

Advice about recitation found in recitation anthologies can be heard as popular and practical renderings of wider debates about the ontological status of the speaking individual in relation to socially identifiable others. Glenn provides a useful summary of some of the key theories of the period that informed ideas surrounding popular and especially comedic mimetic performance. These included Henri Bergson's idea that character-oriented comedy was based on exposing the mechanical uniformity of character types, and the American pragmatist philosopher George Herbert Mead's social theory of imitation as the construction of another self through kinesthetically informed enactment of the other. Such theories opened possibilities for self-conscious speculation on identity as a socially performed phenomenon, the interpretation of a performing character's position in society and culture, and the meaning of human forms of imitation in relation to new mechanical modes of reproduction. These socially informed theories also called attention to the implications of amateur versus professional contexts for mimetic performance, and the emergence of new industries of celebrity and cults of personality.[104] There is no evidence to suggest that the rise of the record industry silenced the home reciter, at least during the first several decades of recorded sound. That said, there is still the implication (keeping Bleackley's advice to aspiring mimics in mind) that while the amateur reciter was positioned as a potential imitator of a diverse collection of sounds and personae, the recording artist represented an authoritative realization of that potential on permanent record.

The spoken records of monologists like Cal Stewart and Russell Hunting were professional manifestations of reading naturally, of "doing" Uncle Josh or Casey or Cohen in an unstudied manner that entailed a transformative immersion into the details of these characters not as generally rendered types but as veritable, particularized personalities. The Jewish dialect sketch, "Cohen on the Telephone" was recorded by various artists over the years, but verbatim from the same script. The same is true for many of the Casey sketches, and for the recitations of canonical poems. In the case of character-based monologues first made famous by individual performers (e.g., Cal

Stewart of "Uncle Josh" fame), the recordings made by later artists can be understood to have been imitations in a double sense: of the character, and of the artist who first developed the mimetically performed identity of that character.

Recorded character monologues, like their precedent recitation anthology texts, were delivered in a manner suggesting that the reciter conceived of his audience as a kind of "family circle." Uncle Josh would tell you slowly (many of his sentences starting with "Well, I'll tell ya . . ."), and with the interruptions of his own giggles, what new silliness had resulted from his engagement with the increasingly technological and savvy world. The Cohen recordings gave the same sense, but often positioned the listener as eavesdropper on his one-sided conversations with people he does not understand, and who do not understand him. The continuity between recitation practice in the home and recitations that one could play in the home was reinforced by the occasional inclusion with early records of transcripts for following along or for "reading along," but also for replication by the listener in his turn after the record had ended.[105] Early talking records thus worked as an extension of the recitation piece, providing both a text to recite and a recorded example of how to recite it.

Mark Morrison has argued that the recitation anthology as a platform for reading in the family circle enabled a mode of performance that was "safe from the shadowy and disreputable theaters" usually associated with "deception and duplicity," transforming public theatricals into a private drama of acculturation. His description of the popular recitation book as domesticated theatre is equally applicable to the early talking record, which brought the voices of the stage, sometimes by one mimetic remove, into the drawing room.[106] The image of the theatre brought into the home in miniaturized form was a popular trope in early advertisements and window displays for the phonograph and gramophone as entertainment media. Cal Stewart's works are an explicit example of the relationship among stage performance, recitation recordings and home elocution, since his stories were published as *Uncle Josh's Punkin' Center Stories* (all of them transcripts of records he had made) even as he continued to write and record new ones, and to perform them on the stage before live audiences. Monologues delivered by foreshortened, caricatured personages worked to enact the confluence between the regional, specific, homey locale, the ubiquitous public stage, and the even more ubiquitous talking record brought home to play on the parlor phonograph or gramophone. This movement between stage, record, and home (and school) would become an important formula for the conception and development of literary recordings for use in educational programs developed by record companies.

The sound-recorded monologue occupies a space between the vaudeville or music hall stage and the domestic fireside or parlor. It is interesting to speculate about the audiences for these recordings, whether they laughed at the ethnic characters or, in a more familiar way, laughed with them—or both. Gavin Jones has asked a similar question about vaudeville audiences of the period, speculating that "ethnic groups within larger theater audiences must have actively laughed at greenhorn stage types as a means to establish their own status in mainstream society."[107] An analogous process of distancing from the dialectical stereotype seems likely as a scenario of reception for such recordings, although different recordings seem to offer different options of positioning between the normative figure and the other.[108]

At times we can hear parameters for an appropriate response to the speaker integrated into the sketch and sound of the recording itself. For example, a Monroe Silver recording, **"Cohen on His Honeymoon,"** provides an audible and occasionally responsive "American"-voiced bystander within the sketch suggesting how we are supposed to laugh in a friendly way at Cohen, who is depicted as one who is *aware* of the comic errors in his speech, and so is not a greenhorn Jew after all, but someone playing a greenhorn Jew with self-conscious comic effect, and with the benefit of one generational remove, one assimilationist step away from Cohen's accent. The speaker in this recording seems conscious of what it means to speak in Jewish dialect, and of how to speak it. It also seems to understand the social significance of *not* speaking in that way.[109] The presence of a "standard" American friend, laughing *with* Cohen at Cohen's errors in speech suggests that it is fine to laugh at an American "playing" the Jew with a shrewd, punning sense of the English language. Without such a framing device, the corruption worked by the Jewish speaker on standard English would not be presented as funny but as disquieting in the Jamesian sense.

Consider a similar example in greater detail. The following is a transcribed excerpt from an early recording of **"Cohen on the Telephone"** as performed by Joe Hayman and which became "a great hit in the popular field" for Columbia Records in 1913, the first in a popular series of "Cohen" recordings that he made in the early nineteen-teens.[110] The same script was used by Monroe Silver and Herbert Samuel Berliner in later recordings of this recitation piece. My emphases have been added to underscore the double entendres:

> I rang up to tell you that I'm your *tenant Cohen*. I say I'm your tenant, Cohen. I ain't *goin'*, I'm stoppin' here. I'm your tenant Cohen—Not *lieutenant* Cohen. I vant to tell you thet last night the vind came and blow down the shutter outside my house. And I vant you to send—I say last night de vind came—De vind, not the devil, the vind. The vind. You know vat shhshhshh [wind sound], like that. Vell that blew my shutter down. Outside my house. And I vant you—I say it blew the shutter out. The *shutter*. No, I didn't say *shut up*. . . . I vant you to send the karpenteh *to mend the shutter*. Not a *tremendous shudder*. . . . I vant you to send the karpenteh . . . the voikman...*to mend* the shutter. . . . Not *two men*, no, vun man, to mend . . . the damedge, the *damaged* shutter. . . . I ain't swearing at you, I'm only telling you. Are you there?[111]

In this Cohen recording, the miscomprehensions due to accent (*"tenant Cohen* heard as *"goin'"/"lieutenant* Cohen"; *"de vind"* heard as "devil"; *"shutter"* heard as *"shut up"*; *"to mend* the shutter" heard as *"tremendous shudder"/"two men"*; *"the damedge. . .* shutter" heard as *"damned* shutter") are clearly sounded out for the listener in a manner that suggests the need for a general translation or explanation of the corruption that is being performed. And yet, through the none-too-subtle double entendres, a lesson about what can be done to words by a speaker also comes through. The performance reveals a complete awareness of vocal performance as an acculturating practice and, at the same time, a sense of the performer's imperviousness to the corrupting effects of the ethnic transfiguration of language. As Sander Gilman has noted, the Yiddishization of certain English words (saying *vindas* instead of the Yiddish word *fensters*) were comprehensible only to people in the Diaspora. Such diasporic Yiddishizations presented the speaker as one who was "both in a society and in transition into a society."[112] A recording artist rendering dialect in this way enacts a speaker who can confidently perform such cultural transition from an already firmly established position within that society.

The repertoire of recitation texts and spoken recordings invited listeners and reciters to experience the potential mutability of the speaking subject through the practice and heard performance of convincingly distinct voices by a single speaker, in this way challenging the assumption of identity as a fixed and irrevocably embodied phenomenon, and suggesting opportunities for social mobility. These same recordings also reinforced specific vocal characteristics as othering ethnic stereotypes. There is no single account that explains the impact of such recordings and recitation pieces in all cases. A vaudeville performer and recording artist like the Scotsman Harry Lauder performed imitations of Scottish characters types that were widely received as "offering a reassuringly 'natur-ral' depiction of Scottishness" and inspired already assimilated Scottish Americans to come out and openly claim their Scottish ethnic heritage,[113] whereas Joe Weber's and Lew Fields's Yiddish-inflected Dutch dialect acts were recognized by audiences "as the embodiment of the immigrant Everyman, and not of any particular ethnic group."[114]

Len Spencer's 1904/5 Edison recording **"What I Heard at the Vaudeville"** captures the complexity of audience positioning within the reception triangle of public stage, home recitation and "talking record" as the recording presents Spencer imitating "The Cardinal, America's popular dialect comedian, Mr. Gus Williams," reciting one of his own dialect compositions, "Only a Lock of Hair," with "orchestral embellishment."[115] The recording is numerous things at once: a staged vaudeville performance (and thus a kind of descriptive record), a mimicry record (in which Spencer mimics Williams who is in turn mimicking a Dutch-German ethnic character of his own composition), and a recorded emulation of a public performance of the kind of recitation piece that the record's listeners might have purchased for home recitation use in one of Williams's numerous, published recitation anthologies, such as Gus Williams' Fireside Recitations (1881) and Gus Williams' Standard Recitations (1882).[116] The poem is presented as an "emotional" nostalgia piece (calling for "shiver" music from the orchestra) until the final line where it shifts from serious to comical ("serio-comic" being a common category used to describe many of the pieces in Williams's recitation compilations). As a descriptive recording, it seems conscious of itself as a phonogenic emulation of a live performance genre (in this case, a staged, sonic reproduction of "what I heard at the Vaudeville"). As a mimicry record, it raises questions about whether Spencer is playing the role of an ethnic (Yiddish-sounding) character of his own devising in the act of imitating the vaudeville performance of Gus Williams as evidence of what he has heard, or whether he is supposed to be in character as Williams on stage from the moment he speaks in accent. The first reading would suggest a record that performs an ethnic audience member performing his memory of a vaudeville ethnic character performance (and thus, functions as a performance of audience reception), whereas the second suggests a more direct mimetic reproduction of a vaudeville performance on record as it happened. Precisely how any given early listener would have heard this recording depended on a wide variety of mitigating factors pertaining to reading, private and public performance, imitation, genre, ethnic identity and cultural positioning that suggest numerous possible protocols for the reception and use of a two-minute talking record.

Early spoken recording artists were not identified simply as specialists in the ethnic personae that they performed but as versatile elocutionists capable of inhabiting different voices at will. Russell Hunting may have become famous for his development of the phonographic persona Casey the Irishman in sketches that would be reproduced by other artists (including Joseph Gannon, Jim White, John Kaiser, and George Graham), but he got his start in the Boston theatre, recorded several poetry recitations during the course of his career, and was sometimes explicitly identified as an "elocutionist" on record labels.[117] An article published in *The Talking Machine World* (October 1917) captures this range of capacities as manifest in a performance he gave at a Pathé jobbers convention: "One of the pleasing events of the evening was the appearance of Russell Hunting, of 'Casey' fame. Mr. Hunting . . . gave several of his popular 'Casey' numbers in his inimitable fashion and then surprised his audience with a dramatic poem which brought back recollections [of] when he was a prominent figure in Shakespearean productions."[118]

Len Spencer, who built his early reputation as a recording artist by interpreting what record companies described as "Negro" material, also recorded the Edison promotion piece "I am the Edison Phonograph" discussed above, speeches by famous historical figures such as "Lincoln's Speech at Gettysburg" (1902), and scenes dramatized from novels such as "Uncle Tom's Cabin (Flogging Scene)" (1904), in which he performs the voices of both Uncle Tom and Simon Legree, and the transformation scene from Dr. Jekyll and Mr. Hyde (in imitation of the scene as it was performed on stage by the actor Richard Mansfield).[119] John Terrell performed deadpan comic routines in a straight "American" voice, but also made Casey recordings, including "A Few Words in Regard to Drinking" and "Casey's Address to the G.A.R." (both n.d.).[120] George Graham's "Colored Preacher," a sing-song delivery of a mock sermon infused with content that would have been insulting to a congregation, appeared in the same series as his "Auctioneer" recording (1900), both performances demonstrating Graham's virtuosity in fast, rhythmic reading, but within different voice-culture contexts.[121] Another recording by Graham, his **"Drama in One Act"** (1896) in which he does a girl's voice, an old man's voice, and a murderer's voice, switching between them seamlessly, displays a key selling point for many early talking records, that is, virtuosic monopolylogueism: the display of the reader's ability to perform multiple voices and sounds in one monologue.[122] Hunting, Spencer, and Graham were all well known for their innovations and skills in performing numerous sounds in a single recording. In fact, Hunting's reputation as a recording artist was established as early as 1891 for his ability to perform "highly dramatic representations . . . with the addition of imitations of railway whistles, bells, galloping of horses, and other sounds, brought to a wonderful degree of perfection."[123]

To replicate the sounds of animals and machines with the human voice brings us back to the illogical question, "What did the voice of the phonograph sound like?" and to the issues of neutrality, purity, and unlimited versatility that such a question evokes in the context of historical sound recording media and early spoken recordings. To mention one last example of a "mimicry" recording, Len Spencer announced at the opening of a 1918 recording made by the performers John Orren and Lillian Drew: "I take pleasure in introducing to you Orren and Drew, vaudeville's favorite mimics. The imitations produced in this record are made by the human voice alone, without the aid of any mechanical device whatsoever."[124] In so prefacing the recording, **"A Study in Mimicry—Vaudeville,"** Spencer not only proclaimed the power and versatility of the human voice with a salesman's "you won't believe your ears" pitch (and the imitations truly are remarkable), but also raised a significant point about verisimilitude and absorption that applies to spoken recordings in general. Implicit in Spencer's statement that the sounds of train whistles, wood saws, barnyard animals, and bird songs appearing on Orren and Drew's recording are produced "by the human voice alone" is the idea that even in such a sound-effects recording, the spoken recording's status as a skilled performance in naturalized mimetic articulation is preserved. The performance of "other" sounds and voices appealed to the listener's ability, as a consumer of culture and as a judge of reality in the context of mimetic performance, to discern the authenticity of a sound.[125] These recorded vocal imitations of bells and whistles represent a human's attempt to replicate nonspeech sounds with a fidelity equaling the phonograph's "indexical" power. The speaker who can mimic a range of sounds and voices convincingly may then underscore the underlying neutrality of his own voice, just as the phonograph's voice was, according to one promotional fantasy, inherently clean. In another sense, though, the technical and cultural distinctions between mechanical replication and human mimicry are further underscored by such recordings, and come to evoke the idea of the phonograph's voice as an acousmatic figure we may try to reattach to historical objects and bodies acting within culturally informed historical contexts.

Reading versus Listening

I have stressed in this chapter the continuum that I believe existed between early spoken recordings and the reader/listener's own practice of recitation, in part to counter the common argument that the early phonograph was received as immediate and definitive of reality, and with the broader purpose of framing some of the key ideological and affective issues—voice, identity, authenticity, mimesis—that informed early spoken recordings, as well as private and public acts of recitation and character performance. My account has attributed to the listener a far greater degree of interactive agency than is commonly granted the "audiobook" consumer today. Many accounts of the talking book, from the moment of this format's introduction to the present, suggest that the mode of absorption resulting from reading as listening, as opposed to reading as deciphering symbols printed on a page, may entail a serious loss of agency on the part of the book reader. As Mladen Dolar has put it succinctly, according to one definition, "Listening entails obeying."[126] The danger of the talking book as it is often described by such critics is that it lulls one out of a true, thoughtful, and empowering literary culture that is identified with print; that it lulls us out of controlling what we absorb, and keeps us from stopping, thinking, and especially from *vocalizing* for ourselves.[127] Vocalization, in this silent sense, is understood as an act of critical interpretation that is built into the act of processing words on the page. These kinds of objections have been catalogued by Matthew Rubery in his rehearsal of complaints made against the "audiobook" in its more recent (post-1930s) manifestations, including claims that audiobook listening "is a passive activity" that does not demand "the same level of concentration as printed books" and removes the reader's control over pace thus disrupting the reader's reception of the work of literature.[128]

If we stick with the audible version of the complete (or only partially abridged) novel, for a moment, which is the main genre that falls under Rubery's definition of "audiobook," the question of vocalization during the reading process is inseparable from the fact of dramatic interpretation. This precedent was already in place in an explicit way in the earliest spoken recordings of narrative fiction, which usually were based on stage dramatizations of popular novels.[129] The spoken recording of the full novel (including narration and dialogue) necessarily entails a concrete "envoicing" narrator, where a printed text demands the reader to perform the vocalization of the text for herself. This act of solitary vocalization or reading is significant in most conceptions of literary experience, for the process of constructing the narrator's voice (let alone the voices of the characters who speak in the novel) is one of the primary values attributed to the act of reading literature; it is sometimes identified as "the main event of literature itself."[130] As Denis Donoghue remarks in *The Practice of Reading*: "the purpose of reading literature is to exercise or incite one's imagination; specifically, one's ability to imagine being different."[131] From this perspective, fiction helps to solve "the problem of other minds, the question of whether we can know anything of the inner lives of others."[132] In its print form, the novel answers that yes, we can. But in the most skeptical accounts of the modern, full-length talking book, the possibility of exercising this form of empathetic imagination is called into question.

In "traditional" print-focused literary criticism, the voice we conjure up for the text in our internal auditorium is identified as a crucial aspect of critical interpretation itself. It constitutes the meaning we find in the text and the subsequent arguments we generate in formulating hermeneutical analyses of literary works. In criticizing an aural text, the disparity between our own voice and that heard in the recording comes to the fore. This disparity between different manifestations of literature is dramatized for us in extravagantly useful ways by early spoken recordings. Consequently, literary recordings and the audiotexts they bring forth invite us to speculate on the vital effects of a literary work's materiality, and of its production in the act of reading.[133] The materiality I refer to includes the media formats and all that they imply for diverse forms of literary production and use, for sure, but it also includes other seemingly invisible aspects of the literary artifact, as well—for example, "the voice" of the work in the wide range of meanings, experiential, practical, and theoretical, that we attribute to the term, and the idea of literary interpretation itself. The literary work's materiality in the sense I am using it here encompasses the historically situated capacities of the generic form of an audiotext as mobilized within the capacity of the media format that defines its status as an artifact to perform, experience, research, and study.

Because the apparent proximity of literary recordings to print books coincides with so many material or "performative" differences between them, literary recordings reveal much about the modes of aesthetic experience produced by particular performative manifestations of literature, and serve to remind us that reading a text, a book, a work of literature is never a simple or quiet activity, but always a technologically informed and culturally rehearsed practice. In the case of early adaptations of fiction to sound—the topic we will turn to next—the problem of empathetic obstruction resulting from the reader's loss of her right to envoice the fictional narrator is not much of an issue, since there is neither space nor time for the subtly immersive techniques of narrative focalization on a three-minute cylinder or disc. The limited storage capacity of early recording media formats demanded the adaptation of audiotexts to generic forms that had limitations of their own, and performance techniques that suited these limitations in wider contexts of reception and consumption. In early adaptations of fiction to sound, instead of fully narrated fictions, we find techniques of character compression, scenic dramatization, auto-narration, transformative action, and, in all cases, techniques of mimetic reproduction that aimed to convince a listener with naturalizing vocal performance that the speaking character or personality was distinctively real, even if, in the case of the mimicry of characters from novels, they were born in fiction. In all cases we hear a sonic performance of the relationship between the particular occasion staged in the recorded selection, and the largely silent fictional world from which that audible occasion was produced.

2 CHARLES DICKENS IN THREE MINUTES OR LESS

Early Phonographic Fiction

THE AUDIOBOOK AS we now think of it was not a material possibility in the early days of sound recording, but this did not inhibit speculation about such literary media artifacts.[1] In 1878, soon after the introduction of the tinfoil phonograph, Edison forecast "a book of 40,000 words upon a single metal plate ten inches square" as "a strong probability," adding that such phonographic books "would preserve more than the mental emanations of the brain of the author; and, as a bequest to future generations, they would be unequaled."[2] Others who witnessed the early demonstrations of the phonograph remarked on the significance of the new medium for the form and delivery of the novel on record. For example, Julian Hawthorne, who covered the literary beat for the journal *America*, speculated in 1888 on how the novel might be "produced on a sort of cooperative principle" when delivered with the technology of Charles Sumner Tainter's graphophone (another manifestation of the wax-cylinder recording machine of the period). The novel, in this ideation, becomes a collaborative operation of audio production, with the author functioning as "a kind of stage manager and dramatist in one," directing specialized actors and elocutionists in the enactment of her or his novelistic scenes and narration.[3] Hawthorne's vision of the audible novel as a full-fledged dramatization with personations and eloquently delivered narration was still a futuristic fantasy in 1888. Edison may have dreamed about having a novel in its entirety (he is said to have referred to Dickens's *Nicholas Nickleby* as his example) on a compact audio record, but it was not until the 1930s, under the initiative of the Library of Congress Books for the Adult Blind project, that books the length of Victorian novels were transferred into the medium of sound.[4] And even then, when Victor Hugo's *Les Misérables* was produced in talking-book format on records that played at 331/3 rpm—much slower than the then commercial standard of 78 rpm—it still ran to an unwieldy 104 double-faced disks.[5] The Edison cylinder and Victor flat disc record circa 1900 had limited affordances for the presentation of the novel as a genre.

This chapter examines some of the earliest adaptations of Victorian literary fiction into sound and focuses in particular on two extended examples that are useful for understanding how early spoken recordings were shaped by precipitant precedent media and forms of literary expression, and how audio technologies of the early twentieth century were imagined for use in teaching "new" kinds of literary experience. The story of early adaptations of Victorian fiction into sound introduces a variety of diverging plot-lines about remediation, all of which can be understood to display the twin logics of immediacy and hypermediacy—transparency and opacity—outlined by Jay Bolter and Richard Grusin, wherein "immediacy dictates that the medium should disappear and leave us in the presence of the thing represented" and yet simultaneously demands that the user take pleasure in the act of mediation by calling attention to the specificity of the new media form in itself and in relation to other media.[6] The oscillation between immediacy and hypermediacy provides clues about how a new medium refashions older and other contemporary media, since the promise of "more immediate or authentic experience . . . inevitably leads us to become aware of the new medium as a medium." Immediacy thus leads to hypermediacy.[7]

Sound-recording technology was marketed for its immediacy (among many other things) from the day it was introduced. The phonographic book was represented as a medium that would allow authors to communicate to future audiences with powerful immediacy and presence.[8] The novelty of the medium lay in its capacity to store and reactivate the effects of authorial presence and literary immersion from one historical moment to another, rather than in the effect of vocalized authorial presence, itself. The voice of the author and storyteller was made available to the Victorian reading public "with all the living reality of the present moment," repeatedly, in the form of "At Home" theatricals and public readings for decades prior to the existence of a talking machine.[9] Any account of the new media claim for an invention like the phonograph—that it supersedes the print-based book in its delivery of vocal presence—must consider the Victorian book not as a silent repository of text awaiting an automated sounding technology but as the locus of what Ivan Kreilkamp refers to as Victorian "performative, mass reading," understood as "a mode of literary consumption that is intersubjective, often occurring communally; vocal rather than silent; productive and active rather than passive and receptive; often occurring in public spaces rather than interior, domestic ones; and—perhaps most significantly—somatically responsive, involving a performance or display of physical reaction."[10]

With this conception of reading in mind, Edison's bequest might seem somewhat unidirectional and somatically delimited; it might sound inflexible, even a little tinny. It is precisely in such qualitative distinctions between mediated modes of literary expression that we can articulate a historicized conception of a medium's relationship with a particular art form. To tell the story of early phonographic novels, both as they were imagined and as they existed, we need to consider the kinds of literary practice that informed them, as well as the literary works that furnished them with content to replay. In doing so, we come to understand the import and function of a medium and of the literary forms it can afford. John Guillory has made this point in a statement that serves to elucidate Bolter and Grusin's argument about hypermediacy: "It is much easier to see what a medium does—the possibilities inherent in the material form of an art—when the same expressive or communicative contents are transposed from one medium to another. Remediation makes the medium as such *visible*."[11]

Early spoken recordings were produced according to diverse models of generic adaptation, aesthetic and social value, display, dissemination, use, and experience. To recall Bauman's terms, the way in which a recorded speech was entextualized, recontextualized, and performed had a significant impact on how it was understood and received by an audience. Approaching recorded performances for their "dynamics of recontextualization" reveals how specific early adaptations of Victorian novels into sound signified differently from each other.[12] If you compare, for example, Len Spencer's recordings made for Columbia Records in 1904 of "The Transformation Scene" and **"The Flogging Scene"** (based on *The Strange Case of Dr. Jekyll and Mr. Hyde* and *Uncle Tom's Cabin*, respectively), "Svengali Mesmerizes Trilby," as recorded by Herbert Beerbohm Tree for The Gramophone Company (later HMV) in 1906, and the numerous Dickens recordings made by Bransby Williams (between 1905 and 1948 for Edison, HMV, Columbia and other companies) and William Sterling Battis (for Victor in 1916), you encounter three different models of recontextualization and remediation.[13]

Spencer's "The Transformation Scene" and "The Flogging Scene" recordings, dramatizations from popular novels, stand as the recordings of a seasoned phonograph performer playing roles on record that he had never played on the stage. It might be more relevant to understand Spencer's recording of this transformation scene (which entails the performance of multiple character voices) in relation to his fame as a master mimic and monopolyloguist, than as a recording from a stage adaptation of R. L. Stevenson's novella. This early adaptation of fiction into sound might be more usefully approached by considering phonographic reading formats than with reference to traditional literary genres. Spencer's "literary" recording may well have been more recognizable as a descriptive sketch than as a fictional adaptation.

The meaning of "descriptive" as an audiotextual format, while wide-reaching, referred to a range of expected sonic elements, including the performance of multiple voices (sometimes by a single speaker) often of different speech dialects, enacting some kind of socially inflected scene (an auction, a journey, an encounter, a debate), with sound effects that both informed and were identifiable because of the framing scene, all delivered in a manner that conveyed spatial movement and depth through the strategic uses of sonic amplitude. Such records might have explicit verbal cues to situate the listener in the scene, or, might rely on sound effects to do that work for the recording. Spencer's recording of **"The Transformation Scene from Dr. Jekyll and Mr. Hyde"** (1904/1908)[14] opens with an announcement of the title (by Spencer, in a clear "American voice") and then moves quickly into the refined Scottish brogue of Jekyll setting the scene with explicit contextualizing information, a sort of CliffsNotes leading up to the moment of transformation that will be portrayed in the recording. Here is a transcript of the recording in its entirety:

> Jekyll: I have ransacked London in vain for the drug which has been the cause of all my misery. Half an hour after I have taken the last drop, [organ music] I shall sink into the terrible [unintelligible]. This, then, is the last time Henry Jekyll can see his own face, or think his own thoughts. I am losing my original self and becoming more and more incorporated with my worse nature. I go to sleep as Jekyll and wake up as Hyde. Will I die on the gallows, or will I have the courage to take this poison? What's this I feel? The demon is coming. Hyde is– Ah, no, not yet, thank God. [Knocking.] What's that? That way all arrive. Can it be my house steward? [Chiming bells.] Ah, those chimes. They remind me of that terrible night when, transformed as I was into that fiend incarnate Hyde, I murdered the father of the woman I loved. [Organ music.] Ah, I must pray—Pray God to keep away the demons. Ah, God, look into my heart and forgive my sins. You were right. I was wrong. Ah, ah the fiend is coming. Yes. Hyde is here!
>
> Hyde: [Shrill throaty noises.] Stop that damned organ! The noise offends me ears! [Cackling laughter.] [Knocking.] They come for me! They're going to take me to the gallows! [High tempo organ music.] But I don't die on the gallows, oh no! [Cackling laughter.] I killed two people already. Here it goes for the third. Jekyll! Jekyll! I always told you I'd kill him. Ah, ah, aaooh [expiring cry].
>
> Poole: [Knocking.] Break in the Door! [Sound of door being broken open.]
>
> Utterson: Dr. Jekyll?! Why, it's Hyde. [Organ music.] Dead.

Accompanied by mood-setting organ music as in melodrama, bell chimes that evoke the distant past as well as the acoustical space of the dwelling where the scene takes place, sound effects of door knocking and battering, and three distinct voices in different accents (those of Hyde, Jekyll, and Utterson the Lawyer ordering Mr. Poole, the butler to break down the door), this recording, while clearly the rendering of a scene from a stage adaptation of Stevenson's novella, communicates all the elements that defined the "descriptive" audiotextual format in the context of early sound-recording culture. These generic elements of this particular kind of audiotext were developed to situate and render a concise series of events sonically. To make this point does not contradict the possible usefulness of the literary generic description of this recording as the dramatization of a work of fiction. But to apply that more traditional, print-oriented generic vocabulary does not fully capture the audiotextual format of the sonic artifact in question.

Tree's **"Svengali Mesmerizes Trilby" (1906)** recording, on the other hand, can be understood as an adaptation from George du Maurier's 1894 novel to Paul Potter's popular dramatization, in which Tree performed the role of Svengali to great acclaim.[15] The record was first advertised in the general HMV catalogue, and soon after listed in the *Records of Unique and Historical Interest* supplement to the general catalogue of 1910.[16] Other artists whose recordings were included in this later, special catalogue included Sarah Bernhardt, Enrico Caruso, Leo Tolstoy, and Lewis Waller. The catalogue was designed to demonstrate "a new role" for the gramophone, given that by 1910 it had "been established sufficiently long" to undertake "the preservation of the art of a past generation."[17] In effect, the Beerbohm Tree recording was presented, almost from its first release, as a sound memento of historical significance. It was sold as one among several of the roles to which Tree applied his distinctive genius, along with Hamlet's soliloquy on death, Falstaff's speech on honor, and Mark Antony's lament over the body of Julius Caesar, all of which were also recorded and released in that same year.

Listening to the recording itself, we hear that it was not the angelic singing voice of Trilby that was captured in the grooves of a ten-inch Black Label flat disc record but the "foreign"-accented voice of Svengali admiring the inside of Trilby's mouth, fantasizing out loud about how he will dominate the world by using Trilby as a vocal instrument through which to communicate his musical genius, and then mesmerizing her for the first time. The bulk of the recording presents a sample of Svengali's accent, which the novel describes as one that turns "a pretty language into an ugly one."[18] When Trilby's voice is briefly heard (possibly rendered by the actress Dorothea Baird, who played Trilby in the Potter production, but we can't know for sure), it is only her speaking voice, the voice of potential that Svengali is musically equipped to discover in her that we hear, and not the realized, ineffable voice of La Svengali singing under her master's influence—not the vocal equivalent of Svengali's cosmic piano. Considered in relation to the novel *Trilby* and its ubiquitous nostalgic impulses and themes, this recording represents the kind of memento that Taffy, The Laird, and Billee, the three musketeers of the brush who were infatuated with Trilby, would have loved to possess—a cylinder bearing the golden time when they were bohemian artists, when Trilby lived among them as some combination of mother, maid, and object of desire—to replay in the present. Or, more accurately, it represents the antithesis of such a souvenir, an anti-memento, insofar as it renders Svengali's voice in lieu of the more transcendent sounds associated with that lost time. The 1906 Gramophone Company recording based on *Trilby* seems in a way designed to resist its status as event by capitalizing on compiling and communicating the fixed social stereotype of Svengali's greedy, foreign-accented voice, rather than the protean voice of La Svengali as it is never fully captured in the text of the novel.

In many ways, the Beerbohm Tree recording is similar to the William Sterling Battis recordings based on minor characters from Dickens, in that it renders a paradigmatic event from du Maurier's story in a manner that is abstracting and particularizing at the same time. Because the monologue provides the most typical verbal and active elements of Svengali by condensing a selection of his verbal ticks from speeches throughout the novel, and by making the speech itself an act of mesmerism, the recording works simultaneously as an abstraction of Svengali, a condensation of all of his most material eccentricities, and a speech act that, in the context of the larger drama of *Trilby*, was at the source of the sublime and protean voice of La Svengali, which can never be described or heard.[19] In effect, this historical literary recording captures the inherent complexity (I am tempted to say impossibility) of the sound recording as a historical artifact. For all of our desire to capture the transcendent essence of past experience, to "preserve the art of a past generation," to capture the sound of the magic that was, what remains instead in this adaptation of fiction into sound, is a grotesque caricature in dialect.

The Dickens records made by Bransby Williams, and then by Williams's less famous epigone, William Sterling Battis, suggest further models of early phonographic literary adaptation and rendering. Williams's long legacy of Dickens adaptations reveals a variety of methods by which fictional character impersonation was calibrated to the affordances of the gramophone and the evolving market for talking records. And while Williams (after Dickens himself) may have been the original Dickens imitator—the better Dickens man, so to speak—Battis's story is compelling inasmuch as it relates to literary history and the newly mediated ways of teaching literature to students that gramophone companies worked to produce.

Talking records of different kinds were usually categorized together in record catalogues up until the second decade of the twentieth century when record companies began to develop their own education departments. These new education departments drew on the recordings in their company's back-list, commissioned new ones, and organized them all into separate "Educational Records" sections at the back of the regular monthly catalogues. Such educational sections began to appear around 1910 as single-page lists featuring a few dozen records, categorized according to the lower educational levels (kindergarten, primary grades, intermediate grades, grammar grades, high school) and with minimal instructions for use.[20] Then, as record companies began to identify schools as a strong potential market for records and record players, they developed more explicit pedagogical arguments for the use of sound recordings in the classroom, produced new records for this purpose, and published discrete education catalogues designed to serve as manuals with suggested listening programs for use by teachers.[21]

As the earliest audio adaptations drawn from works of fiction that were produced specifically for educational purposes, William Sterling Battis's Dickens records are thus a bridge between earlier conceptions of the "talking record"[22] as a novel form of popular entertainment and the later, also pedagogically motivated, category of the "literary recording." A key element of this historical transition from "talking record" to "literary recording" is the identification of the sound recording material with the printed book.[23] The production of Battis's Dickens records, and their inclusion in the Victor educational records catalogue, bring us one step closer in the history of spoken recordings to what we now call the audiobook, although with regard to form and format, they were still a long way apart. The Battis recordings also serve as a useful point of focus for speculation about the particular kind of literary adaptation, excerption, condensation, and rendering that resulted from the earliest recordings produced specifically for such pedagogical use. This is interesting in itself, but my own concern with the pedagogical context relates to the conceptual rationalization and material realization of a new kind of sound recording offered as both supplement to and surrogate for the printed book.

The story of Battis's recordings begins, of course, with Dickens himself, both as a novelist and as an adaptor and performer of his own work, but my discussion of them will move from the Lyceum Stage on which Battis made his reputation as a Dickens impersonator to the transformation of a popular form of public entertainment (with pedagogical motives) into a classroom instrument, with an early form of mechanically audible literature serving as what we now call educational technology, or ed tech. Chautauqua in America, music hall performances in England, record catalogues, actors' memoirs, education theory, and the technology of early sound recording are all involved, as is, with regard to Battis's own contribution, the Harold D. Smith Collection, a rich archive at the National Library of Canada.

Before moving on to the Victor Company's foreign-languages division, Harold D. Smith, a "jobber," or manager, at its offices in Camden, New Jersey, from 1913 to 1935, worked until the mid-1920s in the company's educational department, where he developed Victor's first comprehensive educational catalogue. The Harold D. Smith Collection, consisting of more than thirty boxes, filled with everything from recording ledgers, in-house publications, sales reports, Victor internal and dealer correspondence, advertising materials, pamphlets, and newspaper clippings to Smith's unpublished autobiography, reams of unused stationary, and half-used Victor-stamped pencils, allows us virtually to reconstruct Smith's Camden office, where the spirit of commercial strategy and literary enthusiasm led him to develop a vision of an educational program, using sound recordings, aimed both at selling gramophones and gramophone records and heightening students' experience of literature.

"The system of the fine arts yielded to a new system, the media," in the late nineteenth century, John Guillory remarks, noting that this concept developed over time and has been applied variously to mimesis, rhetoric, communication, instrumentality (means), mediation, and representation, among other things. The Bransby Williams and Battis Dickens recordings are an especially rich field of media study, in which old and new rhetorical concepts converged, and print mediated sound as much as sound remediated print.[24]

From Lyceum Stage...

Attendees of a Chautauqua gathering in 1907 would have waited under a huge circuit tent (capacity 4,000), camped out early for the main event at 8 p.m., when William Jennings Bryan, "the world's greatest orator" (the program announced) was scheduled to deliver his lecture, "The Old World and Its Ways." While waiting they may have payed intermittent attention to some of Bryan's opening acts: Dr. A. Grant Evans lecturing about the "Age of Atheism and Reviving Faith," then the Chautauqua Orchestra giving a brief concert, its third concert of the week since it had played once already on Saturday, prior to The Vitagraph Company's screening of its nine-minute film *A Modern Oliver Twist* (1906, directed by J. Stuart Blackton), and then again on Sunday before the Hon. J. N. Tillman, president of the University of Arkansas, delivered a lecture on the "Life and Personality of Jesus."[25] Still waiting for Bryan, they might have turned their attention to "A Most Humerous [sic] Entertainment of Literary Value" by a "Master of Interpretive Impersonation" and "Literary Life Portrayals"—an act that the program identifies as "Entertainment, 'Masterpieces from Dickens' [sic] by William Sterling Battis, impersonator and dramatic orator.'"[26]

Gazing at the stage, the audience would have seen a regular-looking fellow sit down at a dressing table, apply makeup, don a wig, and gradually, before their eyes, transform himself, first, into "A rough, kind hearted, noble-souled fisherman. Poor and ignorant, but possessing a refinement of thought and delicacy of feeling rare among any class of men" (Daniel Peggoty),[27] then into "a stoutish, middle-aged person in a brown coat and black tights and shoes, with no more hair upon his head than upon an egg" and who says in a distinctively loquacious manner that he finds himself under a "temporary embarrassment of a pecuniary nature" (Wilkins Micawber),[28] and, finally, into a squirmy character of cloying humility and irritating voice who makes great claims to being humble, but proves himself to be as snakelike as he sounds (Uriah Heep).

Following the performance, the audience might have agreed with the *Peoria* [Illinois] *Daily Star* that "Mr. Battis appears to his audience not as an impersonator, but as the real living character"; with the *Henderson* [Kentucky] *Journal* that "the people in the audience felt as if they were in the presence of characters in a Dickens story"; and with *The Lyceumite*'s report that "Mr. Battis has delivered something entirely new to the lyceum. . . . He does not suggest the characters—[rather] they are flesh and blood creations."[29] Having witnessed Battis's character impersonations from Dickens, they might have come away feeling they had just seen "one of the best posted, most thoroughly acquainted and most practical Dickens scholars in the lyceum."[30]

The precedent for an impersonator of Dickens characters like Battis goes back to Dickens himself. As the work of Philip Collins, Edwin Eigner, Malcom Andrews, Ivan Kreilkamp, and numerous others has shown, Dickens's fiction is fruitfully understood as an art of remediation from the moment it first appears in print, and even from a period that precedes print publication. For example, Eigner makes strong claims for the influence of the popular traveling pantomime theatricals Dickens experienced in his youth on the development of "Dickens' ultimate clown, Wilkins Micawber," a character that "eclipsed even Grimaldi's comic creation."[31] And in tracing the influence of the great early professional impersonator Charles Mathews on Dickens as both a writer and oral reader, Andrews notes Matthews's "extraordinary technique of impersonation," his "capacity almost to efface himself in the act of embodying one of his characters" as having contributed to Dickens's mode of creating character in his writing, and performing it in his readings.[32]

More specifically, these one-man performances displayed techniques for creating an intimate rapport between narrator and audience/reader, the constitution of fictional characters with signal character exaggeration, idiosyncratic dialects, speech styles and reiterated tag lines, the use of comic dramatic formulae associated with such theatre practitioners of the 1830s as John Poole and Richard Brinsley Peake, and, especially, the unique literary allure and performative power of the virtuoso monopolylogue.[33] Such performative and formulae-generating techniques characteristic of popular Victorian theatricals were transformed by Dickens into print and would, in turn, influence subsequent adaptations of his novels for public reading.

To the list of models Dickens inherited for his public readings, Philip Collins adds "that of the actor or elocutionist giving Shakespearean or other literary selections, and that of the author giving lectures or readings from his own work."[34] Collins identifies "The Victorian Soloist Tradition" as one context through which to approach Dickens as reader and then follows that discussion with another under the heading "The Performer and the Novelist," which rightly acknowledges that Dickens was more than just a soloist; he was an author reading to his public. As the *Illustrated London News* reported of Dickens's earliest performances, "Mr. Dickens has invented a new medium for amusing an English audience."[35] The novelty of this "new medium"—Charles Dickens reading aloud—seems to have been identified with the way these readings combined virtuosic performance, cultural codes of celebrity, and authorial intimacy. In performance, Dickens cultivated his own sense (and the tangible fact) of what he described as "that particular relation (personally affectionate and like no other man's) which subsists between me and the public," delivering close to five hundred readings from his work to large audiences in Britain, France, and the United States during his lifetime, [36] These readings represented a performative reinforcement of what Dickens worked to establish in other ways through apostrophe and other narrative techniques in his fiction and through his use of the periodicals *Household Words* and *All the Year Round* as platforms for exchange between author and reader. They enacted in theatre the "strength of a faultless sympathy" that George Gissing understood to be the key ingredient to Dickens's "supreme popularity."[37] In short, by functioning as the performative medium for his own fictional characters, Dickens theatricalized the function of reader as a figure for sentiment in circulation.[38] Or, to repurpose a phrase from Garrett Stewart, he functioned as a public figure for private absorption by enacting "an extroversion of the fictional inner life."[39]

In moving from written text to immersion in the performed character, the Dickens public reading might also be understood as the reverse or playback mode of Kreilkamp's description of Charles Dickens, the novelist, as voice recorder.[40] Kreilcamp makes a suggestive claim for the inscriptive medium of phonography, or shorthand, as a key to understanding the means by which Dickens delivered such qualities and techniques of oral utterance to the page. "What is characteristically and newly 'Victorian' about Dickens cannot be separated from what is phonographic in his writing: its urge to vocalize writing and to write voice," Kreilkamp says.[41] Dickens's shorthand skill and its connection to the facility with which he could render (or capture) vivid and immediately distinctive voices for his fictional characters is a familiar element of his biography. As a transcriptive model for writing characteristic voice into fiction, this version of the novelist as voice recorder informs subsequent reality claims made for Dickens's characters and may help explain the emergence of late Victorian Dickens impersonators even more than the precedent of Dickens's own public readings.

Bransby Williams, born the year in which Dickens died (1870), was the most significant one-man Dickens show immediately after Dickens. He became a star of the English music hall in the 1890s with an act that featured imitations of great stage actors of the day, including Henry Irving and Herbert Beerbohm Tree, and then pioneered the development of a repertoire of Dickens characters, which he played on the music hall stage and took on the road.[42] The impact of his work in the early rendering of literary works—whether on stage or through sound recordings and film work—was profound, and among his admirers was Charlie Chaplin who recalled seeing him perform Dickens on stage with the effect of "enlivening a young boy's interest in literature."[43] One would think that the extensive documentation of Dickens as public reader in periodicals like the *Illustrated London News* might have inspired his own Dickens shows, but Williams never mentions Dickens's own performances in the chapter of his memoir entitled "How I Became a Dickens Actor." Instead, Williams credits his career to a belief in versatility as the hallmark of great acting, an early admiration for "wonderful single-handed performer[s]" like Fred Macabe and Fleming Norton, a professional interest in comedic mimicry, and an early love of reading Dickens's novels.[44] It was during his early success as a comedic mimic that the idea of bringing Dickens to the stage arose in his mind:

> During this time I was always reading Dickens's works, and slowly but surely I began to realize what great living characters were all these people of his brain! No mere figures of straw, but real living personalities, who gradually became to the reader his very friends, so to speak. All their little idiosyncrasies, all their sayings and doings, their very temperaments, developed by their own words and actions, lifted then from lay figures in a book into human beings whom we felt were real friends. That is one of the reasons of Dickens's greatness: he has created men and women for us who are as real and living as any men and women who have walked the earth. And the idea seemed to come to me all at once, that if these characters were all this to me, they must also be as well known to the rest

of the world, and that being so, why not present them with their peculiarities, their pathos and humour and tragedy, in the flesh upon stage?[45]

I cite this passage at length because it is so typical of the language that was the rationale for all subsequent Dickens character impersonators, as well as the early Dickens character recordings. The focus now was not on a performance of the narrator or author in relation to his audience, or of Dickens himself, but on the corporeal realization of those immediate transcripts of "real living personalities" found in his fiction, with "their little idiosyncrasies," "sayings and doings," and "temperaments." A new representation of Dickens's power as a novelist was being formalized in Williams's performances. They were nothing less than enactments of the reader's experience of immersion in a feeling of intimate encounter with the characters who emerged from Dickens's brain.[46]

Williams began to make commercial recordings based on his live performances as early as 1905, when Edison released on cylinder a dialect piece entitled "'Is Pipe-Monologue" and his imitation of Sir Henry Irving in **"The Dream Scene from 'The Bells' (Leopold Lewis),"** followed by three Christmas-themed recordings (although all were made in July), "Christmas Eve in Old England—Descriptive," and two more derived from Dickens, one being "Pickwick Papers (Wardle's Christmas Party)" and another entitled, **"A Christmas Carol in Prose (Charles Dickens)— Scrooge's Awakening."** All three Christmas recordings featured a male quartet of carol singers.[47] In addition to over fifty non-Dickens recitation and speech recordings made between 1905 and 1928—including recitations of poems "The Charge of the Light Brigade (Alfred Lord Tennyson)," "The Green Eye of the Little Yellow God (Milton Hayes)," "How We Saved the Barge (Arthur Helliar)," a speech from Shakespeare, "Uncle Tom's Cabin—Death of Uncle Tom (H. B. Stowe)," impersonations such as "The Stage Doorkeeper," burlesque sketches, as in "The Showman," and children's stories like "The Three Little Pigs" and "Puss in Boots"—Williams recorded some fifteen distinct Dickens recordings during the same period, most of them character sketches (Captain Cuttle from *Dombey and Son*, Bill Sikes from *Oliver Twist*, Micawber from *David Copperfield*, etc.), and many of them rerecorded under different labels at different times.[48]

I would like to spend some more time before I return to the story of Battis, with the precedent example of Williams, important as it was, by considering three specimens of Dickens recordings that he made, two of which were based directly on his stage performances, which were done either as recitals or with full stage effects, and a third that seems to have been a phonographic spin-off from the success of his earlier recordings. Williams's first two Dickens recordings of 1905 seem to have been produced as part of a triad of Christmas-themed records, all of which take advantage of having a quartet, the Edison Carolers, in the studio. "A Christmas Carol in Prose (Charles Dickens)—Scrooge's Awakening," captures the third part of a three-part monologue that had become one of Williams's signature stage performance pieces, and matches closely, if not exactly, a later printed version of the monologue, suggesting that Williams did not extensively adapt or transform his performance texts for recording, but aimed to deliver a phonogenic reproduction of one part of the stage performance his record listeners might have witnessed and remembered.[49] The exaggerated use of direct self-narration deployed in Williams's monologue was well suited to the medium insofar as it fulfilled the requirements and generic expectations of the early descriptive record (minus extensive sound effects) by making the scene intelligible to a listener without the provision of visual cues. As the experienced recording artist Russell Hunting described the requirements for depicting a scene in an audio recording, "You must talk as though you were speaking to a blind man, who depends entirely upon sound unaided by sight."[50] Williams's fulfillment of this phonogenic requirement was not deliberately motivated by the context of record making but was already a feature of his dramatic mode of adapting Dickens's fiction for performance on the stage. While there are arguably a few minor additions or changes in Williams's recorded performance that might have been included to help his listener understand the situation and setting of the scene as heard—such as the explicit statement "I must have been asleep" and the addition of a piece of furniture ("me own table") to the verbalized stage set—the self-narrating "tell, don't show" method of the monologue, including occasional self-reference in the third person, works to provide most of the hints and cues required.

Here is a brief comparison of my transcript of the opening lines of Edison and Columbia recordings of "The Awakening" with the text of the third part of Williams's Scrooge monologue as printed in *My Sketches from Dickens*:

> [Edison Carol Singers male quartet singing "God Rest You Merry, Gentlemen"] Mercy! Mercy! Why, why, wha, w-what's this, what's this? *Eh –I must have been dreaming. I must have been asleep.* Asleep? Oh yes, this is me own chair, in which I fell asleep. It's me own room! Then it must have been a dream! Yes, a God-sent dream to save me from meself. May God and this merry Christmas time be thanked for the reformation that shall now begin with Ebenezer Scrooge. (**Edison 1911**; emphasis added)[51]

> [Male and female carolers.] Mercy! Mercy! Why, why, wha, w-what's this? *Why I-I-I-I must have been asleep.* Th-tha-tha-tha-that's me own chair, in which I fell asleep. *It's me own table.* It's me own room! Then the time before me is me own wherein to make amends. A dream, a God-sent dream to save me from meself. May God and this merry Christmas time be thanked for the reformation that shall now begin with Ebenezer Scrooge. (**Columbia 1912**; emphasis added)[52]

> *(Slips out of chair on to knees on floor—continuing the cry for "Mercy!" All lights go up to suggest morning. He is then bewildered and scrambles to his feet and gazes round the room)* Why, what's this? This is my own room—my own chair in which I fell asleep—a dream! A dream! Thank God the time before me is my own wherein to make amends. May God and this Merry Christmas time be thanked for the reformation that shall now begin with Ebenezer Scrooge.[53]

In addition to the tendency of Williams's text and audiotexts to speak what Scrooge feels and acts, a good part of the situating information of the sketch is delivered through Williams's manner of vocal performance. From the opening cries of "Mercy!" articulated with desperate prolongation, the cackling laughter that erupts with his realization that he has not missed Christmas Day, to the speaking of the multiple voices of his conscience as he talks to himself aloud about his coming reformation, his performance of the voice of the public's opinion of him prior to his awakening, to the solemnly buoyant repetition of Tiny Tim's Christmas blessing at the end of the monologue, it is the explicit affective work of Williams's voice, combined with his specific technique of auto-narration—comprised of a generic composite of monologue, soliloquy, and characteristics of a dramatic aside—that render this recording phonogenic within the expectations of an early spoken recording. As an early spoken recording, "The Awakening" could have been identified with several genres, including dramatic recital, descriptive (scene), and celebrity recording.

This penultimate scene of Scrooge's moral progress from miserly curmudgeon to empathetic philanthropist was first recorded as a stand-alone cylinder record, and, as such, it would have been typical of recordings based on fictional sources from this period in focusing on a single scene of transformation, in this case, of moral awakening. But with his Columbia Scrooge recordings of 1912, Williams pursued the moral narrative arc of his longer monologue in a three-part series that was the first attempt in the medium of recorded sound to adapt a published fictional narrative beyond the three-to-four minute limits of the single record format.

As he had developed it for the music hall stage, Williams's adaptation hinged on the performance of three distinct affective stations for the character of Scrooge, each one functioning as a discrete character performance unto itself. As he describes the idea of these stages of transformation in his "Introduction" to My Sketches from Dickens: "In 'Scrooge' (which can be done as a recital) there is first the idea of the man—endeavouring to show the hard faced, bitter old miser before his dream, the horror and fear during the dream, and then the great change in face, body and voice, etc., after the dream; in fact, the contrast to the opening should be a beaming, merry old gentleman."[54] Not quite a full-fledged audiobook, the set of Columbia records based on the complete "Scrooge" monologue, titled according to the transformative sequence that hinges on the morally illuminating ghostly visits—"Before the Dream," "The Dream," and "The Awakening"—converts the affective illustration of moral progress, so pronounced in the visual, staged version of the monologue, into a depiction that sounds the transformation in Scrooge's voice and, at the same time, explicitly narrates the moral lesson of the affective sounding that is heard. As with the original stage monologue, the recordings were presented as intensified affective and didactic exempla devised from Dickens's novella, a published text that haunts and informs the dramatized scenes as a more granular fictional fabric that contains the affective and moral message within it.

Neither excerpts nor summaries, Williams's stage monologues and sound recordings functioned as intensive enactments of the real feeling and message that a capable reader could find in Dickens's original text.

The weaving of intensely rendered affective speech with explicit didactic statement worked to reinforce the connection between the immersive and moral qualities of fiction. In this sense, the recordings function as audible renditions of presumed reader experience and understanding. So, explicit pronouncements concerning the didactic import of the story (from "The Dream" recording, in this case), such as "This spirit will show me what I may be if I do not reform" and "I am afraid to learn it [the name on the gravestone] but I must; I must for the lesson it will teach me," are reinforced by Scrooge's desperate, screaming, "No! No! I'll see no more. I've seen enough! Eh-No! Eh-No! [high-pitched screaming] MERCY! MERCY! Aaaah! Aaaah!"[55] Together, Williams's sequence of "Christmas Carol" records converted Dickens's fiction into a sonic morality fable that tells and screams in mutually reinforcing ways.

In 1908, Williams made another, single-sided HMV flat disc recording entitled **"A Christmas Carol—Bob Cratchit Telling of Scrooge (Dickens),"** probably because of a request to provide alternative Dickens content for another record label. On it Williams came up with a character speech delivered by Scrooge's abused clerk, Bob Cratchit, in a manner that refers directly to the Edison record "The Awakening," which was already in circulation. I have transcribed it thus:

Well, well upon my word. Wonders will never cease! *Fine thing*! [high-pitched]. I left my master, Ebenezer Scrooge alone in his office on Christmas Eve, growling like an old bear. He said Christmas was all a Humbug, and I was a pickpocket because I wanted Christmas Day with my wife and my little ones. [Laughs.] And now, today, I went to business a few minutes late, expecting him to bite m'head off, instead of which he [unintelligible] on me, shook hands with me, and wished me a Merry Christmas and a Happy New Year. He laughed and he cried so that I though he'd gone mad. [Laughs.] And then he told me that he was an altered man. That he'd been a bad and wicked old man, but thanks to a dream he got his senses again. He made me sit down and drink his health! [Unintelligible] drinking old Scrooge in health. [Laughs.] He told me he fell asleep on Christmas Eve and three spirits appeared before him. The first was the Ghost of Christmas Past which showed him what a waste his life had been. Then, the Ghost of Christmas Present showed him a wicked, grasping old miser, alone, while everybody else was happy. Then, the Ghost of Christmas Yet to Come showed him if he did not alter he would die alone and uncared for. And others would spend his money and laugh at his memory. Then he awoke and he found it was all a dream. [Laughs.] And he believes it was sent as a warning to save him from himself. So now, the old miser Scrooge is dead, and a new Scrooge lives. [Laughs.] And he's begun well. He's begun by giving me a holiday. Imagine Scrooge giving me a holiday. [Laughs.] He's doubled me salary which is more wonderful still! And instead of cursing Christmas, he blesses it. What will my wife say, I wonder? She won't believe it. Well, well, the spirit of Christmas and charity and peace and good will have not visited old Scrooge in vain. Fancy old Scrooge no longer a miser, but benevolent and good; and he's going to care for the widows and the orphans. [Laughs.] Well I must run home now with the good news to my little wife and little ones, and they'll never believe it. I know they won't, bless 'em. And my poor little crippled Tiny Tim. He sends his message to all the world. A merry Christmas to all, a happy new year, and may God bless us, everyone.[56]

Here Cratchit renarrates the final paragraphs of Dickens's story, after Scrooge has wished him a merry Christmas "with an earnestness that could not be mistaken."[57] The conceit of address in the recording is peculiar, since it is a speech that does not have an explicit context to refer to in Dickens's *A Christmas Carol*. The high-pitched exclamation "Fine thing!" (see italics in the transcript above) might initially suggest his wife or one of his children responding to Cratchit's exclamation "Wonders will never cease!" and thus as the audience for the speech, but the content of the recording indicates that he is rushing home to tell his family the story we are hearing, and the high-pitched exclamation is understood as an eruption of Cratchit's own excitement from the encounter. The recording functions as a privileged, extemporaneous account of Cratchit's response to Scrooge's transformation, an "insider interview" with a character from a Dickens's story. The monologue provides a clear explication of the moral point and impact of Scrooge's awakening. reinforcing the moral of Williams's earlier recording. The record is also a form of self-conscious merchandising that does not simply adapt a scene from the original fiction to a new medium but adds content and offers new perspectives from fictional characters concerning scenes we are familiar with either from the published story or from Williams's own dramatized adaptations. From a contemporary perspective,

Cratchit's monologue may seem familiar to us due to its similarity with those off-scene, fourth-wall-breaking interviews with a character that we find in self-consciously filmed docu-comedies (like the TV series *The Office*), interviews in which a character shares his or her feelings about something that has just happened *within* the four walls of the mimetic drama. In this instance, Bob Cratchit would be taken into a side office at Scrooge and Marley and asked how he felt about the unexpected kindness Scrooge had just shown him, a scene of kindness that is also depicted in the final John Leech illustration to appear in the 1843 Chapman and Hall first edition of *A Christmas Carol*.[58] Not quite narrational diegesis, the Cratchett speech does summarize and color the dramatic events of the Scrooge story, but also adds new, supplementary mimetic content to a fiction that is no longer defined exclusively by a plot, but has begun to develop a narrative shape determined by a consumer's record collection.

The third specimen of a Bransby Williams Dickens recording is in many ways the most typical of his Dickens character sketches, in that it is an explicit attempt to bring a Dickens character to life "in the flesh upon stage," or, in the case of this **1906 Edison cylinder "Wilkins Micawber's Advice,"** in voice on record.[59] The aim in this recording is not to communicate a narrative arc or transformation (as in the "Scrooge" recordings), nor is it to add content to a familiar fiction, but simply to perform a fictional character (Micawber) in all of his discursive particularity as he might be overheard speaking in real life to another fictional character, David Copperfield. The addressee in this case is clear, since the monologue opens, "My dear young Copperfield," and the speech that follows is drawn primarily from chapter 12 of *David Copperfield*, with the integration of a phrase or two from elsewhere in the novel, some repetition of phrases, and a little filler to make the entire speech coherent. In short, it is a monologue made from the speech of a single scene (of advice-giving and departure) from the original novel.

Although Williams claimed to have invented the field in 1896, many other Dickens character impersonators followed, and, by 1909, Williams estimated that there were sixteen men and one woman who impersonated Dickens characters. What seems odd now is Williams's insistence on the originality of his art, and his dismissal of later Dickens impersonators as mere copyists of his original mode of imitation: "In 1896 I was the only actor presenting Dickens on the stage, now there are many imitators; and what is more strange, they are so indifferent to the fact that they are copyists, that in course of time they think they have been the originators themselves."[60] Williams identified the originality of his own impersonations with the way he adapted the texts of Dickens for performance and with the realization in performance of "what Dickens meant or what he intended to convey."[61] His adaptations of speeches by Scrooge and Bob Cratchit from *A Christmas Carol* can thus be understood as Williams's interpretation of the moral and affective meaning of Dickens's story, pursued with license, not only to encapsulate and render a scene in performance, but to elaborate, clarify, extrapolate, and invent. It was such qualities of his work as an interpreter of Dickens that Williams had in mind when he identified his own original-ity as compared to other impersonators. Among the supposed interlopers were Battis, Frank Speaight (whose 1909 Dickens season was advertised in *The Dickensian Magazine*),[62] and Mortimer Kaphan, who prepared his "realistic portrayals of Dickens' characters" for performance "in the theatre, drawing-room, society entertainments, colleges, clubs, seminaries, lodges and schools," and whose own recording of Micawber would be released by Pathé Records in 1917.[63]

While working on his educational catalogue for the Victor Talking Ma-chine Company, Harold D. Smith studied clippings concerning all these Dickens impersonators, Bransby Williams included, and the latter was also the model based on whom William Sterling Battis's own work as a Dickens impersonator was judged: "Mr. William Sterling Battis is doing for Dickens in America what Bransby Williams has done for the novelist in England," W. B. Matz remarked in the *Dickensian Magazine*.[64] Precisely what Battis was doing, and could do, for Dickens in America was of great interest to Smith as he formulated the rationale for teaching English literature with the aid of gramophone records.

. . . to Early Ed Tech

The listening programs developed by record companies during the 1910s–20s aimed to create a more powerful experience of literary works. Such programs embodied in rhetoric (if not in actual artifact) some of the key principles articulated by John Dewey in works like "My Pedagogic Creed" (1897) and *Schools of Tomorrow* (1915) concerning the importance of primary experience and social encounter in education. Dewey argued that an education must attend to the "vital impulse" in the child to learn by experience or risk being "'academic,' 'abstract,' in the bad sense of these words." He held that teaching with textbooks alone repressed "the impulses of the child toward action" and resulted in "an external presentation lacking meaning and purpose as far as the child is concerned."[65] Dewey's idea of "Learning by Doing" was translated by opportunistic gramophone companies, and by their educational department directors in particular, into a rationale for using new technologies like sound recording and film in the classroom as a means of teaching literature so that it could be delivered to students as lived experience. Harold Smith's *A New Correlation* (1915), which has a substantial pedagogical introduction, and notes and suggestions running throughout the record listings, argued that recitation and music recordings could be used, as he put it, to lift "a seemingly dry subject from the black and white of the printed page into the realm of human interest."[66] Smith's argument took the Deweyan tenet that "knowledge that is worthy of being called knowledge . . . is obtained only by participating intimately and actively in activities of social life"[67] and identified the gramophone with such active, social participation.[68] According to Smith, the gramophone allowed "the bond of sympathy" to be "established between [English students] and the character in [a] story."[69] Dewey's statement in Article Three of "My Pedagogic Creed" (1897)—that "the social life of the child is the basis of concentration, or correlation, in all his training or growth"—suggested a model for Smith's development of the "correlation" method of teaching literature through correlating books with musical selections and recitation recordings as a means of establishing an affective and sympathetic "social life" between students and the poem, play, or novel they were studying.[70] The speciousness of Smith's argument is my concern only insofar as it reveals the distinctiveness of the medium he was promoting. My main interest is in the nascent conception of literary interpretation that arose, and with the formal implications of these adaptations of Dickens onto audio disc.

An examination of pedagogical journals from the period reveals a concerted effort to realize an integration of the study of literature with "a real preparation for participating in a real society," a goal for students that could be accomplished only by "having them do real things."[71] As Elmer W. Smith put it in a 1917 address he gave to The National Council of Teachers of English, published in *The English Journal* under the title "The Advance Movement in English," the new "method has come to include real conversation, real speeches, real letters, real articles on real subjects, the reading of real literature; that is the literature that grows out of the real life they are living."[72] The movement Elmer Smith described was concerned with making the aesthetic sensibility that he believed could enrich the lives of all citizens in a democracy as accessible to as many people as possible. "We must win as many as we can to the life beautiful," he argued, by making "the bait tempting" through the implementation of "widely varying methods by which to teach expression, and a scheme of attractive activities, such as dramatization, journalism, speech-making, . . . and all the rest, all in the interest of popularizing and socializing English study."[73] The Victor Education program was on top of this new trend in education, as their advertisements in the back matter of key pedagogical journals demonstrate.

In the same issue that published Elmer W. Smith's address, alongside advertisements for textbooks such as Antoinette Knowles's *Oral English: Or, The Art of Speaking* (designed to teach "students how to prepare what is worth hearing"), and Cornelia Carhart Ward's *Manual for the Use of Pictures in the Teaching of English, Latin and Greek*, was a full-page advertisement asserting that "according to a report unanimously adopted by the National Council of English teachers The Victor [gramophone] and Victor Records are a necessary part of the equipment of every English classroom." The advertisement included a list of ten recorded recitations by William Sterling Battis, "to be introduced at the proper time during the recitation . . . to illustrate and vitalize the lesson."[74] Victor ran a full-page advertisement for its Christmas-themed teaching records in the December 1919 *Journal of Education*, including recordings of Christmas carols, Handel's *Messiah*, a Bible reading by Harry E. Humphrey, and a four-record series of "Scrooge" recordings by Battis, arranged according to the four ghostly visits (as opposed to Williams's before, during, and after trilogy), bettering Williams's three-record rendering of the Victorian novella by one flat-disc record.[75] Advertisements such as these continued to appear well into the 1920s.[76]

The selection of recorded "character impersonations from the leading novels of Charles Dickens" (as these recordings were described in a pamphlet about *Victrola's in the Schools*) represented a prototypical manifestation of Elmer Smith's idea of an attractive activity for the study of English, and of Harold Smith's idea of marketing the gramophone as social experience in the classroom, through the synecdochal concentration of lengthy narratives into refracted personations of minor characters.[77] It was an approach that stood in interesting contrast to the Hepworth Company's film *David Copperfield* (directed by Thomas Bentley, 1913), which was advertised as "an immortalized visualization of Dickens's masterpiece"[78] and, as Joss Marsh notes, "set British film on a long and fruitful course of preoccupation with production design"[79]—that is, with reproducing the world and setting of Dickens in all its elaborate material detail, as opposed to the people of Dickens in all their essential, characteristic traits.

One elocutionary model informing these Dickens recordings was what the late Victorian natural elocutionist Samuel Silas Curry referred to as the "dramatic instinct" in the oral performance of literature, which he associated in his 1896 book *Imagination and Dramatic Instinct* with insight into and the sympathetic assimilation of a literary character.[80] Such sympathetic characterological absorption, realized through an act of oral performance, was a form of literary interpretation, he argued. It was precisely this kind of interpretive work that Williams identified as the source of his originality, and that informed *The Platform* magazine's identification of Battis as a Dickens scholar.[81] The primary difference between performing this active mode of literary interpretation and the experience of listening to it being done in one of Battis's Dickens recordings was that the model of engagement in the latter was not one of sympathetic immersion with the speaker (an "assimilation of the character" of Uriah Heep or Micawber)[82] but of inhabiting the invisible space of David Copperfield (the narrator) as the minor character addresses him. The listener is positioned as the recipient of characters observed and heard, but without the responsive capacity that a narrator possesses simply as a result of his ability to narrate.

The Dickens recordings Battis made for Smith—the only recordings in the Victor catalogue based on a novel (all the other recordings were either of poems or scenes from plays)—were simultaneously a more blatant and more

e010788099

Figure 4. Photograph of Victrola used in classroom teaching. Victor Record Co., *The Victrola in the Schools*. Brochure, 1918. Library and Archives Canada, Harold D. Smith fonds, MUS 113, vol. 3, file 85.

estranged version of Curry's conception of literary interpretation. They were more blatant because the characters that Battis (and other contemporary Dickens impersonators) "interpret"—all minor characters—came already foreshortened, pre-processed, and dolloped into their distinctive molds, in which the extremity of their attitudes and the liquidity of their motives had hardened into a "substantive physical phenomenon."[83] They came with the physiognomic traits and linguistic tics that had rendered them "over-significant" in relation to the protagonists of the novels from which they emerged seemingly alive.[84] They were more estranged because the listener was disingenuously positioned in the space of interlocutor, but, like Ebenezer Scrooge in audience with his younger self (only without the visuals), the listener could not respond or evoke a response from the speaker. So, while the recordings may have been marketed as providing a more immediate, immersive, "real," and socially profound experience of a fictional character, the fixed action pattern of the Victor record, the fact that it turned in one direction at the right speed and that its grooves were uniformly spaced to play only one set of audible vibrations again and again—betrayed its inflexible materiality as a medium. The same might be said of the fact that these records based on Dickens novels were short, only about three minutes' long.

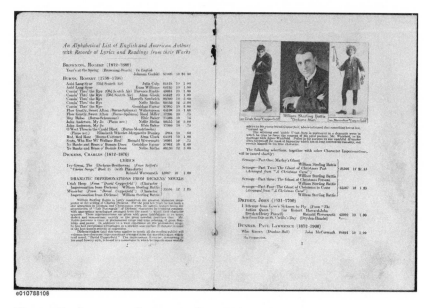

e010788108

Figure 5. Catalogue pages depicting William Sterling Battis "Dickens Man" recordings. *Victor Records Suitable for Use in the Teaching of English Literature*. 1916. Library and Archives Canada, Harold D. Smith fonds, MUS 113, vol. 9, file 253.

While the original suggestion of intimate encounter with "real" Dickens characters—with the suggestion of analogy to Dickens's own public readings—were embedded in the Battis Dickens recordings produced by Harold Smith, formally these records are altogether different from the texts Dickens prepared for reading. Dickens's performances generally lasted three hours rather than three minutes. Further, when Dickens prepared his texts for public reading, he usually did not "introduce any substantial new material, nor did he often change the order in which episodes had occurred in the original novel or story." Even in the case of an exception, such as the changes he made to *David Copperfield* in preparation for performance, which involved an atypical amount of "condensation and rearrangement, conflating into one episode passages from various chapters, raiding various chapters for happy phrases or speeches (by the Micawbers, for instance), and drastically reducing the length of the narrative retained," this abridgment was still designed for a two-hour reading as opposed to a three-minute recitation.[85] As Smith worked with Battis to develop these recordings, the primary issue that arose in their correspondence was compression—how to bring out the essence of the character in a recorded monologue of no more than three minutes in duration. Battis worried about "how it will be . . . difficult to reduce" his monologues and what may be lost if they "attempt to cut too much."[86] But Smith was adamant, and the result was a character collage consisting of the key sentences and tag lines—the most markedly identifiable idiosyncrasies of speech—that best represented the "person" of a minor character from across a Dickens novel. Although J. Hillis Miller once noted that "it is impossible to give appropriate space to Micawber," expansive space was precisely what Smith and Battis did not have available to them in their project of adapting this character to a 1916 Victor flat disc record.[87] The medium's limitations shaped a tightly woven, discursive audiotextual collage. More than simple excerption, the Battis recording was an engagement with the constraints of the Victor twelve-inch disc in the form of an intensive selection of the most typically particular (a paradoxical formulation, I know) speech acts of a Dickens character.[88]

The label of **Battis's Micawber recording**—the B-side to his performance of Uriah Heep—describes it as a "Character impersonation from Dickens: Micawber (from 'David Copperfield')."[89] While beginning in a mode of address similar to the recorded monologue as performed by Bransby Williams (a record that was no doubt one precedent model), Battis's monologue consisted of sentence fragments (and the rare complete sentence) procured from at least five separate chapters (36, 35, 12, 41, and 11) of David Copperfield (whereas Williams's monologue was drawn mainly from two pages in one chapter of the novel). These passages in Battis's monologue were reassembled without regard to the narrative chronology of their appearance in the novel and were grafted onto other passages that are sometimes paraphrases of quotations from the novel and sometimes the product of Battis's own sense of what Micawber should say. These discursive fragments (each in its own way characteristic of Micawber's distinctive vocabulary, syntax, and speech patterns as they appear in the novel) were then strung together as if Micawber were speaking a unified monologue in real time. It is the bullion-cube method of character impersonation, packing the already salty, potent flavors of a minor character's speech into a neat, performable package.

The most explicitly identifiable occasion for this collaged Micawber discourse as compiled by Battis is Micawber's imminent embarcation on the study of the law (through the influence of Uriah Heep). However, the more general sense of occasion that arises from such discursive grafting is simply that of departure in any one of the various instances of leave-taking that give Micawber occasion to speak in Dickens's novel: departure for the debtor's prison, departure for Plymouth (where Mrs. Micawber's family lives), departure for Canterbury (to work for Uriah Heep), departure for Australia to begin a new life. The occasion of the speech in this contrived monologue is both particular and general, just as Micawber's character as manifest in his eccentric manner of speaking is simultaneously compressed and verbose. Insofar as the monologue functions as both an abstraction of Micawber and a condensation of the verbal eccentricities that make him a distinctive literary representation of an imagined human being, it can be seen as the materialization of a typical Dickensian minor character, already caricatured because of its constriction to an extremely reduced space, which emerges out of this delimiting flatness as distinctively singular.[90] This condensation is imposed on a character who already resembled an impersonator's performance when originally fixed into print by Dickens, if not even before that, as a pre-Dickensian iteration, in the monologues of the impersonator Charles Matthews.

The recording medium achieved the illusion of neutrality by erasure—its own limitations and the generic nature of the occasion combining to erase discursive condensation—and by putting the listener in the position of interlocutor. Automation was a third strategy. From the beginning, sound recording was presented as the automation of writing, thus supposedly bypassing (actually concealing) the fact and process of production. Kreilkamp's account of the phonographic identity of Dickens the novelist as voice recorder explains the cultural logic of such automation as it relates to the medium of shorthand. In the case of these early Dickens-character recordings (and as manifest in the rhetoric surrounding the marketing of early sound recordings in general), we are presented with the automation of voice capture *as if* the voice that has been captured is itself the voice first heard in Dickens's head, written by Dickens on the page, read by Dickens live to an audience, and so forth. In short, the rhetoric of automation attributed to the technology of sound recording worked to instantiate the fictional act that had been recorded as a kind of immediate rendering of the fictional imaginary. Harold Smith's interest in Battis's Dickens character impersonations for his catalogue—which otherwise consisted only of poetry and drama recordings—was based on this sense that the major achievement of Dickens as a novelist could be grasped in the sharp dints and expressive singularities of his most paradigmatic minor characters and delivered within the limited format offered by sound recording in 1916.

Like the modern-day MP3 file format, which models human hearing so that it can remove as much audio information as possible and still trick the ear into believing that it hears a sound with high fidelity to its original source, William Sterling Battis's Dickens recordings are strategically patchy constructions made of discursive bits webbed together piecemeal in a syntactical structure that hides the gaping holes and implies the delivery of a complete character. Jonathan Sterne suggests that as cultural object, the MP3 format, designed to achieve mass popular use, can be seen as "a celebration of the limits of auditory perception."[91] By analogy, these earliest examples of fiction-based literary recordings are a test case for the limits of the formal category of the talking novel, which, after all, implied a rich, immersive encounter with the text through the medium of sound.

3 ALFRED, LORD TENNYSON'S SPECTRAL ENERGY

Historical Intonation in Dramatic Recitation

IN THE FIRST two lines of Tennyson's "The Charge of the Light Brigade," only four words are used. Like the repetition in Poe's "The Bells" ("Of the bells, bells, bells, / Of the bells, bells, bells, bells, / Bells, bells, bells—"), the repetition of whole lines in Tennyson's poem raises specific questions about how to read, intone, and sound "Charge," and more general questions about the purpose and significance of reading poetry out loud as a mode of literary interpretation. So what could the modern, post–New Criticism reader possibly learn from reading this particular Tennyson poem out loud? Jerome McGann has noted that the reception history of the poem reveals how it "has not merely fallen out of favor . . . but . . . has come to seem mildly ludicrous, slightly contemptible." McGann focuses on "the historical events," "their ideological significance," and Tennyson's "attitudes towards these matters" as primary reasons for the decline of "Charge" from critical favor.[1] The poem's historicity—that it is a period piece—has allowed it to serve an aesthetically compromised example in contrast to Tennyson's "deeper, more universal" poems (this last phrase from Cleanth Brooks's *Well Wrought Urn*, quoted by McGann). In addition to these reasons, the formal, metrical choices and dramatic repetitions that informed Tennyson's approach to this kind of commemorative battle poem, and the thoroughly declamatory treatment of the historical event, must also have had much to do with the decline of "Charge" as a poem we can relate to. In great part, its galloping dactyls did "Charge" in.

The dactylic meter of the poem seems to invite a fast and furious reading, and led to the attitude expressed by R. M. Milnes that "Charge" is a "real gallop in verse, and only good as such."[2] In other words, the poem has been unable to shed its function as a recitation anthology mainstay, the embarrassment of which was already declared by literary speech and expression theorists at the turn of the nineteenth century. By the first decades of the twentieth century, recitation selections of the kind discussed in chapter 1 came to indicate poor taste and vulgar interpretation in part because they were so often *occasional* pieces. Further, the selections served as explicit examples for rehearsal in the delivery of assonance, consonance, weighty repetition, strong rhyme, and markéd meter. "Charge" was a Victorian recitation anthology favorite, appearing in compilations fewer times only, it seems, than Poe's "The Bells." The most popular recitation pieces, in addition to appearing frequently in anthologies, were also those most often parodied in a manner that simultaneously capitalized on and mocked those predictable, overtly metrical, formulaic elements of the poem that made it so popular.

To pause for just one more example of such a recitation parody (to go with J. E. Frobisher's parody of "The Bells" discussed earlier) the following piece, "The Charge of the Lightning Judge," contributed by Ray Porter to Henry Soper's *Scrap-Book Recitation Series* of 1882, makes my point by seeming to capitalize on the effect of dactylic meter in Tennyson's poem as a means of framing the theme of this poem about a court stenographer who is racing to transcribe speech. Porter's poem does not replicate the dactylic meter of "Charge" (instead it consists of an uneven combination of iambs and anapests), but uses the metrical pace of "Charge" to signal that the reciter should attempt to read his own (more tripping than galloping) lines in urgently rhythmic haste. *Stenos* the stenographer finds that he can't keep up with a motor-mouthed judge and "soon" has fallen "fifteen words behind" in his transcription of the judge's speech. Poor *Stenos*. The mouth is faster than the pen. But, as the poem progresses or romps awkwardly along, *Stenos* begins "to catch the judge's *style*," to recognize his rhetorical and rhythmic speech patterns, and consequently is able to match "phrase and sign-word" at a steadier rate:

> The first that came into his head were groups
> Of hooks and circles, and then the loops,
> Now a phrase brings him up close, or perchance
> Carries him two or three words in advance.
> And so page after page, away he sped,
> Sometimes behind, and sometimes ahead,
> And when they reached the end,—do you mind?
> The *Judge* was fifteen words behind.[3]

As a comment on the predictable nature of rhetorical forms and the power of phonographic scripts to capture them, the parody narrates a stenographic triumph in comic contrast to the martial blunder of Tennyson's original. But the running joke of the parody seems to be on the fatal combination of predictable popular sentiment with forthright verse form in Tennyson's "Charge." Once such a poem gets moving, the parody seems to suggest, its form and fate are inevitable, and the rhythm and rhyme drive the verse forward at a premeditated rather than meditative pace. The metrical charge of the poem subsumes the poetic experience; or so the joke of the parody goes.

There have been few contemporary critical attempts to prove that "Charge" demonstrates "a level of artistic sophistication . . . exceeding that of an ordinary 'gallop in verse.'"[4] McGann's reading in *The Beauty of Inflections* is one example, and still the most sophisticated, inasmuch as it has a well-articulated theory of criticism—summed up for our purposes in the concept of "critical sympathy"—behind it.[5] J. Timothy Lovelace makes another kind of attempt in *The Artistry and Tradition of Tennyson's Battle Poetry*, contending that "Charge" is imbued with Homeric and Virgilian epic significance.[6] For a more formal (i.e., New Critical) kind of defense of the poem's sophistication at a psychological and emotional level—for the argument that we can still find "Charge" as an autonomous aesthetic object legitimately moving, and not just full of clopping metrical movement—Lovelace refers us to a close reading of the poem in 1972 by Christopher Ricks, who described "Charge" as "a stirring poem, the more so for anyone who has heard **the recording of Tennyson reading it.**" Ricks says:

"Tennyson's voice swoops upon *knew* with an emphasis at once awed, exasperated, and half-incredulous at the immediately culpable folly of *some one* (the effect in the recording is riveting)." Ricks's reading of Tennyson's oral performance of the poem stresses the dramatic voice of the narrator/poet, his incredulity at the event, and his particular sense of privilege to make reply, which runs parallel to the soldiers' obligation not to.[7] In drawing on the Tennyson recording as the source of his own close reading of the import of voice in the poem, Ricks is conflating the New Critical idea of voice (as abstract unifying force) with the dramatic conception of speaking voice as formulated by oral interpretation critics of the late nineteenth century and after. He is raising a New Critical question of oral interpretation. This kind of critical gesture by a late twentieth-century literary critic will come across as eccentric, but it was not an unprecedented thing to do.

The New Criticism may have worked generally to silence oral interpretation as a critical method by transposing the literal voice of an interpretive poetry reader into a silent, critical concept of "voice" (something to be found in a poem), but literary interpretation in the sense that pre–New Criticism critics such as Samuel Silas Curry and C. C. Cunningham meant it, was still alive in some quarters of the academy (albeit in theatre or communications departments rather than English departments). In the mid-1960s, critics like Don Geiger and Wallace Bacon, figures now all but forgotten in literary studies, were adapting New Critical methods of reading canonical literature to oral performance.[8]

In *The Sound, Sense, and Performance of Literature* (1963), Geiger acknowledges Samuel Silas Curry as *the* nineteenth-century critic who understood the characterological and dramatic nature of all oral interpretation.[9] Extending Curry's argument about Browning's dramatic monologues to all modes of poetry, Geiger contended that in every poem there is a speaker waiting to be voiced by an interpretive reader. He used Curry to reimagine the New Criticism as a method of literary, interpretive performance. In *The Dramatic Impulse of Modern Poetics* (1967),[10] Geiger borrows the New Critical idea of the poem as a self-sufficient system, as language coming to terms with itself (through abstract New Critical concepts like "contrast" and "ambiguity"), but then adds to it a less-championed New Critical idea, quoting Cleanth Brooks and Robert Penn Warren's *Understanding Poetry*: "All poetry involves dramatic organization . . . every poem implies the speaker of the poem . . . the poem represents the action of such a person."[11] If we take Ricks's reading of the "voice" of the poem a little further, then, and approach "Charge" in the spirit of Geiger's adaptation of Curry's idea that oral performance consists of "the spontaneous realization of ideas in living relations, and of motive and manifestations of character,"[12] we are left with an interesting audiotextual interpretation. The imagination required to read and hear the poem according to Curry's method as adapted to our contemporary critical perspective, is both performative and historical in nature. It calls for us to imagine how Tennyson's manner of speaking his world might speak to our own, out loud. What I have in mind as an interpretive approach in this chapter is something like the critically sympathetic method of reading that McGann articulates in *The Beauty of Inflections*, but without glosses, citations, footnotes, or a developed argument; only with inflections.

Critics like McGann and Natalie Houston have remarked that the idea of the all wondering "world" imagined in Tennyson's poem initially consisted of those who were united on a mass level in their affective response to the event by reading the accounts of the battle in the *Times*.[13] "The poem in many respects is a distilled interpretation of the popular reaction to the charge as that reaction was expressed in the newspapers," McGann observes.[14] Moreover, as Tennyson revised the poem, he erased the observational context from the scene, resulting in "a self-enclosed text that exhorts the members of an unspecified and unified ideologic world," Houston notes.[15] Through revisions the recognizable viewing perspective and speaking voice are abstracted and generalized. One important example of this kind of revision is Tennyson's decision to return to the more abstract closing stanza that he had used in the *Examiner* version of the poem, after he had temporarily changed it for a more specific scenario of telling the story of this battle in the version he published in *Maud and Other Poems* (1855). So, the instantiation of an ambiguity of vision (and voice) can be found in Tennyson's removal of a revision from the last stanza of the poem, which went from

> Honor the brave and bold!
> Long shall the tale be told,
> Yea, when our babes are old—
> How they rode onward.

(*Maud and Other Poems*, 1855)

to

When can their glory fade?
O the wild charge they made!
  All the world wondered.
Honour the charge they made!
Honour the Light Brigade,
  Noble six hundred![16]

The (re-)removal of "long shall the tale be told . . . " from the last stanza is one instance in a larger procedure of revision that distills out occasional details, and delocalizes the character of the speaker in the poem. Tennyson's replacement of a specific reference to Captain Louis Edward Nolan who issued the order to charge ("Forward, the Light Brigade! / 'Take the guns,' Nolan said") that appears in the first, *Examiner* version of the poem with an anonymous command in later versions ("'Charge for the guns!' he said") is another example. Such revisions separate the agents and speakers in the poem from particular, historical individuals, and remove the spectator and the domestic circumstance of the recitation as oral memorialization, rendering the "voice" of the poem ambiguously omniscient and assertive of a universal act of nobility, at which "All the world wondered."

The oral performance of the poem according to an updated version of Curry's method of dramatic instinct—a sympathetic method of interpretation that seeks to find and perform the voice of a poem's speaker—requires a sympathy first with the poem's initial attempt to capture the unified affective response of British newspaper readers in 1854–55, and with the localized affective response of the poetry pamphlet readers in 1855, and then with the poem's will to move beyond any traces of particularity by establishing a less actual and identifiable perspective and voice for the event. In this case, it requires a vocal interpretation that captures the erasure of many of the historically specific frames noted by McGann that initially shaped this battle as visible spectacle, including the erasure of the spectacular language of W. H. Russell's journalistic reports of the battle in *The Times*, the erasure of Captain Lewis Nolan as original speaker of the command to move forward, the erasure of the quoted prospect views of the allied troops who observed the battle in astonishment at what they were seeing, erasure of

Tennyson's appropriation of a French "tradition of military art" that positions these English soldiers as figures in a romantic Napoleonic tableau,
the erasure of military class politics, and the attempted redemption of the
English aristocracy as legitimate spiritual leaders of the nation.[17] And, in
addition to all these erasures, it demands more than anything a vocal performance that captures the erasure of Tennyson's own imagined collective
view of the event, his idea of how the patriotic citizenry would have seen
it and then continue to tell of it. In short, the instinct that would need to
be dramatized would result in the vocalization of Victorian ideology itself,
that set of ideas, beliefs, ideals, assumptions, and motivations that, if voiced
in a single speaking character so as to articulate the spontaneous realization of that character's ideas in living relation, motives, and ethos, would
sound like, *what?* Some voice of objective memory that suffused descriptive concreteness, lyric musicality, and epic authority into something else
altogether, something without the culpability of ordinary sentiment, but
sentiment sprung "from a deeper, more universal cause."[18]

A late Victorian elocutionist like Canon James Fleming (of and from
whom we shall hear shortly) described "reading and speaking by word,
without any regard to the sentiment" as "reading mechanically," stating that
"when we read without feeling, we are inclined to speak on one note of the
voice only, in monotone."[19] Reading without feeling but for patterns of sound
and meaning, for "a musical organization" or "the principal of complexity"
(critical categories used by F. R. Leavis and Cleanth Brooks, respectively,
to interpret T.S. Eliot's *The Waste Land*),[20] might also describe the effect of
New Critical approaches to poetry that translated dramatic voice into the
formally unifying "voice" (read: structuring force) of the poem.

The dull flatness that natural elocutionists like Fleming would identify
with certain mechanical methods of elocution as a result of the disconnect
between performed affect and the intellectual and affective context, and
the abstract conception of "voice" as an organizing principle that informs
a New Critical vocabulary, are, arguably, performed by many modern and
contemporary poetry readers as a subtle alternating use of flat or monotone
intonation with a repeated pattern of falling cadence to organize poetic
phrasing, a technique that has been identified with the intonation of "poet
voice," a contemporary style of reading that is often performed, sometimes

vilified, and rarely explained historically as a particular style of reading poetry out loud.[21] Marit J. MacArthur has identified this style of poetry reading as *"monotonous incantation*, a version of the neutral style that performs an understated sincerity" with three predominant qualities: (1) repeated falling cadence within a constrained pitch range, (2) flattened affect evoking an earnest tone, and (3) the subordination of elements of the printed text such as line breaks and punctuated syntax to "the prevailing cadence and slow, steady pace."[22] MacArthur identifies this style of reading with characteristics that define recitation within the frame of Christian (especially protestant) liturgy and consequently identifies "poet voice" as the sound of a secular, academic ritual.[23] As one example of a neutral style of reading, "poet voice" may well have a genealogy in certain forms of antiphonal liturgy, and the possibility suggests an exciting range of possible ways we might correlate patterns heard in the performance of poetry with other kinds of public reading, whether they are identified explicitly as modes of performance, or not. If we understand the prevalence of "poet voice" and other variations on this neutral reading style as an effect of the rise of the New Critical method of literary interpretation, for example, we may also begin to understand "the lack of spectacle, drama and dynamic range" that Charles Bernstein uses to define the contemporary poetry reading as a typically "anti-performative" and "anti-expressivist" phenomenon.[24] "Poet voice" as a reading style that "represents the half-realized dream of a secular church for academia" may be just the performative mode necessary for a modern performance of "Charge."[25] Try reciting the opening line of "Charge" with the intonations of the poet voice, that is, in this rise-and-fall-poetry-voice way:

/   —   \   /   —   \ /   —   \   \   -
Half-a-league, half-a-league, half-a-league, onwards . . .

It may be interesting and certainly is humorous for the contrast it performs between a martial occasion paced with dactyls and a mode of intonation that means to render all occasions uniformly grave and lyrical, but the exercise alone does not capture the kind of reading I am trying to imagine and describe here. My aim is to have us hear a reading style that not only voices the rhetorical protocols and goals of the Victorians in delivering their verse aloud, and the historical motives that informed such choices in performance, but a reading that sounds our own, present critical preference for reading in silence, and the implications of that preference for how we now listen to poetry that was designed to be read out loud as an interpretation to be heard.

Elocution, Interpretation, and Literary Performance

Modes of recitation that combined prescribed vocal actions with gesture and facial expression were once an important part of the experience and study of literature. Elocution was a prescriptive, performative practice developed in the eighteenth century as a method for a public reader (usually other than the author) to convey to the hearer the meaning of the writer. It was, in the words of John Rice (as he put it in his work *An Introduction to the Art of Reading* [1865]), a method for "converting Writing into Speech."[26] The process of this conversion involved a self-conscious performance of natural expression. As Jacqueline George has put it, in elocution, "The reader must be at once self-consciously constructed and perfectly natural, adhering to the proper rules for reading—pronunciation, pitch, pauses, gestures—without revealing his reading to be a performance, as such."[27] The reader, in short, attempts to function as a good (that is to say, natural, immediate) vehicle of delivery between text and audience. In this sense elocution is all about interface. George has usefully sketched out some models for the structure of this interface, depicting relations among the participants in the public scene of reading as "quadrangular, mediated by the text and determined by the participant's various engagements with it."[28] Similarly, Ben McCorkle, has shown how "the elocutionary movement and belletristic tradition of the nineteenth century's New Rhetoric worked in tandem as parallel educational and cultural forces in order to naturalize the printed page . . . [and to render] the print interface invisible to an increasingly literate society via the remediation of handwriting and oral speech."[29] Such an understanding of elocutionary practice may explain some of the discourse surrounding the phonograph as a less burdensome instrument for reading aimed at "the leisure reader seeking to relax after a day's work" without having to engage the eyes or mouth.[30]

It seems counterintuitive to us today, when we examine the pages of elocution manuals, with their extensive categories and instructions for vocal manipulation, bodily gesture, facial expression, and symbolic systems of annotating texts for performance, to think of them as handbooks for the naturalization of print. We are estranged in significant ways from understanding what an elocutionary model of reading meant in the nineteenth century: what it meant in relation to print media and written composition, social decorum, and the models of perception and the mind that informed the particular kind of communication circuit it aimed to achieve. In considering recorded literary recitations in relation to models of elocution and oral reading we begin to understand how complicated it can be to hear the historical resonance of any early recorded literary performance. The difficulty of recognizing the traits of a performance model, or understanding why a poem or dramatic selection would have been performed in a particular way, is largely due to the fact that the oral interpretation of literature is no longer a significant part of English literary pedagogy, and has not been for many decades.[31]

Most accounts of the history of reading literature out loud begin with the influence of the eighteenth-century English elocutionists and their growing interest in how to train and use the voice and body for the purpose of successful expression in reading. The interest in elocution defined as training in oral reading developed from the study of classical rhetoric and poetics, in particular, Aristotle's interest in *euglōssia* (ευγλωσσία), or eloquence, and the interest of Cicero and Quintilian in *pronuntiatio,* the right management of the voice to express various emotions, and *chironomy,* the laws of expressive gesture.[32] The English writers who came to call themselves elocutionists were mostly either involved in the theatre or else grammarians and lexicographers, which suggests that elocution in the eighteenth century arose in relation to ideas and opinions surrounding the theatre at the time, and as an extension of the rhetorical interest in style (also known as *elocutio)* into *pronuntiatio* (the use of voice for the expression of text).[33]

The story generally continues by noting that two schools of elocution emerged in the eighteenth century representing opposing pedagogical philosophies, these being the natural and mechanical schools. The founding fathers of these schools are identified as Thomas Sheridan (natural) and John Walker (mechanical). These schools that signal a stark and essential binary are, in fact, best understood as a plastic and permeable set of descriptive categories used to identify and demarcate a variety of differences between methods of reading from the eighteenth century into the twentieth century. This is not to say that the categories are not meaningful but that they come to mean different things at different times and within different theorists' vocabularies. The distinction in the broadest sense often signifies a differentiation between methods that favored the use of extensive prescriptive (mechanical) rules and accompanying notation for the instruction and direction of reading as opposed to methods that sought to keep such prescriptions and symbolic notation to a minimum, the latter being deemed more natural in their orientation.[34]

There are some other core elements of difference between Sheridan and Walker that are worth noting and that continued to inform later debates about the oral performance of printed text. Sheridan identifies the source of the unfortunate dominance of artificial versus natural habits of reading in the modern revival of the ancient, "dead languages" and its preoccupation with writing over speech: "From that period, the minds of men took a wrong bias. Their whole attention was employed in the cultivation of the artificial, to the neglect of the natural language. Letters, not sounds; writing, not speech, became the general care."[35] The "natural" language is thus located by Sheridan in the sounds of common speech, and the function of elocution is to release the capacity of the reader to remediate the artificial language of print into the natural language of speech. Speech is endowed with this natural quality according to Sheridan in part because it makes the imitative connection between words and the sounds of the natural world audible. Certain "mimical" words, for example, "contain a power of expression from a natural resemblance" to the sounds of animals in nature, and thus the pronunciation of a text depends in great part on a reactivation of the natural, sonic resemblances inherent in the printed word.[36] Walker's approach, on the other hand, bases a system of methods for proper reading on certain established rules of grammar and rhetoric and their print analogues in the form of printed punctuation and sentence forms. Walker's rules for reading thus unfold from a set of abstract principles and in this sense are identified as mechanical rather than imitative of natural speech.[37]

An important common thread that runs through this continuum of natural to mechanical elocution guidebooks is their assertion of a general antithesis between reading and theatrical performance. In *A Course of Lectures on Elocution*, Sheridan notes the regrettable manner of reading for an effect of "pomp and solemnity" that people engage in due to a falsely held assumption that "public declamation" ought to be in everything "different from private discourse." It is "the vice of the stage," he continues, that has given rise to the distinction between "Theatrical Declamation, in opposition to that of the natural kind," and that has led "public speakers" to wax "Theatrical."[38]

In *Lessons of Elocution* (1779), Scott argued for the need to teach reading as opposed to acting on pedagogical grounds, not so much because he associated acting with unnatural theatrics, as Sheridan did, but because "it is plain, open, distinct and forcible pronunciation, which school boys should aim at; and not that quick transition from one passion to another, that archness of look, and that *jeu de theatre*, as it is called, so essential to a tolerable dramatic exhibition, and which actors themselves can scarcely attain. In short, it is speaking, rather than acting, which school boys should be taught."[39] While the motives informing the development of distinctions between natural versus theatrical declamation, and between speaking and acting, may differ significantly from elocutionist to elocutionist, such a separation of reading from theatrical performance plays an important role in establishing the oral interpretation of a work of literature as a unique activity, a distinct genre of communication, or, to use Bernstein's phrase, "as its own medium."[40] With its recurrent stress on the difference between speech and print, on the one hand, and between public reading and theatrical stage acting, on the other, early elocutionary theory worked to define the proprietary boundaries of the literary reading.

The development of elocutionary methods for reading short poems, selections and speeches excised out of their dramatic context, with a stress on the conversion of print into a more "natural" delivery of the author's meaning, via voice, provided the groundwork for the many different manifestations of oral literary interpretation to come, all the way up to the early literary sound recording. We have already discussed the ways in which texts adapted for the media of early sound recording were aware of the need to compensate for the loss of visual information through the integration of supplemental sonic cues, whether by explicitly narrating the actions and objects that define the scene—like Scrooge telling us he has just woken up, and what furniture surrounds him—or by the inclusion of sound effects (created with instruments and tools, or by the human voice) to evoke sonically the material world of the speakers heard on record. Vocal actions based on established elocutionary protocols may have evoked similar supplementary visual effects for the listener due to the common association of particular techniques involving the manipulation of pitch and amplitude in speaking with bodily gestures, postures, and facial expressions. Literary interpretation in the elocutionary context involved the speaker's use of the voice and the body as a coordinated expressive apparatus. This leads us to ask the interesting question: What is the status of bodily gesture in a sound recording? Clearly we cannot see the gesture that accompanies a given vocal action. Can we hear it? Of course, none of these visual cues of expressive gesture accompany the sound-recorded performance (except, possibly, in the form of a catalogue image), so the gestural elements of elocutionary performance are either signaled to the listener by the voice to be imagined or are simply absent. However, as Carrie Preston has shown, for many late nineteenth-century theories of performance, there was an integral relation between bodily gesture and the production of emotion in the performer, "an idea of the primacy of physiological response that would be the basis of the James-Lange theory of emotion in the 1880s."[41] The pose of the speaker would help produce an emotion that could, in turn, be heard in the vocal performance. Because posing the body produces the emotion in performance, the recording of the literary reading can also be understood as communicating the affective result of the pose in voice. With this possibility in mind, certain poetry recordings that were informed by elocutionary theory can be understood as having sounded gesture-inspired or gesture-produced emotions. Further, it is equally possible that for those versed in some of the most basic and common protocols of elocutionary expression, the sound of a vocal action would evoke a bodily gesture, the voice thus providing sonic cues for a visualized choreography of expressive movement and gesture.

The stress on gesture in literary performance gained momentum during the nineteenth century through the work, teachings, and students of the French expression theorist François Delsarte, who developed what he called a "semeiotics" or "science of organic signs" that "postulated a natural-spiritual-physical correspondence between gesture and meaning."[42] The potential of gesture as opposed to voice for expression was taken to an extreme in the work of Delsarte, which explored the possibilities of "wordless expression" through the enactment of sequential emotive poses.[43] James Naremore and Roberta E. Pearson have discussed the "limited lexicon" of gesture in the Delsartean system of performance as manifest in early cinematic productions,[44] noting that the "connection between acting and speechmaking" that dominated acting and performance pedagogy in the nineteenth century, "began to disappear at the turn of the century as drama became increasingly visual, representational and responsive to the tastes of a larger audience."[45] In the case of cinematic representation, the grand and formulaic signifying gestures that characterized much acting in silent films were gradually replaced by more subtle, granular approaches to filming and editing physical actions and expressions, with the use of filmed and then interspersed takes that were framed from multiple angles and distances.[46] Commenting on the impact of new media technologies on the presentation of gesture in performance, Naremore notes how the microphone used in electrical recording worked to tame and naturalize "the vocal instrument, detheatricalizing language in much the same way as close-ups [in film] detheatricalize[d] gesture."[47] In the context specifically of recorded vocal performance, the electrical recording process, with the microphone in front of it, suddenly allowed for far greater subtlety in the use of volume, affective tone, and timbre in vocal delivery, so singers could now croon, actors could whisper, and readers could emote with new kinds of unmelodramatic nuance.[48] The shift from acoustic to electrical recording and the greater storage capacity of sound recording media were among the factors that transformed the way literary works were performed. With changing technologies and new audiences came new theories and expectations of oral interpretation.

To understand the slow movement from elocutionary to modern reading, we must trace the gradual identification of physical gesture accompanying vocal actions as undesirable, mechanical aspects of reading out loud, and the motivations for their erasure from acceptable literary performance.[49] Delsarte's ideas established their legacy and helped push along the eventual dissolution of prescriptive elocutionary methods, through the influence it had on the establishment of the academic study of speech education in

America, and most notably by its assimilation into the work of the speech theorists Geneviève Stebbins and Samuel Silas Curry.[50] Stebbins stressed the physical side of Delsartean interpretation and classical form as the structuring model for gesture and performance. Her 1885 work, *Delsarte System of Expression*, for example, depicted a series of poses drawn from classical sculpture to serve as paradigms in elocutionary delivery. She attacked rival theories of interpretation by arguing that art does not arise from imitating nature, per se, but from the studied approximation of superior (usually classical) types that reveal embedded essences.[51] Curry's approach was an anti-theatrical method of interpretation that valued the interpreter's "imagination" of how the speaker of a text would think and feel in natural response to the circumstances informing action in a given scene. Both Stebbins and Curry identified their methods as *natural* approaches to expressive performance, both vilified "elocution" as an outdated, mechanical method of rant and affectation in performance, and although they proposed distinctive approaches to performance, they both laid claim to the term "expression" to describe the new (anti-elocutionary) discipline of literary performance. Stebbins and Curry thus represented one more phase in an ongoing dialectic that periodically proposed to counter artifice with nature, the mechanical with the natural, or, in this particular case, elocution with expression.[52] Overall, this anti-elocutionary wave of literary performance theory focused on nonprescriptive ideas of expressive interpretation that stressed naturalized scenarios of imaginative dramatization. Curry, in particular, devoted much time to the development of a key concept that would be the cornerstone of ideas surrounding "natural" vocal interpretation for decades to come.

For Curry, correct oral expression of literature hinged on the reader's ability to assimilate the perspective of the speaker in a poem by "dramatic instinct," which he defined as "the spontaneous realization of ideas in living relations, and of the motive and manifestations of character."[53] According to him, the poetry reader approached the poem as a repository of character in action, and through the practice of his method, "the personality of the speaker . . . [entered] into an instinctive assimilation of the character" that was alive there.[54] True expression for Curry depended on "the sympathy of the thinking mind" in the form of a complete assimilation of the speaking character's point of view, which would then become manifest.[55] As he explains in *Imagination and Dramatic Instinct* (1896), the possible ways of rendering a passage

> illustrate the fact that consciously, or unconsciously, the reader adopts some point of view for each phrase, and so determines his feeling and expression. It is a definite point of view, which makes expression dramatic. The ability to vary the point of view, and the instinct to conceive the right one in any specific case, is a most important element of all forms of vocal expression. The instinct that conceives a point of view is one of the most important in the human mind. It is as important for success in life as for attainment in reading and speaking.[56]

Curry later developed this theory of interpretation as a form of immersion and assimilation of literary character further in a book on Robert Browning and the dramatic monologue.[57] Throughout his published works Curry stresses his main point that "expression is not exhibition."[58] That is to say, the "isolated execution of specific external acts is most antagonistic to the true spirit of dramatic instinct" which aims to unify the expressive manifestations delivered in performance with the reader's sympathetic understanding of the characters whose speech he performs. Character in speech is unified, and yet, to recall a term from Erving Goffman, the changing "footing" of that character is how it becomes dramatized in speech performance.[59]

Curry's idea that as readers we "identify ourselves sympathetically with character" is similar to the English diction teacher Elsie Fogerty's idea that oral readers must "act as interpreters, as executive artists." Author of one of the most important books about reading poetry, *The Speaking of English Verse* (1923), Fogerty identified Victorian parlor recitation and prescriptive elocution as the primary impediments to achieving "executive artist" status.[60] From the late 1920s on, interpretation would become a new word for the practice of reading aloud. In some contexts, it would replace "elocution" and "recitation," both of which had undesirable associations with unanchored and flamboyant effects, vulgar literary taste, and false literary understanding, as opposed to the newer methods of oral interpretive expression, which sought by arduous technical training to achieve *impersonality* (rather than destructive "personal self-assertion"), so that the character of a great work of literature could be experienced and communicated.

This approach to the oral performance of literature was extremely popular. The specific advice on developing the instrument of one's voice might vary, but the basic concept of the interpreter's role remained the same in most of the writings on diction published in England and the United States between 1920 and 1940. "The reader's speech, voice and body must become as mirrors through which his hearers see and understand the author's meaning, moods, and motives, whatever they may be," Margaret Prendergast McLean asserts in her book *Oral Interpretation of Forms of Literature* (1936). [61] C. C. Cunningham's influential *Literature as a Fine Art, Analysis and Interpretation* (1941) similarly recommends: "The body and the voice of an oral reader should be like the pen and paper of the creative artist—mere instruments with which he works. . . . They should in no way attract the attention and arouse the curiosity through either the visual or the aural sense." [62]

Theories and methods of best converting writing into speech varied significantly from the eighteenth to the mid-twentieth century, but consistently sought the most "natural" means of delivering a literary work to an audience, with the performer functioning as the immediate interface. As older elocutionary methods lost their effectiveness, the expressive apparatus (the technology of the prescriptive elocutionary notation system, and the elocutionist's physical execution of that system) became increasingly visible (one might say, hypermediated) to the listener, and, was in turn replaced by a new theory and method that seemed to meet the requirement for immediacy. The trajectory of literary interpretation—which seems always to have been motivated by a desire to eliminate the interpreter's body from the circuit of literary communication—moved with a kind of inevitability from prescribed gesture and vocal action to the unassuming performance of an interpreter's sympathetic identification with the work's character, and thence to silent acts of written critical analysis wherein "voice" no longer meant something one heard in the air.

Teaching literature prior to the 1940s was in many ways a noisy affair, but by the time Cunningham published *Literature as a Fine Art* in the early 1940s, a new method of literary interpretation, which we have come to call the New Criticism, was already establishing itself as an alternative to the oral and experiential pedagogical methods I have been describing. Elsie Fogerty's school was still in business (it still is, as a matter of fact), [63]—but the skills she taught were now finding use primarily on stage and screen, rather than on the poetry podium or in the literature classroom. The New Criticism as a method of interpretation was for the most part aggressively antithetical to performative interpretation. René Wellek and Austin Warren's *Theory of Literature*, for example, argued that oral recitation could result in a dangerous distortion of serious literary study, that "we must . . . distinguish between performance and pattern of sound" and that "a real science of rhythmics and metrics cannot be based only on the study of individual recitals."[64] As Andrew Elfenbein has noted, "in place of oral recitation, the New Critics reappropriated 'voice,' a unique, intangible entity conferring authenticity and pre-existing unity on a particular text or career."[65] With this inaudible concept of voice, which "has since become virtually omnipresent in literary, cultural and composition studies," the New Critics introduced a silent abstraction of the elocutionary idea of voice with which, for a brief period, dramatic recitation was competing as a viable mode of literary interpretation.[66] This is not to say that performative reading has ever been eliminated from literary pedagogy, although its place within the curriculum has arguably changed from being a form of interpretation to an act that supplements creative expression. If, as Raphael Allison has said, the New Criticism "treated the poem as an object imbued with ontological grace"—that is, as an artifact with coherent presence, there, on the page— attention to historical literary performance troubles and even disrupts that conception of the poem as an autonomous literary entity.

Dramatic Interpretation with Musical Accompaniment

For a period, oral interpretation was deemed a valuable means by which to develop one's emotional and intellectual understanding of literature. Reading theories and styles varied but in each case led to the delivery of a distinctive literary sound generated by the voice of the speaker. We can hear these historical examples of literary sound on the records produced during the early periods of sound recording, many of them developed or organized specifically for the purpose of literary study. Among a variety of proposals for the use of recorded audio to teach literature, listening programs developed by record companies sold the idea that recordings of literary recitations combined with selected musical corollaries might create a more powerful experience of literature for the student. This idea brought two kinds of sound together under the rubric of the literary. Harold D. Smith's program and catalogue *A New Correlation*, for example, deployed "music as a vehicle of poetic thought" by incorporating musical accompaniment with recorded recitations.[67] None of William Sterling Battis's Dickens monologues in Smith's catalogue, discussed in chapter 2, featured recitation with musical accompaniment, however. This was reserved for a few recorded poetry recitations.

Recordings that integrated music and sound effects with poetry reading emerged from a practice of "literary and musical entertainments" that became popular in the late nineteenth century and continued into the twentieth. These programs of piano performance, solo and duet singing, and readings were performed at home, in churches, clubs, and civic buildings. While the musical performance and literary recitation were most often discrete events on a program, Marian Wilson Kimber's research has shown that "musical selections were often heard in an individual's [reading] program, functioning as prelude, postlude, or interlude between numbers, providing rest for the speaker and time for audiences to reflect on a poem," and, further, that sometimes "musical improvisation or previously composed music could be used to accompany speech."[68] Suggestions for particular combinations of text and music were advertised and published in periodicals of expression, and in 1897 the relative value and potential of "musically accompanied recitations" was debated and discussed by scores of contributors across multiple numbers of *Werner's Magazine*, with responses to the question posed ("Do you believe in musical recitations?") ranging from "I do not" to "most emphatically yes."[69] Such debates focused on whether musical accompaniment could add to the emotional impact of the performed poem, or whether music was antithetical to the expressive goals of recitation because it distracted the listener from the genuine emotion of the spoken poem.

Record companies took the affirmative position on the question and explored how music and literature might be mixed together for pedagogical effect by the development of listening repertoire from their backlists and by producing new recordings. The correlation programs of record companies, developed and explained in education department teaching catalogues such as Smith's *A New Correlation* and Milnor Dorey and Louis Mohler's *Literature and Music: A Manual for Teachers and Students in School and Home* (Columbia Graphophone Company), imagined the use of all manner of records for the purpose of enhancing a student's experience of literature.[70] Such manuals advertised the credentials of their compilers, and Dorey and Mohler are identified as holding M.A. degrees from Harvard and Columbia University, respectively, while S. Dana Townsend, compiler of *The Victrola in Correlation with English and American Literature* (1921) is listed as A.B Columbia University.[71] These authors suggested the creation of "[m]usical settings" for teaching "the poems of Longfellow, . . . Tennyson, Browning, Scott, Burns and Kipling" in a manner that would "help emphasize the close kinship between poetry and music."[72] The development of "musical settings" for literary works entailed the selection of appropriate records from the company's catalogue. So, for teaching Longfellow's "Hiawatha" the instructor was advised to play "[r]ecords of American Indian songs, sung by real Indians" and "selections on Indian themes with the rhythmic tom-tom effect" to help "add to the romance of this story," and "The Village Blacksmith" might be "further elaborated by the use of music with imitative anvil effects."[73] In a slightly less instrumental vein, Dorey and Mohler outlined principles for using a combination of music and poetry to powerfully appeal to the students' emotions, arguing that the "inter-relation of poetry and music must never be considered as a complete, scientific co-ordination," but "the power of *Suggestion* is ever present in both, and through that beautiful and potent alembic the mind and heart may be reached."[74] The goal was to create "musical settings" that "adequately harmonize[d] with the spirit and thought of the poems."[75]

The selection of music and other contiguous sounds to play during the course of studying a poem was meant to enhance, not distract from, the power of the text, just as the oral interpreter's vocalization was supposed to convey the meaning and emotional message of a poem notwithstanding that the reader was delivering words from a printed text. It is possible that the correlation of musical compositions with poetry reading alleviated the need for overly expressive or musical vocal techniques in the reading voice itself. While there is no sonic evidence of an extreme segregation of voice from expressive musicality, the weight of atmospheric expression in this genre of recording had been shifted to a large extent onto the orchestra from the voice itself. What we do hear in such recordings is that sonic frequency-based expressivity functioned by reciprocity between music and voice. The orchestra did sometimes function as an emotive supplement, while the voice continued to perform with complementary elocutionary musicality.

The catalogues and manuals discussed above suggest many correlations of sounds with texts, but the philosophy of correlation is best heard in the genre of sound recording often described as a "dramatic recitation with musical accompaniment." In many ways, this genre of recording belongs to the slightly longer generic recording tradition of the "descriptive sketch"—in the most basic sense, a recording that contained scene-setting sound effects—except that the combination of speech and nonspeech sounds was now framed as specifically literary in its motivation.[76]

Orchestral accompaniment in such recordings was intended to reinforce the mimetic effect of the setting and actions communicated in the narrative poem, and appropriately assigned instrumental music was meant to correlate with the emotionally resonant intonations and actions of the speaker's voice as heard in her elocutionary delivery of the poem.[77] For example, in **Rose Coghlan's dramatic recitation of Tennyson's "The Charge of the Light Brigade" (1909),**[78] recorded for the Victor label, the production of the recording and the manner in which it integrates voice and music evoke what we might call Victor's distinctive literary sound, as compared to that of Edison, which tended to underplay the use of mimetic sound effects and make sparing use of melodic accompaniment.[79] Coghlan's "Charge" was first commissioned by Victor for its general catalogues, and it was advertised in Victor catalogues under the heading of "dramatic recitation" as early as 1910. The recording only made its way into the catalogues of records "suitable for use in the teaching of English literature" a few years later.

This recording, which integrates orchestral accompaniment into the recitation meets the requirements for a full-fledged elocutionary and orchestral dramatization (with mimetic and emotional effects). The musical accompaniment works as sound-effect backdrop, and parts of Coghlan's performance of the poem are characteristic of the delivery, not of an elocutionist, but of a stage actor (which she was) performing for an audience in a large public theatre. The goal of the rendering of the first five stanzas

120   **RECITATIONS**

A Dramatic Recitation by ROSE COGHLAN

NUMBER   SIZE

31728   **The Charge of the Light Brigade**
                                    Tennyson   12

The Victor has induced Miss Coghlan
to recite Tennyson's famous poem, and the
result is one of the most dramatic and thrilling records imaginable.

The Victor controls exclusively Miss Coghlan's rendition of this selection on disc records.

ROSE COGHLAN

Dramatic Recitations by EDGAR L. DAVENPORT

Incidental music by Victor Orchestra

We take pleasure in announcing two splendid numbers
by this popular actor—Deprez's beautiful poem, "Lasca," in
which Mr. Davenport describes the cowboy's love for the Mex-
ican beauty, the wild ride for life before the maddened cattle,
and the final tragedy as Lasca sacrifices her life for her lover;
and the famous "Jim Bludsoe," which is delivered in fine
style by Mr. Davenport.

4701   **Jim Bludsoe**   John Hay   10
31529   **Lasca**   Deprez   12

DAVENPORT

Figure 6. Record catalogue description of "A Dramatic Recitation by Rose Coghlan."
Victor Records Catalogue, July 1910, 120.

in this recording, in the context of correlation pedagogy would have been
to make the historical event of the poem as actively present to the listener
as possible, to make the poem "dramatic and thrilling," as the catalogue
puts it (fig. 6). For example, the command to the soldiers to move forward
is followed by trumpet flourishes that would have been typical of a British
brigade in the Crimean War, and the lines on the cannon fire that greets
the six hundred are followed by kettledrum rolls. These sound effects are
arranged to be heard in between the recited lines. The goal of the recitation
with musical correlation in the final stanza of the poem, where the orches-
tration is melodic and swells in volume along with the speaker's voice, was
to capture the seriousness, the universally acknowledged, grave wonder of
the event just dramatized, as she delivers the penultimate lines painstak-
ingly slowly (taking about thirty seconds to deliver twenty-seven words)
with extensive prolongation of selected words:

When can their glory fade?
O the wild charge they made!

All the world wondered.
Honour the charge they made!
Honour the Light Brigade,
    Noble six hundred![80]

In listening to Coghlan deliver this final stanza with the orchestra supporting her, we can understand dramatic recitation as a powerful, hybrid form of art in performance, drawing on elocutionary technique, dramatic performance, historical and descriptive interpretation, and a kind of vocalization that verges, in the end, on singing. The record mobilizes a full range of sonic media in the service of literary interest and excitement.[81]

The audiotextual format of the Victor recitations with orchestral accompaniment influenced subsequent American recordings of "Charge," including those released by **United Talking Machine Co. in 1913**[82] and **Emerson Phonograph Co., ca. 1917.**[83] The United Talking Machine release, recited by Edgar L. Davenport, imitates the Victor orchestral accompaniment extensively, with bugles at the start, kettledrums for cannon in the middle, and a more solemn horn outro, only in this instance, the bugle call played at the end is "Taps," which had been associated with the American military since the Civil War.[84] The performance in the Emerson recording is unattributed, and may have been delivered by a less-seasoned recording artist given the way the speaker seems to need to speed up his reading at the end (despite the text's demands to slow down and linger in sadness and gravitas) to fit the poem onto the record. Even the orchestral arrangement (which is, again, imitative of the Victor approach, and of the United adaptation) must hurry its delivery of "Taps" by playing over the speaker through the last stanza. This last recording was marketed among a series of "Patriotic Selections" released under the Emerson label, in this instance, "Charge," Americanized and integrated into a list alongside U.S. Army and Navy Bugle Calls, and such titles as "American Patrol," "All American March," and "Stars and Stripes Forever."[85] The pedagogical motives behind the inclusion of recitation recordings like "Charge" in Victor's education catalogue and the multimedia production of their delivery of "literary" works seem absent in Emerson's "Patriotic Selections," where it is not a new kind of literary sound that is being conveyed but the sound of American military patriotism.

All these recordings were produced in the United States, albeit in some instances with artists, like Rose Coghlan, who had begun their careers on the British stage before moving to America. Recitation records produced in the United Kingdom usually lack the kind of orchestral accompaniment heard on Victor and Edison records.

Tennyson's Spectral Energy

Tennyson's "Charge of the Light Brigade" was also recorded between 1907 and 1912 by the British Victorian actors and elocutionists **Canon James Fleming**,[86] **Lewis Waller**,[87] and **Henry Ainley**.[88] According to John R. Bennett's list of vocal recordings from English catalogues, Waller and Fleming first recorded "Charge" on ten-inch Gramophone and Typewriter Co. Black Label "Concert" records in 1906. (Fleming also recorded Poe's "The Bells" on two separate records—verses 1–3 on one disc, and verse 4 on another—in the same year.) Waller recorded "Charge" again on a ten-inch Black Label record in 1911 (now marked as Gramophone Company Ltd., with the "Once more unto the breach" speech from *Henry V* 3.1 on the other side of the record).[89] Henry Ainley released his acoustic recording of "Charge" ca. 1912 on a ten-inch double-sided Gramophone Company Plum Label record with his recitation of "The Day," a forceful, angry World War I poem by Henry Chappell blasting the Kaiser, on the flip side.[90] Ainley later recorded "Charge" again with the benefit of electrical recording technology.

In Britain, "Charge" was a regular part of variety stage shows,[91] touring costume recitals,[92] and benefit entertainment programs.[93] It was also occasionally recited before or following dramatic productions, sometimes as an "anniversary reminiscence," as when the actor Walter Steadman (in the uniform of the 10th Hussars) recited "Charge" at the Britannia Theatre in commemoration of the Crimean War in 1889.[94] It was recited by men and women, amateurs and professional actors on a regular basis throughout the latter half of the nineteenth century and into the twentieth. It was such a common recitation piece for so many different kinds of occasions that it was also an effective text for comical treatment. As with the dialect adaptations of "Mary Had a Little Lamb," comic actors would make use of "Charge" as a device to imitate "the manners, voices, and dialects of various people reciting" a widely known text, the poem thus functioning as a generic vehicle by which to replicate socially identifiable speech mannerisms.[95] In some cases, it was deployed for comedic ends to accentuate the methods of delivery favored by those who performed the poem seriously. For example, at a benefit entertainment for a children's hospital, the burlesque specialist Arthur Playfair performed imitations of the distinctive acting styles of Herbert Beerbohm Tree, Charles Wyndham, and Weedon Grossmith reciting "Charge," arousing "much enthusiasm in an audience that was not naturally demonstrative." As a *Morning Post* reporter described the effect of these comedic imitations: "Everything is wickedly exaggerated, and yet everything seems perfectly true. They are not 'as large as life and twice as natural,' but much larger than life and no less natural. They are unique."[96] The exaggerated theatrical method deployed in these comic imitations revealed the seam between performativity and natural expression that the serious elocutionist aimed to conceal.

Given the ubiquity of "Charge" as a stage recitation standard, it is not surprising that all three of these British-produced recordings of the poem were recorded by individuals who had professional expertise in public performance, and who had performed "Charge" on the public stage before recording it. Lewis Waller and Henry Ainley were well-known actors of the late Victorian and Edwardian theatre. Waller had been reciting Tennyson's poem in public since 1899 at least, when he was listed in *The Stage* as being scheduled to read the poem at a fundraiser for widows and orphans, and then as having performed it a month later at a "War Fund" matinee benefit at the Albert Hall, a reading that *The Era* said was delivered "with all his accustomed fire."[97] Such public performances continued even after the records were released, suggesting an ongoing cycle of mutual promotion between live recital and recorded recitation. In July 1915, Waller performed "Charge" live in a "Grand Gramophone Concert" in Middlesbrough, North Yorkshire, that also included a live performance by Enrico Caruso.[98] Waller's 1906 recorded recitation of the charge was noted in the theatre paper *The Sketch* as an example of the growing influence and seriousness of the gramophone as an instrument of the arts, on the same page as a listing of Waller's latest theatrical production at the Lyric Theatre.[99] The recordings by an actor such as Waller functioned as an extension of his professional work on stage.

Noted throughout his career as a superb elocutionist, Henry Ainley also established himself in the theatre before going on to successful work in film and radio. , and the BBC preserved some of his broadcasts as examples of fine diction.[100] This aspect of Ainley's talent as a performer was recognized in a 1931 review of his later recording of "Charge," which noted: "Henry Ainley is generally regarded as one of our finest male elocutionists and after hearing the 'Charge of the Light Brigade,' 'A Chant of Love for England,' and 'The Bells,' I am not prepared to dispute that conclusion. Of the three, I liked best the first, 'The Charge,' which he recites more quietly than most elocutionists, but not without intense effect."[101]

Ainley's 1931 recorded performance of "Charge" to which the reviewer refers sounds subtler and calmer because it was made using electrical recording technologies with a microphone rather than through a horn. Ainley had originally recorded "Charge" acoustically ca. 1912. His delivery in the later electrical recording suggests an awareness of the potential for subtlety in amplitude that an electrical recording environment with microphones calibrated to transduce acoustic energy into electrical energy could provide. In contrast, Waller's declamation of the poem captured acoustically in studio, is done in a manner that suggests declamation in a large hall before a large audience. The performance methods respectively associated with "fiery Waller" and "elocutionary Ainley" thus inform what we hear in their recordings, as does the technology (acoustic vs. electric) with which the recording was made.

While not a stage actor like Waller and Ainley, Fleming was a renowned preacher and public speaker and led what he called "the penny readings," a series of after-work recitations for working men designed to be "elevating and instructive."[102] Some of these readings and his sermons were transmitted via "the electrophone," which was, in the late 1890s, a "modern application of the telephonic principle as a means of establishing communication [by wire] between a popular theatre or opera house and one's private drawing-room."[103] Fleming had been lecturing on and reciting the poems of Tennyson in public as part of his pedagogical and missionary practice for at least twenty years before he produced his recording of "Charge." As an 1878 article in the *York Herald* reports, Fleming presided at "An Evening with Tennyson" under the auspices of the York Church of England Union of Young

Men, at which he discussed Tennyson's biography, critical reception, and his personal appreciation of Tennyson's poetry over the years. The evening concluded with Fleming's reading of a selection of poems. The purpose of the reading was understood to be illustrative of the lecturer's critical and appreciative observations about Tennyson's work. So, Fleming's argument that "there was in Tennyson a wonderful study of melody and music, . . . was illustrated in 'The Bugle Song' from 'The Princess,' which the lecturer read with fine effect."[104] The audience of the 1878 lecture and readings is described as having been "spellbound" by Fleming's recitation style. The grand finale of the evening was Fleming's recital of "Charge," the *York Herald* noted, "which was given with rare power and force. In conclusion, Canon Fleming pointed out that every young man had a duty to perform, and in eloquent language urged them to perform that duty, and to take for their motto not only 'Onward,' but 'Upward.' It should be their ambition not only to work below, but to rise above, and to rise every day to the service of God."[105]

The elocutionary prowess that Fleming displayed in his readings and lectures served to sound the possibility of upward ambition and mobility that he was preaching through his public discussion and performance of literature. Due to Fleming's popularity as a public reader of literature, he made a few recordings (that of "Charge" being an extant example). Fleming was also the first Whitehead Professor of Preaching at the London College of Divinity, and published his college lectures in book form as *The Art of Reading and Speaking* (1896),[106] which gives some sense of Fleming's own theory of reading in relation to the recorded performance that we have.

What, aside from researching the contexts in which the individual artists performed, can we, as literary historians, do with such recordings? More specifically, how can we extract useful information from them in relation to contextualizing information obtained from the analysis of printed texts?

Linguistics as a discipline, and the digital tools used by linguists for phonetic analysis, can help us develop methods for approaching historical literary recordings. Praat, open-source software designed to "do phonetics by computer," which provides a means of visualizing and analyzing a variety of properties of speech, at various granularities, with highly accurate results, is the tool I will use here.[107] Praat suggests ways in which we might immerse ourselves in the signal of historical voice recordings to find new formal and prosodic properties, but although useful for rendering aspects of the sound wave graphically, it is specialized and ponderous. It remains up to the literary scholar to interpret that visual information, to decide how it might be a significant formal representation of performance in relation to the literary historical contexts that seem most relevant or interesting to the project of interpretation. I will focus primarily on the elocutionary context (discussed in a more general sense above) that informed the performance of Tennyson's "Charge" at the turn of the nineteenth century by considering how graphic visualizations of these recorded readings, and the visible pitch contours, in particular, might help us describe and say things about the formal characteristics of different elocutionary modes of delivery of this particular poem during this historical period.[108]

In saying I am interested in examining an elocutionist's pitch contours, I am actually saying that I am interested in discovering what a computer rendering of an isolated linguistic concept like "pitch" might reveal about how Victorian elocutionists chose to read Tennyson's poetry out loud. The annotation approach I have taken with these early recordings of "Charge" has been to work from categories of vocal action as described in a large sampling of elocution manuals published between 1800 and 1922, and then to apply certain ubiquitous categories to speech effects heard in the recordings themselves. My analysis of these recitations of poems using Praat is here limited to some basic prosodic details, roughly divided into the three overarching categories of pitch, duration, and amplitude. Again, such categories are abstractions of far more complex phenomena. Intonation, manifested by pitch, is an auditory property that correlates with the fundamental frequency (fo) of a wave form, but must also involve certain qualities of amplitude and duration. Stress is manifested by an increase in pitch, length (duration), and loudness. The acoustic correlate of the auditory property of loudness is intensity, which may consist of basic amplitude, but is often accompanied by other sonorant features as well. When deployed in certain combinations these sonorant features result in prosodic (not syntactic) phrases indicative of shifts within a reciter's delivery.

Tremor

Take, for example, the prevalent use of a combination of tremor (vibrato) and prolongation (holding or extending a uniform vocal sound) in Waller's

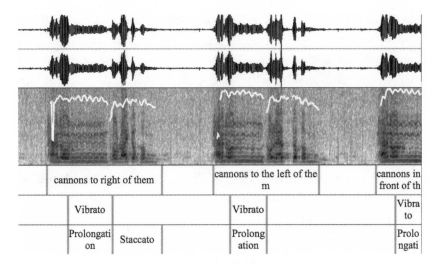

cannons to right of them		cannons to the left of the m		cannons in front of th
Vibrato		Vibrato		Vibra to
Prolongati on	Staccato	Prolong ation		Prolo ngati

Figure 7. Praat interval annotation showing tremor and prolongation pitch contours in Lewis Waller's recitation of "The Charge of the Light Brigade"

delivery of the lines "Cannon to right of them." We can see the vibrato clearly in Waller's pristinely squiggly pitch contours (fig. 7).

Waller deploys vibrato here as if to represent the fury of the cannon fire, but he actually does so almost all the way through his reading, giving the entire performance a frantic and relentless feeling of distress. The persistence of Waller's high volume delivery with tremor and prolongation was a mark of his vocal power and the "'phallic' performing skill" for which, James Naremore says, he had become known.[109] This is an unorthodox use of the effect (according to Victorian elocution manuals), where vocal tremor is meant to be used sparingly to express "the condition of suffering, grief, tenderness, and supplication."[110] Fleming and Ainley, on the other hand, in accordance with the advice of the manuals, reserve their use of vocal tremor for the expression of tenderness and grief. This is most audible in their delivery of the final stanza of the poem, lines already considered in the context of Coghlin's dramatic recitation, above:

> When can their glory fade?
> **O the wild charge they made!**
> All the world wonder'd.

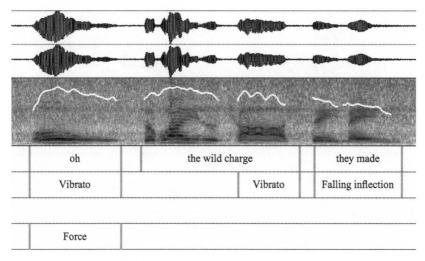

oh		the wild charge		they made
Vibrato			Vibrato	Falling inflection

	Force	

Figure 8. Praat interval annotation showing tremor and prolongation pitch contours in Canon Fleming's recitation of "The Charge of the Light Brigade"

> Honour the charge they made!
> Honour the light brigade,
> Noble six hundred![111]

Note in the visualizations provided how the line cast in bold is performed by Fleming (fig. 8) and Ainley (fig. 9).

In the recordings of Fleming and Ainley, the technique of vocal tremor (or vibrato) is implemented uniquely at this important moment in the poem. Remember, this is the universalizing moment of reflection on the significance of the action that has just been narrated. From the standpoint of elocutionary technique, the deployment of vibrato here functions as a sonic signal for the listener to engage in what the reception context assumes will be received as natural, communally felt sentiments of wonder and admiration. Tremor deployed appropriately sounds the sentiment meant to be experienced on hearing "Charge" read well. It does not (or may not) sound that way to us anymore, of course, but it clearly once triggered a powerful sense of the glory of the British nation.

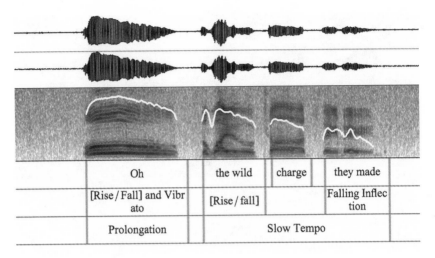

Oh	the wild	charge	they made
[Rise / Fall] and Vibrato	[Rise / fall]		Falling Inflection
Prolongation		Slow Tempo	

Figure 9. Praat interval annotation showing tremor and prolongation pitch contours in Henry Ainley's recitation of "The Charge of the Light Brigade"

Force

Vocal force, apparent most obviously in the peak amplitudes of the wave form itself, is a rich and complex category, to which Victorian elocution manuals paid a great amount of attention. In one sense, this category of vocal action pertains directly to the contextual factors of audience and venue. It is a scaled property to be applied in proportion to the scale of the venue in which a speech is delivered, as Robert Fulton and Thomas Trueblood, authors of *Practical Elements of Elocution* (1893) illustrate in their suggested exercises for the practice of the scales of force in elocutionary delivery:

> Give the words "*I'm nearer my home to-day than I ever have been before*," in **Subdued** Force on a scale for different auditoriums seating **50, 500, and 5000 persons** respectively.
>
> In the same way give, "*Fellow-citizens: It is no ordinary cause that has brought together this vast assemblage*," in **Moderate** Force; "*Has there any old Fellow got mixed with the boys? If he has, take him out, without making a noise*," in **Energetic** Force; and "*Forward the Light Brigade! Charge for the guns!*" in **Impassioned** Force.
>
> Give the sounds **ee, oo, ah**, and the words **on, ile, aim** through **all the Degrees** of Force in appropriate scale for different auditoriums.[112]

Fulton and Trueblood develop numerous categories to describe the qualities and gradations of the many possible degrees of force, and provide visual scales and charted figures to illustrate their idea of force as an elocutionary technique (fig. 10).[113] Their working scale of the degrees of vocal force—divided into the four levels of subdued, moderate, energetic, and impassioned—is presented as a relative range in relation to the properties of the speaking venue and the individuality of the speakers, each of whom will have "a certain **range** in Degrees of Force which is measured by his own scale."[114] This last point is significant for distinguishing between amateur and professional orators, and Fulton and Trueblood warn against the "strained and unnatural effect" that arises when "minor actors" attempt to "imitate their 'star,'" whose range of force functions is far greater than that of minor imitators.[115] Force as an elocutionary ability could be admirable in itself, even without extensive subtlety in its deployment, as in the case of the critic's admiration for Lewis Waller's talent for "fiery" delivery, which is, in great part, a compliment on his ability to generate substantial volume or force while delivering a speech.

Beyond the basic issue of generating the degrees of force necessary to be heard within different acoustical contexts, Fulton and Trueblood proceed to map out their theory of the relationship between degrees of force and the expressive potential of sounds according to the "Mental, Emotive and Physical laws governing the production of speech notes."[116] Having already provided a "Multiplication Table of Expression" earlier in their book, in which they link voice qualities (orotund, aspirational, guttural, etc.), expressive forms (effusive, expulsive, explosive) and their expressive effects (solemnity, gaiety, grandeur, etc.), they here proceed to outline the possibilities in executing these effects within particular ranges of vocal force (fig. 11).[117] The basic point is that some emotions cannot be credibly expressed at certain volumes, that is to say, within certain degrees of vocal force. The normal timbre and effusive vocal form required to express solemnity, tranquility, and pathos (as the final stanza of "Charge" demands) can only be achieved within a subdued to moderate range of vocal force. The rage of Othello upon his discovery of the villainy of Iago, on the other hand, would demand a Guttural Explosive delivery that can only be achieved at a degree of Energetic and Impassioned force. The mismatching of vocal quality, forms, and degrees of force were

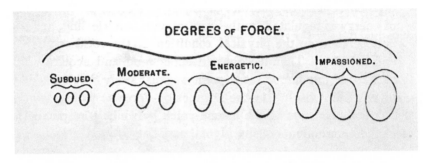

Figure 10. Detail depicting "degrees of force" in vocal expression. From Robert I. Fulton and Thomas C. Trueblood, *Practical Elements of Elocution* (Boston: Ginn, 1893), 148.

effective in acts that comically mimicked such techniques of elocutionary delivery, and the maladjustment of scale in relation to emotive intent was a sure sign of a poorly developed vocal culture.

I will not pretend to understand all the hairs the elocution manuals are attempting to split with their different qualifications of quality, form, and force. What seems clear in Fulton and Trueblood, and in other elocution manuals, is that a sharp command, such as that in the line "'Charge for the guns!' he said" demands an Impassioned degree of force from the reader.[118] It must be delivered loudly. I have annotated the words that are spoken proportionately the loudest within each of the recordings, simply, with the tag 'Force', and this annotation reveals that each of our three readers fulfills the elocution manuals' prescription to deploy substantial force in a sharp command.

In this moment of command that I have isolated for interpretive listening, we can hear the sound of transition from purely formal elocutionary protocols of literary performance, as articulated in manuals like that of Fulton and Trueblood, and the theories of dramatic interpretation that became prominent at the end of the nineteenth century in the work of Curry and others. The sound of this performative transition is especially evident in the way Fleming and, especially, Ainley perform the difference in quality between the explosive command and the narrator's attribution of that demand from another vocal footing with the words, "he said" (fig. 12).

Canon Fleming's idea, articulated in *The Art of Reading and*

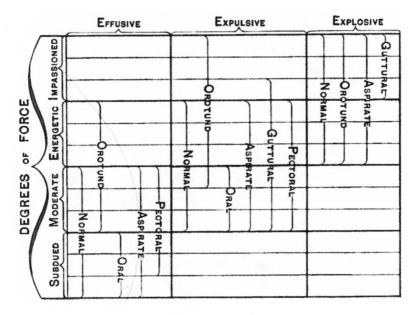

Figure 11. Chart depicting vocal force, form, and quality. From Robert I. Fulton and Thomas C. Trueblood, *Practical Elements of Elocution* (Boston: Ginn, 1893), 153.

Speaking (1896), that "the standard of good speaking is to express one's self, just as one would in earnest conversation," entailed a recognition in performance of this kind of distinction between the voice of the narrator and the voice of the speaker within the poem.[119] This was a facet of his idea of what it meant to read "naturally." It is a point that Curry stresses as well in developing his idea of discerning "purposes in expression" as a key aspect of realizing a sympathetically imagined oral interpretation. Curry includes an exercise in *Imagination and Dramatic Instinct* that is designed for the reader to practice conceiving and assimilating the different aims that motivate the speakers inherent in the array of contrasting excerpts provided. Within the context of this exercise, by which the student may practice expressing "a great many purposes, such as to teach, to warn, to encourage, to apologize, to reprove, to rebuke, to inspire, to arouse," etc., the inclusion of the line, "'Forward the light brigade! Charge for the guns!' he said," clearly aligns the quoted command with the imagined speaker's purpose "to arouse to battle," and clearly delineates this motivated

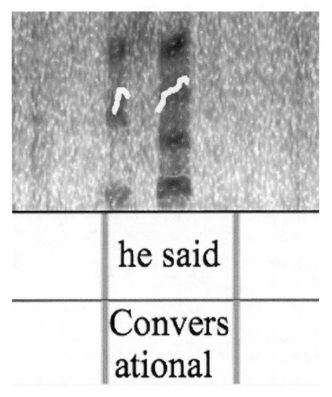

Figure 12. Praat interval annotation showing pitch contours in Henry Ainley's delivery of the words "he said"

expression from the narrator's purpose to situate the commander's speech within this purposive context.

The performance of distinct motives informing the voice or voices heard within a poem would become a cornerstone of many later theories of literary interpretation and performance, from Curry (1890s) to Geiger (1960s). The explicit delineation of those dramatic expressions of purpose from the situating voice of the narrator is one categorical example of the principle of oral literary interpretation. When Fleming and Ainley read the line, "Charge for the guns! *he said*" (my italics), we hear such a distinction clearly. This principle is enacted even more explicitly by the two American reciters of "Charge" I have mentioned, Davenport distinguishing between the command and the narration strongly, and the unknown speaker in the Emerson recording omitting the narrator's "he said" from his reading, altogether, focusing his interpretation on dramatic utterance alone, without narration.

While we do not see many broken pitch curves of the kind I have isolated in figure 12 in Victorian elocutionary recordings, when they do appear we know we are looking at the complexities of pitch variation linguists identify with natural or conversational speech intonation.[120] Natural speech intonation appears as broken lines and fluctuating frequency patterns because conversational, semantic-oriented speech is typically characterized by dramatic changes in pitch, enacted on a constant basis for the purpose of semantic and emotional intelligibility. The contrast between solid-state pitch contours (which will still vary significantly depending on the application of such expressive techniques as prolongation, tremor, force, etc.) and the variable fragments that represent natural speech (in the linguistic sense of the term) illustrates the sonic association of purposeful, expressive speech with the enactment of literary character, and conversational speech as a subtle disguise of the voice behind the action of the literary work. The vocal performance of this delineation of character from narrator, banal and obvious as it may sound to us as experienced silent readers of fiction with quotation marks and narration, is meaningful for its presentation of the narrator's voice in the form of intimate, everyday, interactive speech.

Ending this chapter with an observation about the rupture of elocutionary reading by the jagged pitch curves of conversational speech might suggest a gradual, historical movement toward the identification of elocutionary naturalism with the vocal actions of what linguists identify as "natural" speech patterns. Or, to put it conversationally, the trajectory of my discussion of early recorded poetry readings might seem to suggest that poetry reading as a practice becomes increasingly conversational in tone as we move deeper into the twentieth century. There may be some general truth to such an observation. This would help explain recent accounts of the contemporary poetry reading as its own anti-theatrical, "anti-performative," and "anti-rhetorical" medium.[121] Such a transition can be explained in part by the gradual historical shift from oral to silent, analytical interpretation of literature in the classroom. Such an interesting claim about the historical transformation of the forms of literary reading (out loud) from prescriptive and elocutionary to dramatic, natural, and conversational warrants further research in the form of distant listening to and analysis of a large data set of historical literary audio. The next chapter will, however, instead consider one modern poet's experiments in reading his own poetry as an attempt to find a way beyond antiquated elocutionary methods without succumbing to the aesthetic and philosophical perils that a poetry comprised of everyday voices, and everyday speech patterns, has seemed to present.

4 T. S. ELIOT'S RECORDED EXPERIMENTS IN MODERNIST VERSE SPEAKING

BETWEEN ACTORS AND elocutionists reciting Tennyson into horns and T. S. Eliot reciting his own poetry into a microphone, a new style of literary performance emerged. Still, we can refer to something called T. S. Eliot's Victorian voices as a starting point for this chapter's discussion of the emergence of modernist verse speaking. When I say "T. S. Eliot's Victorian voices," I am not referring to Victorian sources for Eliot's poetry and criticism.[1] Nor will I be discussing at any great length Eliot's own critical discussions of voice in poetry, insofar as he used that term to explore the efficacy of some key generic categories that we often apply to poetry, such as the lyric, the epic, the epistle, the dramatic monologue, and dramatic verse. Eliot's lecture to the National Book League in 1953, "The Three Voices of Poetry," a revised version of which was later published in *On Poetry and Poets* (1957), is, in fact, dripping with Victorian categories, antitheses, and poetic examples. The opening sentences alone suggest the influence of John Stuart Mill and Robert Browning: "The first voice is the voice of the poet talking to himself—or to nobody. The second voice is the voice of the poet addressing an audience, whether large or small. The third is the voice of the poet when he attempts to create a dramatic character in verse."[2]

The first of Eliot's two voices are developments of Mill's famous binary from his essay "What Is Poetry?" where he notes, asking our pardon for the antithesis, "that eloquence is *heard*; poetry is *over*heard. Eloquence sup-poses an audience," whereas the peculiarity of poetry lies "in the poet's utter unconsciousness of a listener."[3] Eliot identifies the first voice with "a poem that is neither didactic nor narrative, and not animated by any social purpose," and mentions later "the enjoyment of *overhearing* words which are not addressed to us."[4] Mill's idea of eloquence is roughly equivalent to how Eliot describes epic, as poetry "that has a conscious social purpose—poetry intended to amuse or instruct." Epic manifests "the voice of the poet addressing other people," Eliot says.[5] About half of the "The Three Voices of Poetry" is devoted to discussion of one Browning poem or another (with some D. G. Rossetti thrown in for good measure). Eliot's discussion of Rob-ert Browning's dramatic monologues is a pivot point here, because it marks the first moment when Eliot's three voices collapse into each other, this collapse being the ultimate point of Eliot's essay. The dramatic monologue is representative for Eliot of the (second) "voice of the poet in non-dramatic poetry which has a dramatic element in it."[6] This awkward category is the most pertinent moment in Eliot's essay as far as my meaning of "Eliot's Victorian voices" is concerned, because it attempts to describe the voice of the poet as both lyrical, musical, nonpurposive, *and* performative, dra-matic, instrumental, all at once. I return later in the chapter to something approximating this idea of hearing "the dramatic" in nondramatic poetry. Yet this idea of a voice that is "non-dramatic with a dramatic element" is still not exactly what I am getting at when I refer to "T. S. Eliot's Victorian Voices" as the place to begin an account Eliot's eventual realization of a post-elocutionary style of literary performance.

I mean, instead, the Victorian verse-speaking voices that I believe Eliot heard in his head and that functioned as antithetical models for his own vocalizations of his poetry. One of the major assumptions that will allow my chapter to proceed is that the key voices in which Eliot spoke his poetry—I will be focusing on his recorded readings of *The Waste Land*—were articu-lated against Victorian ones. That is to say, against the kinds of readings and recitations that we have been considering up to this point. The primary elocutionary models against which Eliot voiced his verse were well estab-lished by the end of the nineteenth century. Eliot did not read poetry like a Victorian stage actor or elocution instructor. In the recordings he left us, his readings sound nothing like those of Len Spencer, Bransby Williams, William Sterling Battis, Rose Coughlan, Lewis Waller, Canon Fleming, or Henry Ainley. *Those* readings either approached the speeches they delivered as modes of character interpretation within a recognizable context of address, or according to a formula, however heavy or light, of structured elocutionary expression. Eliot's experiments in reading his own poetry, and the recordings he produced through such experimentation, work to eschew such techniques and to replace them with modes of intoning speech and character that were more in line with his own poetics.

Eliot's circumstance of reading his poems into a microphone for their transcription onto disc represents an opportunity for us to understand his own interpretation of voice and tone in *The Waste Land*, and how he wished to reframe the original contexts of address that might be attributed to the wide array of utterances presented in the poem "within a more expansive whole."[7] Still, I aim to make the case that the voices Eliot does speak in are audibly knowledgeable of a great variety of verse-speaking methods and modalities, and, further, that some of the more archaic, discredited—to our ears, embarrassing—methods, which were identified with "mechanical" tenets of elocution, are deployed, among other more obvious methods, by Eliot in odd and subtle ways, for specific effects that have nothing to do with the original aims of such schools of elocutionary thought. So, by "Eliot's Victorian voices" I mean that in his recordings of *The Waste Land,* Eliot voices knowingly within a range of modalities that transform techniques of Victorian elocution into something else; something decidedly modern.

Beyond their not sounding Victorian, Eliot's poetry recordings are distinctively different from the dramatic and character-elaborating theories of interpretation, audible in the recordings made of his poetry by an actor contemporary to Eliot, Robert Speaight, of whose manner of reading Eliot approved, but did not emulate. Speaight was a regular reader of poetry for the BBC. He appeared in and then recorded a speech from Eliot's *Murder in the Cathedral* for HMV in the 1930s, and released his own recordings of *The Waste Land* and *The Four Quartets* in the 1950s.[8] In 1942, Eliot wrote to a BBC producer that he was "highly pleased" with Speaight's performance of "East Coker" on the air and recommended Speaight should the BBC wish to produce and air a reading of "The Dry Salvages." Eliot cared about the precedent that a "first reading of a new poem" would set for that poem's reception and understanding.[9] He cared how his poetry was read out loud. He did not believe that there was a single way to read a poem out loud, but he did believe that some ways were superior to others. Eliot's own ways of envoicing the poems he wrote are interpretations that articulate his ideas about how best to intone personality and character as it functions within the formal and ethical structures that modern verse affords. This chapter will seek to explain how Eliot experimented with ways of vocalizing his poetry in an iterative process of recorded performance, and will situate these experiments within a wider discursive context surrounding "verse speaking" (as it was called at this time) that may have informed Eliot's understanding of what he was trying to accomplish when reading his poetry out loud. The story best begins with an understanding of the recording context in which Eliot's early recorded experiments in rendering *The Waste Land* in his own voice were made.

Audiographical Context

Most of us, if we have heard a recording of T. S. Eliot reading his poem *The Waste Land*, are familiar with the 1946 Library of Congress recording, in which he performs his poem primarily (except for the "nerves" and "pub" dialogues in "A Game of Chess") in what I would describe as his robotic liturgical voice.[10] Less familiar to us is a series of non-commercially-released recordings of the poem that Eliot made in 1933 to "instantaneous discs" (made either of acetate cellulose-coated aluminum or just aluminum) under the auspices of William Cabell Greet's American and English dialect series, which this Barnard College professor of English developed for the purpose of teaching pronunciation and elocution.[11] As later institutional documentation of the collection indicates, what had been known as the "speech recording library" since the 1920s became a division of Columbia University Libraries in the mid-1960s and now forms a part of the recorded sound section of the Brander Matthews Dramatic Museum Collection owned by Columbia. Dubs of the early instantaneous disc recordings were made to magnetic tape in the 1970s, and these tape reels are held at the Library of Congress.

The director of the Brander Matthews Museum, Thomas F. Kilfoil,[12] who presided over the collection around the time of its integration into the Columbia Library, provided this succinct history of its development in a letter to an inquiring researcher in 1966:

> [It] began in the late 1920's as the Speech Laboratory, originated by faculty members of the departments of English and Physics. The main objective in the early years was to collect American dialect samples. Instantaneous recordings were cut out on aluminum discs, as students, faculty members, and others read a standard passage and briefly described their formative speech environments. Prof. Harry Morgan Ayers made instructional records in historical dialects. Recordings of visiting poets reading from their own works were added when possible. Radio broadcasts, especially those of literary, social, or political interest, became another source of instantaneous recordings. Local ceremonies and those in which prominent members of the University took part were recorded as well. Between one and two thousand discs have survived, to some degree at least, from this early period.

> The National Council of the Teachers of English published some of the recordings made by Prof. Ayers and the poets. Linguaphone and at least one other publisher issued a series selected from the American dialects recordings.

> By the time, late in the 1940s, when recordings of poetry and drama began to be available in number, our division had abandoned the practice of making its own instantaneous recordings. The commercial releases which we have acquired since then far overbalance the early home-made recordings.[13]

As Kilfoil's account indicates, an offshoot of the Speech Lab recording activities was a poetry recording project by The National Council of Teachers of English in collaboration with the journal *American Speech* (which William Cabell Greet edited), and Erpi Picture Consultants, Inc. (a company that specialized in educational talking pictures).[14] The recordings of visiting poets that were made included records by W. H. Auden, Robert Frost, Vachel Lindsey, Harriet Monroe, Edgar Lee Masters, and Gertrude Stein, in addition to those of Eliot. Some of the poetry recordings made were treated, at least within the pages of *American Speech*, as phonetic specimens to study in tandem with the regional dialect recordings Greet collected for the purpose of correcting students' speech.[15] The Frost recordings and three by Stein were made commercially available for use by teachers in the classroom as early as 1936.[16] There is no indication that the Eliot recordings were made available in the same way at that time.[17]

Richard Swigg notes how different the 1930s Eliot recording of *The Waste Land* is from the later 1946 recording. In contrast to the "monotonous fatalism" of the 1946 Library of Congress *Waste Land*, Swigg remarks that the 1933 recording enacts the kind of "passion and urgency" that must have led Virginia Woolf to record in her diary after hearing a private reading of the poem in June 1922, six months before it was published, that Eliot "sang it & chanted it, rhythmed it."[18] Swigg's observations of the differences between the 1933 and 1946 recordings are valuable, but also raise some basic questions about the nature and status of the recordings in question. If we examine the discs of the recordings that Eliot made, and listen to the transfers that were made from each of those discs to magnetic tape, and then to digital WAV files, it becomes clear that there is no 1933 recording of *The Waste Land* in any singular sense, but rather, twelve two-sided disks (of approximately five minutes of sound per side) containing multiple and often extremely distinct experimental renditions, performances, rehearsals, let's call them *takes*, of each section of the poem. To be more precise, the discs contain five different versions (or in some instances, dubbed duplications from acetate to solid aluminum disc) of "The Burial of the Dead" and "Death by Water," and three each of "The Fire Sermon," "A Game of Chess," and "What the Thunder Said" (see table). What we mean by Eliot's 1933 recording of *The Waste Land* depends on which take of a particular section of the poem we are referring to.

Electrical disc-recording technology combined elements of the earlier acoustic recording process (in which a record was engraved ready for listening on the spot using a stylus connected to a diaphragm) with the electrical transduction of the acoustic signal, at the encoding stage (via a microphone), the transmission stage (via electrical signals sent to a magnetically calibrated engraving-needle cartridge), and the decoding/reproduction stage (via an amplifier and loudspeaker).[19] The presence and sensitivity of the microphone, and the limited yet real means of controlling the amplitude of the signal it sent to the engraving cartridge added new kinds of sensitivity to the process of voice recording, or, in this case, of poetry record making. The increased

T. S. Eliot's 1933 instantaneous disc recordings of The Waste Land

---

[Five versions of "The Burial of the Dead"*]*

402A Burial of the Dead (tape 30 A)

403A* Burial of the Dead (tape 30 A)

404A* Burial of the Dead (tape 30 B)

404.1A Burial of the Dead (tape 30 B)

405.1A Burial of the Dead

(poor audio quality, not duplicated to tape)

[Three versions of "A Game of Chess"*]*

402B Game of Chess (tape 30 A)

403B* Game of Chess, Part 1 (tape 30 B)

404B* Game of Chess, Part 1 (tape 30 B)

405A* Game of Chess Part 2 (tape 30 B)

405B* Game of Chess Part 2 (tape 30 B)

405.1 B Game of Chess Parts 1 & 2

(Poor audio quality, not duplicated to tape.)

[Three versions of "The Fire Sermon" +
 two versions of "Death by Water"*]*

406A* Fire Sermon Part 1 (tape 30 B)

406B* Fire Sermon Part 2 (tape 30 B)

406.1A* Fire Sermon Part 1 (tape 30 B)

406.1B* Fire Sermon Part 2 / Death by Water (tape 30 B)

406.2A* Fire Sermon Parts 1 and 2 (tape 31 A)

406.2B* Fire Sermon Part 2 / Death by Water (tape 31 A)

[Three versions of "Death by Water"*]*

407A* Death by Water (tape 30 B)

406.1B* Death by Water (tape 30 B)

406.2B* Death by Water (tape 30 B)

[Three versions of "What the Thunder Said"*]*

407A* What the Thunder Said Part 1 (tape 30 B)

407 B* What the Thunder Said Part 2 (tape 30 B)

407.1A* What the Thunder Said Part 1 (tape 31 A)

407.1B What the Thunder Said Part 2 (tape 31 A)

407.2A What the Thunder Said Part 1 and 2

(tape 31 A [poor quality])

---

amplitude of the voice signal that was possible with amplification of that signal prior to engraving, and a broader frequency spectrum captured by the microphone, altered the range of vocal actions an interpreter of poetry could deploy. For Eliot, the electrical instantaneous disc recorder seems to have been approached as a mechanism to be tested for its capacities in rendering vocal amplitude and timbre, and for its relative effectiveness in capturing nuances in pronunciation and tonal register. In listening to the various takes Eliot recorded, one can hear him testing the possibilities and limits of the recording technology with which he had the opportunity to engage.

Instantaneous disc recording had the added benefit of producing a record that could be played back immediately, allowing, in the case of Eliot's early poetry recordings, an iterative process of performance, immediate playback listening and experimental adjustments of vocal action in relation to the affordances of electrical recording, and his aesthetic goals in the interpretation of the poem. He could try out different versions and then quickly select the take he most preferred. Upon examining the material artifacts left from Eliot's acts of recording, we can see traces of his judgments concerning the different recorded performances he produced. For example, a note in pencil (and likely in Eliot's own hand) on the sleeve of one of the recorded takes of "Sweeny among the Nightingales" notes Eliot's determination that this particular take was "not distinct enough" and "unsatisfactory."[20]

Something else that I have noted in my listening to these early Eliot recordings is that some of the takes among the 1933 recordings seem to be exactly the same as parts of the recording released by the Library of Congress in 1946. From listening closely to the 1933 and 1946 recordings over an extended period of time, it becomes audibly apparent (and visually apparent from a comparison of the wave forms) that the 1946 recording is most likely an edited fusion of the "best" takes (more about what "best" might mean later) recorded in 1933. In matching the digitized audio of the 1933 and 1946 records, there are occasional, fractional differences in the "speed" of the two digitized sources, most likely attributable to slight calibration differences occurring during one or more of the processes of rendering. Scenarios of the migration of the audio signal of the 1933 recordings across media formats include: (1) instantaneous disc ca. 1933 to 78 disc ca. 1946–49, (2) instantaneous disc to magnetic tape ca. 1972, and (3) magnetic tape to WAV files ca. 2008.[21] Within each scenario, the precise speed of the record and tape players and recorders in question would have to have been exactly the same to avoid even the slightest time differences between the playback speeds of the digitized files. As we do not have the precise specifications by which the various media migrations were pursued in all cases, our digitized versions of these recordings hover somewhere in status between hard copies and audio apparitions of the literary recordings we are studying. With speed adjustments, and adjustments to some variation in pause lengths between audible phrases, using digital audio software, the 1946 recording and certain takes from the 1933 recordings seem to match up exactly, which is especially apparent in a multitrack, stereo presentation of the two files, with 1933 panned to the left ear and 1946 panned to the right (fig. 13).[22]

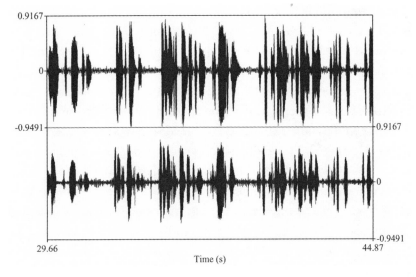

Figure 13. Multitrack comparison of wave forms, T. S. Eliot reading "The Burial of the Dead" (detail) from 1946 78 rpm record (top) and 1933 instantaneous disc (bottom)

From an evidentiary perspective, my claim that the later Library of Congress release of *The Waste Land* is a compilation of certain takes from a larger cluster of recordings made in 1933 raises the question: To what extent can one use analysis of a digital audio signal as the forensic claim about material media migration. The bibliographical leaflets inserted within the 1946 album suggest the possibility of such a compilation recording based on the extant recordings of 1933, noting that the album contents were "selected and arranged by the consultants in poetry in English and issued by the Library of Congress under a grant from the Bollingen Foundation."[23] The Library of Congress received a first grant of $10,500 in January 1946 to prepare five albums of five double-sided 78 rpm records of twentieth-century poets reading their own works. It is not clear who would have made the final selection, although William McGuire's work on the role of the Library of Congress poetry consultants indicates that Louise Bogan (the LC poetry consultant for 1946) spent much of the month of February listening to poetry recordings that already existed as a form of research and preparation, and that "the work of auditing, consulting, listmaking, technical preparation, and text compiling continued through the tenures of the next two Consultants

[Karl Shapiro and Robert Lowell, respectively] before the albums were published, in 1949."[24] McGuire suggests that Bogan and Allan Tate may have persuaded Eliot to record some poems at an NBC studio in New York, but also suggests that Lowell's letters "inviting poets to record or rerecord" attracted few respondents, and that Eliot was not among the poets who came to record during Lowell's year as Library of Congress poetry consultant.[25]

Based on the audible evidence, combined with this other information, it seems likely that Eliot's album consisted of a mixture of old and new recordings, with *The Waste Land* being a compiled and mastered version of his previous experiments. Eliot's Library of Congress album consisted of *The Waste Land* on three records, "Ash Wednesday" on two records, and "Landscapes: I. New Hampshire; II. Virginia," and "Sweeney Among the Nightingales" on the fifth record. Given Eliot's later concern for making recordings that were satisfying to him, it is likely he indicated at some point in time which of the 1933 takes he felt were, to his mind, most successful and worthy of public release. He certainly had much to say about the financial arrangement that was proposed for the release of the album, declining a single flat rate of $50 per record (for a total of $250) without subsequent royalties, and eventually negotiating a royalty of $250 per five hundred records pressed. This was more in line with the arrangement he had recently made around his recordings of the *Four Quartets*, for which Eliot received, in his words, "the usual gramophone royalty from the HMV Gramophone Company."[26] As of the mid-1980s, Eliot's Library of Congress recordings had sold over 10,500 copies, in 78, LP, and cassette form, and have brought more to the Eliot estate since then via the Apple Music store and other such online vendors, where this same selection of 1933 recordings can be streamed or downloaded by users (for a subscription fee) as *The Waste Land—Read by T. S. Eliot—EP*, EP designating, skeuomorphically in the context of iTunes, an extended-play release of about twenty-five minutes, not quite the length of a full LP record album.

The possibility that the 1946 Library of Congress release of *The Waste Land* on three 78 records consists of cleaned-up, de-crackled selections culled from the 1933 instantaneous disc recording session suggests a mastering and cleaning up of the sound of the recorded poem in more than just the sense of arrangement and audible noise reduction. I argue that Eliot combines a particular conception of the voice-recording machine with ideas prevalent in New Critical approaches to literary interpretation—ideas that he, himself, influenced[27]—as a means of expunging accent in any corrupting, dialectical sense, from his reading, and focusing his vocal performance of *The Waste Land* on cultivated forms of tonality instead. If we take Michael North's idea that dialect, for Eliot, "is a flaw, a kind of speech impediment, a remnant of the inarticulate that clogs his language and stands in the way he attempts to link his own individual talent with tradition"[28]—then a consideration of Eliot's experiments in how to vocalize his poetry must be attuned to a method designed to navigate (if not to remove altogether) such impediments, and to realize a delivery that escapes the parochial markers of regional accent by developing a disembodied conception of vocal tone. Knowing, as we do, that Eliot's first recordings of *The Waste Land* originated from a collection of recordings made by a collector of American dialects, Eliot's performative motivation to displace demarcating accent with universal tone sounds all the more resonant as an aesthetic project. In my reading of Eliot's recordings, I provide a series of elocutionary or "verse speaking" contexts that explain how Eliot imagined the voice of modernity as simultaneously oracular and disembodied, musical and mechanical, communal and local. The contexts surrounding such a conception of oral delivery can be read into the history of how *The Waste Land* as an aural artifact was produced, and can be heard in the recordings themselves.

Leaving the relationship between the 1933 recordings and the 1946 Library of Congress release aside for a moment, I want to focus on the variety of performance techniques that can be heard in the 1933 recordings. The different takes of the 1933 recordings *are* remarkably different from each other, providing audible examples of experimentation in tempo, amplitude, intonation patterns, and varying degrees of dramatization and methods of avoiding it. One version of "A Game of Chess" (402.1B) is over half a minute longer than another recording of the same section (403B) and substitutes meditative/colloquial voicing with a more urgent, incantatory style of delivery. One version of the Pub scene from "A Game of Chess" (405B) is far more "dramatically" rendered, with a much more developed cockney accent, and greater character play than the other versions. For example, just following the lines, "You ought to be ashamed, I said, to look so antique. /

(And her only thirty one)" [II.156–57], Eliot adds a "harrumph" of exasperation. He has really gotten into character in this take. One version of "What the Thunder Said" (407.1A) is nearly sung, slowly and distinctly, in shifting and clearly identifiable musical pitches, and this in fact turns out to be the performance integrated into the 1946 recording. Another take (407) of this section is racing and urgently incanted with strong shifts in volume, ranging from whisper to more than occasional screaming, and with hardly any pauses between line breaks. One take of "Death by Water" (406.2B) provides a far more straightforward narrator's voice telling the story of Phlebas the Phoenician that works its way up to melody in the delivery of the lines "Gentile or Jew" (this is the delivery heard in the 1946 recording), whereas another take (407A) opens with melodic delivery as if it a sailor's song is being sung from the start, a sea shanty about Phlebas.[29]

I will return at the close of this chapter with a closer listen to some of these different takes as illustrations of several key techniques in vocalization that Eliot deploys. First, I would like to speculate in a more general way on their significance. What are we to make of these varied experiments in recitation captured onto disc? What contexts beyond that of the recordings' production help determine their significance? In the spirit of Eliot's own early experiments in poetry recording, the rest of this chapter will proceed as a series of interpretive takes on Eliot's multiple recorded readings of *The Waste Land*.

TAKE 1—Phonographic Transcript versus Gramophonic Lament

One way to understand Eliot's 1933 recordings of *The Waste Land* is to hear them as an experimental step on the way to the calculatedly numb or mechanical delivery of his "definitive" recording of 1946—the one he allowed to be released commercially for the next thirty years of his life.[30] There are as I have said sections from these early readings that seem to have been used to produce what we now have commercially available as the 1946 recording. And in the materials held at the BBC Written Archives Centre in Reading, there is information concerning Eliot's recording of another poem, "Ash Wednesday," that indicates both Eliot's aspirations to achieve definitive recitations of his poems, and to help us understand his procedure of achieving such master recordings. Eliot recorded "Ash Wednesday" for the Library of Congress in 1946, but, dissatisfied with that American recording, negotiated terms with the BBC to re-record the poem in 1951. Rayner Heppenstall, the producer in charge of this particular project, remarked in memos that Eliot "seemed anxious to achieve a perfect and definitive rendering of 'Ash Wednesday'" and that he wanted "to hold more than one recording session, hearing each section of the poem played back before he went on to read the next one."[31] If some of the takes from Eliot's 1933 recordings of *The Waste Land* represent failed attempts to achieve the solemn version of 1946, the multiple excised takes of that earlier version sit like misfit pieces abandoned on the way to constructing a vocal rendering that worked via the medium of the gramophone record. These early parts do not work for Eliot because they are too quirky, too human-sounding, too dialectical, too affective, or, too musical, too experimental in their alterations in tempo and pitch, and so not adequately dry, objective, or mechanical.

This interpretation treats *The Waste Land* more as an indiscriminate transcription recording capturing random and diverse sounds of life and culture to be played back than as a poem to be read. In Eliot's recordings of it, we are, in effect, listening to a transcript of the trials and tribulations of (Western) history through the media technologies of modernity. "Poetic discourse competes here with Edison's waxed cylinders and Emile Berliner's blank records," Juan A. Suarez comments. "It aspires to total inclusiveness. . . . The present quickly melts into the past; colloquial discourse transmutes into literature; and [Eliot's female character] Lil blends with *Hamlet's* hapless character."[32] This kind of reading is valuable starting place, for it converts Eliot's "allusions"—a dominant concern of analyses of the printed poem—into voices. Early responses to Eliot's poem all commented on the mediation of his poetic personality through literary allusion. "The poetic personality of Mr. Eliot is extremely sophisticated," a *TLS* reviewer observed in 1923. "His emotions hardly ever reach us without traversing a zig-zag of allusion." Suarez suggests that the poet is not so much "sophisticated" as "phonographic," and that we should think of Eliot's "quotes from a score of authors" (in the language of the *TLS* review) as voices, rather than as literary quotations.[33]

Even if we adopt this idea of *The Waste Land*, however, we are left to deal with Eliot's preferred, less affective mode of reciting the poem. The poem is not simply played back; it is *read* back to us as we play back the recording of Eliot's recitation. The reading reinstills the element of performance as a different kind of mediation (a human elocutionary one) into the resounding of what Suarez describes as a "data bank of mechanical-memories detached from self and psychology."[34] If we approach the poem as an indiscriminate record, when we listen to Eliot's recitation of the poem (the 1946 version), we must be listening to an elocutionary performance of mechanical play-back. With this ear, even the unpurged colloquialisms sound infused with mechanical apathy. The symbols of canned-ness used to communicate a disenchanted culture (the typist's "food in tins" [III.223] and later, her "automatic hand" that "puts a record on the gramophone" [III.254–55]) are given their correlating tone of voice. "He Do the Police in Different Voices"—well known to be the original, abandoned title of the poem—might be translated, in this instance, to mean, "He Performs the Hegemony-Enforcing Medium in All Its Power to Falsely Suggest Multiplicity and Difference." Or, more succinctly, "He Do the Gramophone."

But the robotic liturgical delivery of the 1946 release performs more than just tinny automatism. It sounds a complex, paradoxical experience of the mechanically mediated and decorporealized voice, as it is heard *through* the technology of the gramophone, as simultaneously reduced, demysti-fied, familiarized, automatized, on the one hand, and excessive, sublime, uncanny, and autonomous, on the other. Partly what I am referring to when I say Eliot's delivery is robotically liturgical, or, maybe even better, me-chanically oracular, is Stephen Connor's point (in his cultural history of ventriloquism, *Dumbstruck*) that mechanical "technologies of voice are actualizations of fantasies and desires concerning the voice which predate the actual technologies."[35] The idea here is that the voice that is reduced, demystified, and automatized by technology results in an unexpected excess in the form of an ideational resurgence of the uncanny powers of autonomy that characterized pretechnological fantasies of an all-powerful, superhu-man voice: the voice of oracles and gods. As Connor argues, vocal acoustic technologies enact processes of both disenchantment *and* enchantment. This application of Connor's ideas about ventriloquism to Eliot's mode of reading are in line with other critics' attempts to characterize Eliot's poetic method of voicing worldly and otherworldly perspectives simultaneously. Charles Sanders identifies the "distinguishing trait of Eliot's rendition of the inarticulate superfluous man" to be "its ventriloquism," that is to say, "his self-conscious manipulation of the 'dummy' as a deliberate, elaborate, often parodic piece of theater, in a space whose dimensions are both of and not of this world; in which all time is collapsed; and in which, after his example, it grows more difficult to separate lyric from dramatic poetry (if we ever could before), the speaker from the listener, the 'construct' of the poems from the associations evoked within and all about us."[36]

More recently, Omri Moses has thought a way out of this binary by arguing that Eliot's conception of "poetic voice constructs several different, but overlapping relations of address," some that are "exhibited *in* the circumstantial, dramatic or fictive context set up by the poem" and others that "appeal to perspectives *outside* these contexts."[37] *The Waste Land* as a lyric/epic/dramatic poem constructed of multiple, resonating voices speaking in incompatible tones and from incongruous contexts demands a reading voice that does them justice. It requires a tone of voice that does not get lost in the din of the crowd, or drown it out, but, on the contrary, has a capacity to sound an ostensible babel in tones and frequencies that capture the larger circumstance informing the complex history of human communication, character, and life. That greater tonal mode would resound the significance of particularized utterances in new ways, according to an alternative context of vocal address. Such a tone would, potentially, give those particularized utterances new life. With this model in mind, Eliot's recorded delivery of *The Waste Land* may be understood to evoke a disenchanted voice with undertones of self-conscious knowledge and hope. Or, to use the terms found in so many early interpretations of Eliot's printed poem, Eliot delivers a dry and sterile voice seeking new tonal means for authentic feeling to well up again.

The sterility enacted vocally as an absence of socially motivated intonation would, in the reading of the present interpretive take be meant to sound the automatization of a once reflexive, vivacious, shared culture. Read in relation to Eliot's well-documented interest in specific forms of popular culture, in the art of the music hall and vaudeville (this last term from the French *voix de ville*—the urban, as opposed to, say, the *urbane*, voice), the machine-voice delivery can be heard to enact a declamation of what has been lost in the transition from the vital, participatory music hall era of Marie Lloyd, where "the working man . . . joined in the chorus" and "was himself performing part of the act," to a new era where live performance "has been replaced by a hundred gramophones," and "the working man now will receive without giving, in the same listless apathy with which the middle and upper classes regard any entertainment of the nature of art."[38] These last passages are quoted from Eliot's essay "In Memoriam: Marie Lloyd," published in the *Criterion* in the early 1920s. Eliot believed strongly in music hall performance of a certain era as an art form that was powerful for its ability to engage all classes of society. Eliot's memorial essay on Lloyd, in which he calls her "the greatest music hall artist in England," bases its claim on an argument that asserts her ability to express "that part of the English nation which has . . . the greatest vitality and interest." His assertion of Lloyd's preeminent status rests on his claim for "her understanding of the people and sympathy for them, and the people's recognition of the fact that she embodied the virtues which they genuinely most respected in private life."[39] Barry J. Faulk argues that the Eliot who wrote this essay was mourning "the loss of a compact which had permitted intellectuals to redeem the popular and exert enough authority to make this recognition of difference matter." In short, he was lamenting a working "formula for cultural hegemony."[40]

Eliot recognized the importance of new communications technologies in making such a cultural formula operable. We may productively consider Eliot's early experiments in recording his poetry in the context of his life-long engagement in public broadcasting, which took the form, not only of recitations of poems on the air, but of talks explaining the English literary tradition to a wide public. Michael Coyle's account of Eliot's career as a BBC broadcaster suggests that Eliot understood the radio talk as a distinctly popular genre, a genre that had great potential in shaping "a mass audience into an intellectual community."[41] The airwaves as a communications platform were, in effect, Eliot's musical hall stage. This was especially the case prior to the institution of the Third Programme in 1946. After the emergence of this new program—which BBC Director William Haley called "a programme for the educated rather than an educational programme"[42]—Eliot became the voice of culture on a channel that was distinct from the other bands making their way into the ears of a stratified British public. Juxtaposed with the vision of culture represented in *The Waste Land*, Eliot's early work for the BBC represents a vision of community-building that might serve as reparative of the cultural fracture that is voiced in the poem. This might also explain why he did not feel that modern verse could effectively be presented on the air for widespread public broadcast. In his own radio presentations and discussions of poetry, he focused mostly on works that predated the seventeenth century, as if the "dissociation of sensibility" he identified with the metaphysical poets was still in effect, and would not be helped by broadcast presentations of contemporary poetry that reinforced such a split between thought and feeling.[43]

Eliot's arguments about the transition from participatory, interested music hall entertainments to mechanical film and gramophone entertainments in the Marie Lloyd essay, and his avoidance of modernist poetry in his early BBC radio work, are a comment on the nonparticipatory nature of new entertainment media—and raise the question of how *The Waste Land* as a poem, and Eliot's experiments in performing that poem, might be addressing this same problem. While the poem certainly uses metaphors and similes of canned-ness to communicate a disenchanted culture (the food tins, automatic hand, and gramophone), one might read into the poem other, more performative and participatory elements that harken back to parlor recitation and late Victorian elocutionary culture. To do the police in different voices in one sense means to read aloud the condition of modernity *as* Betty Hidgen perceives Sloppy reading the newspaper in Dickens's *Our Mutual Friend*, and yet, it can also mean to read *for* someone (*for* the pleasure of Betty Hidgen in the parlor), *for* their entertainment or ultimate edification. To *do* the police in different voices *for* someone means to participate in an interlocutory event, a performance for the sake of the audience's pleasure in seeing itself reflected in that performance. Eliot's multiple recordings of *The Waste Land*, and especially the 1933 recordings with their multiple, experimental takes of each section of the poem, may just stand as records of his attempt to realize a new way toward such a form of participatory performance—a *reading for*—for a series of isolated voices who speak in nonparticipatory ways, who speak without hearing each other. In other words, even as he is delivering a recitation of voices that are speaking from the fixed or grooved source of the gramophone record, he is doing these voices of mechanized individuals with experiments in timbre and intonation that aim to demechanize the isolated voices of gramophonic modernity.

If so, Eliot's approach to rescuing such voices from isolation was not to resituate them into dialogical contexts but to emphasize the detachment of socially motivated, semantic intonation as an overarching aesthetic tactic and performative structure. Reenacting on record the vital exchange of sympathy and recognition that Eliot so admired in Lloyd was no longer possible. While *The Waste Land* as a poem constructed of textual excerpts might, in one sense, be understood as the phonographic poem par excellence, comprised of an extensive, eclectic album of phonographic genres and literary adaptations (speeches, scenes, sketches, voices, sounds, and recitations), a Bransby Williams approach to recording *The Waste Land* would not do. Dramatization, mimicry, or mimetic performance were not aesthetically feasible categories with which to frame the reading techniques necessary in a recorded performance of this work. A new mode of recorded performance, one that subsumed the individuated quirks of voice and intonation into a broader vocal purview and tactic, was needed. In experimenting in his performance of *The Waste Land*, Eliot worked to figure out how to speak in a voice that did not emanate from a person but from something that captured the nature and import of the medium with which he was engaged.

Mark Morrison has identified the idea of natural delivery as a mode of reading that conveyed "the sort of impersonality that allows the presence of the author to speak through the reciter."[44] As Morrison notes, this "pure voice" delivery "helps elucidate modernist critical and aesthetic categories like those that preoccupied Eliot in his early criticism—the purity of language, impersonality, and verse drama."[45] Eliot's idea, articulated in "Tradition and the Individual Talent," that "the poet has not a 'personality' to express, but a particular medium," or, rather, an "impersonality" that he cannot reach "without surrendering himself wholly to the work to be done" had its equivalents in verse-recitation and elocution manuals of the early 1900s, which increasingly advocated that the reader enact a similar "impersonality" in relation the work he or she was reading aloud.[46] While there is nothing inherently "natural" about natural elocution, nothing inherently

"pure" about the pure voice, the idea of natural vocal delivery has had identifiable meaning, primarily by contrast with so-called mechanical modes of
delivery, in the history of rhetoric. Eliot's developing ideas about speaking
verse worked to transcend this historical binary by vocalizing the formal
unity of a poetic work as an aesthetic entity, rather than by attempting to
voice the characters whose localized perspectives are articulated within that
unified entity. I will unpack this assertion in my final two takes.

TAKE 2—Speaking Verse on the BBC

By the early 1940s—when New Criticism was well on the rise, if not already in its full ascent—questions about the purpose of verse speaking were
necessarily raised again, this time by pitting the dramatic manner of reading associated with Elsie Fogerty's trained actors against some other way
that would be deemed more appropriate for nondramatic poetry. Fogerty's
methods of executive interpretation had been dubbed mechanical, reci-
tational, distorting in their turn, and a new roundtable debate about why
and how verse should be read ensued. In 1941, the BBC producer Christopher Salmon asked Eliot for his opinion about a roundtable discussion
series called *Well Versed*, involving writers, actors, and elocutionists, which
Salmon put on to stage a public debate about how verse should be read
aloud. Participants included the writers Cecil Day Lewis, Robert Nichols,
and James Stephens, the actors Catherine Lacey and Robert Speaight, the
voice educators Gwynneth Thurburn and Marjorie Gullan (the latter a
strong advocate of choral speaking in the schools), and Thomas Hunt, who
played the role of the "everyday listener" in the midst of these assembled
experts. Individual shows in this series had titles like: "How Should Poetry be Read?"; "Must Poetry Make Sense?"; and "Is Verse-Speaking a Lost
Art?" These discussions articulated the terms and concerns that would have
been informing Eliot's own approach to reading verse, whether his own, or
that of the poets he frequently talked about on the BBC, such as Richard
Crashaw, George Herbert, and John Dryden. These radio discussions set up
a series of oppositions that seem especially relevant to the performance of
a poem like *The Waste Land*. They positioned everyday speech against poetry, communication against communion, meaning against music, action

against meditation, and expressed a general concern for the status of poetry in the minds and ears of a more general public.

In the *Well Versed* roundtable, the "everyday listener" Thomas Hunt asked, "Why can't people read poetry in their ordinary voice, and carry over into it the tones they use every day?" Cecil Day Lewis defended the importance of the "special voice" used for speaking verse, because poetry "has a lot to do with incantation . . . and in that respect poetry is like the voice of a priest." Robert Speaight argued that "reading poetry's a problem of communication," a matter of keeping "the attention of the people." And the poet James Stephens focused on the importance of "rubato" (rhythmic flexibility in phrase or measure) for verse speaking and argued that "the public has got to learn that they must listen to poetry as they listen to music."[47]

In his report on these talks, Eliot challenged their apparent assumption that there was a single, right way to read a poem and then proceeded to articulate his own understanding of a verse recitation. He argued that a printed poem and a read performance of that poem are distinct works of art, and that a reading consists of a combination of three key elements: the printed poem, the performer's understanding and interpretation of it, and the qualities of the reader's voice. He lamented actors' tendency to overdramatize nondramatic verse and to expunge everything but dramatic elements from dramatic verse. And he underscored the need to explain to listeners that different kinds of verse should be interpreted in different ways by a variety of readers, and that even the same kind of verse should be read out loud in a variety of ways.[48]

Eliot's primary concern in his report to Christopher Salmon was that the audience not be deterred by the *Well Versed* series from trying to appreciate poetry. His suggested remedy was to stress the desirability of rendering a single poem in diverse ways and of explaining the value of doing so to general listeners by making the analogy to music, to different adaptations of the same score. Eliot found himself "strongly in agreement with Stephens," the poet, as opposed to the actor, Speaight, on the question of how poetry should be read out loud, implying that he thought there was a right way to read poetry, notwithstanding his assertion that poetry can and should be read in different ways. Eliot allowed the BBC to produce *The Waste Land* dramatized by Geoffrey Bridson in 1938, but he so disliked it that he denied a request to produce a second dramatization submitted by Bertram Barnaby in 1958,[49] and the Bridson experience led to what Terence Tiller called "the ban" of Eliot's publishers and executors "on multi-voice performances of *The Waste Land*."[50]

Eliot's refusal of further multi-voice dramatizations of the poem was due to his idea that *The Waste Land* is a poem, and not a play to which specific parts might be assigned to audibly distinct actors. He does not seem to have minded a more straightforwardly dramatic delivery of the poem by a single actor's voice—why else would he have given Robert Speaight permission to record the poem? In his delivery of *The Waste Land,* Speaight makes far greater effort to deliver the possible voice divisions in the poem as emanating from realized individual characters than Eliot does in his own recorded performances of it. In Speaight's performance, the "nerves" section is dramatically grounded as an exchange between a husband and a wife (with the wife's questioning voice rendered in a higher pitch, verging on Monty Python drag), the Shakespeherian Rag is sung, and in the pub scene, Speaight far out-cockney's Eliot. You can hear this characterizing approach even in Speaight's rendering of the opening portion of the poem. These are far more socially grounded voices than the ones we hear in Eliot's recording.

Eliot's dislike of a multivoiced rendition of *The Waste Land* can also be explained with reference to the categories of poetic voice he enumerates in "The Three Voices of Poetry" (1953–57): "the voice of the poet talking to himself—or to nobody," "the voice of the poet addressing an audience, whether large or small," and "the voice of the poet when he attempts to create a dramatic character in verse."[51] It is especially evident in his awkward description of dramatic monologue as the "voice of the poet in non-dramatic poetry which has a dramatic element in it."[52] This hybrid description of the poet's voice brings us back to his agreement with Stephens. In a BBC talk that he gave in 1937 called "On Speaking Verse," Stephens held "that tonally there are three different kinds of verse, and that each of these demands a different speech, adjustment and attack. There is a form generically the epic which is to be uttered in a fashion approximating gravely modulating speech. There is a form, the lyrical, which without being sung, approximates to singing. And there is an intermediate form which is come to by a subtle balancing of phrase against phrase."[53] The three forms Stephens outlines here—spoken, sung, and balancing verse—approximate the range Eliot deploys in his recordings of his own verse.

Although there are obviously different voices to be done in *The Waste Land*, much of the experimentation in the various takes of the 1933 recordings has less to do with finding the individuated voices of characters in the poem—less to do with *doing* voices—than with finding the correct tempo, pitch, and incantatory rhythm that would best allow the variety of voices already written into the poem to cohere as a vocalized movement of poetic composition. There *are* voices more pronouncedly "done" (e.g., the "harrumph" at II.156–57) among the lost takes of 1933, and even a few in the 1946 recording. But Eliot seems to have left that approach to the actor, for the most part. His own approach and ultimate focus was on tonal patterns that would allow his poem to be received, not as a play, but as a series of themes with their own recurrent vocal registers, a "musical composition of ideas."[54]

Eliot's experiments with pitch, amplitude, duration, tempo, and caesura in the 1933 recordings attempt through vocal leitmotiv to give formal precision to a din of disparate dramatic scenarios that are in fact written into the poem. This approach to reading transmutes character in a manner that suggests an oral performance of New Critical tenets. The spirit of Samuel Silas Curry's idea from *Imagination and the Dramatic Instinct* that oral performance consists of "the spontaneous realization of ideas in living relations, and of motive and manifestations of character" seems alive in Eliot's multiple attempts in 1933 to render *The Waste Land* in voice, minus one key element, the final motive to ground speech in character. Eliot's experiment stresses the more formal elements of vocalization as a means of organizing "ideas in living relations." The issue of "motive and manifestations of character" are addressed by such formal elements not as sources for dramatization but as audible renderings of "verbal imprecisions" and "approximate thoughts and feelings"—these last two phrases being from Eliot's "Choruses from the Rock"—that evoke Eliot's version of New Critical formalism, oralized in *The Waste Land* recordings.[55] Character is set within, and infused by the overarching structure that emerges from his deployment of rubato, tempo, monotone, misplaced intonation, and drone, all of which add up to a performance of *The Waste Land*'s "patterns of sound."

The drama of *The Waste Land* as Eliot works to render it has to do simultaneously with the impossibility of making all the voices fit into a single realized character, and the recuperative, restorative power of poetry incanted to do just that. The late Victorian elocutionist Canon Fleming described "reading and speaking by word, without any regard to the sentiment" as "reading mechanically," stating that "when we read without feeling, we are inclined to speak on one note of the voice only, in monotone."[56] Reading without feeling (but for a "music of ideas" [I. A. Richards] or "musical organization" and "unity" [F. R. Leavis])[57] might also describe the effect of New Critical approaches to poetry that translate dramatic voice into a unifying force of formal cohesion. "The ideas are of all kinds: abstract and concrete, general and particular; and, like the musician's phrases, they are arranged, not that they may tell us something, but that their effects in us may combine into a coherent whole of feeling and attitude and produce a peculiar liberation of the will," as I. A. Richards explained what he meant by a "music of ideas."[58] Alternating authoritative epic speech, lyrical modulation, and localized dramatic scenario, Eliot's recordings render both the abstract conception of "voice" and "music" as an organizing principle that informs New Critical vocabulary, and the dull flatness resulting from the disconnect between performed affect and intellectual and affective context that natural elocutionists like Fleming identified with mechanical methods of elocution. These distinct modes of speech are ultimately both subsumed into a pervading sense of incantation or meditation voiced by nobody in particular—which is to say, by the gramophone as autonomous oracle.

TAKE 3—T. S. Eliot's Asemic Phrasing

What do some of these experimental tactics deployed by Eliot in rendering *The Waste Land* in his own voice look and sound like? We can focus on some of the key prosodic elements that I have been describing above (rubato, tone, amplitude, intonational phrasing, caesura, musicality) by thinking of Eliot's recordings with attention to his use of phrasing, intonation, and stress, and by observing the nature of visualized contours of pitch and patterns of amplitude. Not much can be said about pitch curves and amplitude patterns without first defining the domains in which the patterns take place. Like natural speech, a recorded literary work has natural prosodic divisions—domains that appear to denote complete intonation patterns. Unlike natural speech, they may not always be motivated by the goals of semantic communication, but by aesthetic goals, and expressive aims that differ from the desire to be intelligible in a straightforward sense. As an example of the prosodic divisions of natural speech, a typical declarative sentence will have a high then falling intonation. The declarative intonation curve will be confined to the prosodic domain that encompasses the sentence. I am using the term "phrase" now to refer to these domains, without making any theoretical claims, linguistic or literary, about the status of the phrase, other than to note that phrases in these literary speech acts are generally separated by salient, acoustically measurable pauses.[59] Phrases as I observe them in Eliot's recorded performances are delineated solely on the basis of the recorded speech act and not by the graphic divisions of the poem on the page. Lineation and punctuation found in the printed text are, in the first instance, irrelevant. Consequently, preconceived notions about poetic structure as it pertains to such typographical cues are superseded by acoustic evidence.

And yet, while poetic lineation and punctuation are left behind, the syntactical integrity of the poem-text emerges as a potential element of contrast with our observations about vocal intonation and amplitude heard in the recordings. To track a literary performance for the purpose of critical analysis, it is productive to imagine a tiered descriptive enterprise, each tier representing a different way of visualizing or arranging the text of the poem in relation to the features heard in performance. No single tier exists without the other, but in combination, they can provide a rich sense of the prosody of a performance in relation to the printed poem. One can imagine eventually developing a graphic representation of all sorts of prosodic patterns, which could result in lineation (or text-gridding) of the poem based on phrasal caesura, intonational patterns, amplitude patterns, and formant or other sound patterns. And one can imagine, further, a gallery of aesthetically and critically interesting ways of visualizing salient patterns beyond the linear text and grid. But my foray into illustrating some of the claims I have been making about Eliot's recorded experiments in reading *The Waste*

Land will be limited to just a few interesting techniques discoverable in the audiotext using a simple tiered, time-line-based visualization structure.[60]

Some of the terms that come to mind in listening to and annotating Eliot's readings have to do with Eliot's peculiar uses of intonation in relation to the syntactic or semantically meaningful sentence phrase. With some descriptive license, I have settled on the term "asemic phrasing" to describe a cluster of Eliot's poetry reading tactics in comparison with natural speech intonation. A seme being the smallest unit of meaning, "asemic phrasing" describes methods of phrasing that disrupt, contort, or undermine the semantic resonance of spoken words as compared to natural speech intonation. Where the prosody of talk and reading commonly works to hinge speech to meaning, asemic phrasing aims to unhinge.[61] Forms found in Eliot's earliest recordings of *The Waste Land* that I identify as "intonational drift," "excessive intonation," and "lazy" or "truncated intonation" ("lazy phrasing") merit this description of his use of nonsemantic phrasing. These are, in effect, performance-oriented literary prosodic categories that I find useful to describe what Eliot is doing in his peculiar manner of rendering a difficult modernist work. What do such categories describe? Typically, an intonation curve should start and end with the semantically meaningful sentence. The sentence is the largest prosodic unit and it is supposed that an intonation curve should not exceed the largest prosodic unit. But in Eliot's experimental readings of *The Waste Land* we encounter numerous examples of intonation curves that exceed the sentence (examples of what I am calling excessive intonation curves) or clipped curves that break the normal semantic phrase into smaller nonsemantic units (truncated intonation curves). Further, we often find apparently "appropriate" semantic intonation applied out of synch with the recognizable semantic phrase. I have identified this as Eliot's technique of intonational drift. Overall then, it is fair to say that Eliot's intonation curves in his recorded performances of *The Waste Land* are, to a large degree semantically uninformed, and they are so on purpose. I am interested in how the relation of the pitch curve to the sound phrase is skewed from the semantic phrase in these different instances of what I am calling Eliot's asemic phrasing.

Semantically typical forms of intonational phrasing correspond to James Stephens's category of "speech verse," with an intonation that is

"modulating" and communicating meaning through modulation. This char-
acterizes Robert Speaight's 1956 recording of *The Waste Land* for the Spoken
Arts label in its entirety.[62] A visual clip from Speaight's recording (fig. 14)
illustrates what I am calling semantically *informed* intonation. In looking
at the software-generated visualization of his spoken performance, we can
see the fragmented appearance of the pitch contour data. Natural speech
intonation appears as broken lines, and fluctuating frequency patterns. We
see a graphic rendering of dramatic changes in pitch, reinforcing the point
that I made in the previous chapter that semantically motivated natural
speech intonation manifests in broken rather than solid state pitch contours.

Eliot's recorded poetry-reading style reveals the patterning of three dominant modes of intonation. The first is natural speech with regular sentence
intonation in which the intonation works in harmony with the semantic
motives of the text. The second is a form of melodic intonation in which the
intonational delivery becomes, sometimes not so subtly, outright singing.
Crucially, in these instances the intonation does not seem to be driven by
semantic motivations and sentence boundaries are not obeyed. The third is a
speech-melodic pattern, in which the first and second types are interspersed
within the same phrase. These categories that are audible as speech patterns
in Eliot's poetry reading find some parallel in Stephens's three categories
(speech, song, and balance verse), as if Eliot, in his reading of *The Waste
Land*, was trying to score out a reading that works with variations between
all three categories.

If we compare the visual clip of Speaight reading from *The Waste Land*
with one of Eliot's recorded 1933 performances of the same section, the
opening lines of "Death by Water" (in this case, take 404.1A [fig. 15]), we can
see and hear a good example of melodic intonation leading into a mixture
of speech-melodic intonation, at the end (when he speaks the words "and
the profit and loss"). The first phrase, "Phlebas the Phoenician, a fortnight
dead," can be scored out musically as a rendering of an embedded melody
with the notes C (extended for a period) then B and A. The second phrase,
"Forgot the cry of gulls, and the deep sea swell," also melodic, moves up
one tone to the musical notes, E (extended) D and C. The rendering of
the melody in the second phrase diminishes as we move toward the third
phrase, "And the profit and loss," which is no longer melodic, but semantic

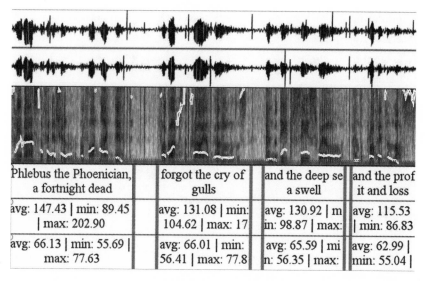

Phlebus the Phoenician, a fortnight dead	forgot the cry of gulls	and the deep se a swell	and the prof it and loss
avg: 147.43 | min: 89.45 | max: 202.90	avg: 131.08 | min: 104.62 | max: 17	avg: 130.92 | m in: 98.87 | max:	avg: 115.53 | min: 86.83
avg: 66.13 | min: 55.69 | max: 77.63	avg: 66.01 | min: 56.41 | max: 77.8	avg: 65.59 | mi n: 56.35 | max:	avg: 62.99 | min: 55.04 |

Figure 14. Praat annotated visualization of Robert Speaight reading from "Death by Water" section of T. S. Eliot's *The Waste Land*. LP record, *Poems of T. S. Eliot* (New Rochelle, N.Y.: Spoken Arts, 1956).

in its orientation. This varying speech-melodic delivery is typical of many sections of Eliot's recorded readings of the poem.

I will move toward a conclusion of my observations about some of the most prevalent characteristics of Eliot's vocal actions in his recorded readings of *The Waste Land* with two examples of Eliot's asemic phrasing, one illustrating excessive intonation curves, and another illustrating truncated intonation curves. The first example, taken from Eliot's 1946 recording (a passage from "The Burial of the Dead," also take 403A from the 1933 recordings) shows him extending the phrase almost without interruption for ten seconds, and without any significant intonational variation (fig. 16). Here the semantic sentence is not divided to render it meaningful. Eliot's phrase is a sonic solid-state drone, and has little to do with the communication of meaning in any traditional sense that we associate with natural speech. This technique is used extensively throughout his reading of the poem, and most prevalently in his various recorded takes of "What the Thunder Said" and "The Fire Sermon," where Eliot practices the possibilities of phrasal

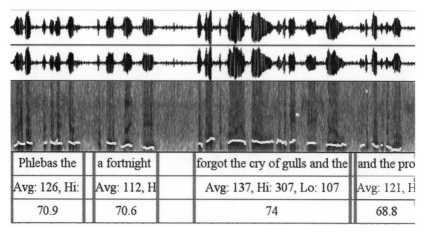

Phlebas the	a fortnight		forgot the cry of gulls and the	and the pro
Avg: 126, Hi:	Avg: 112, H		Avg: 137, Hi: 307, Lo: 107	Avg: 121, H
70.9	70.6		74	68.8

Figure 15. Praat annotated visualization of T. S. Eliot reading a take of "Death by Water" from *The Waste Land*, recorded in 1933

extension to a great variety of extremes, pausing only briefly between uniformly intoned extended phrases, and differentiating between the last and the next phrase with only a slight alteration of the primary, intoned note that drives the next phrasal cluster that is, again, uniformly intoned.

Finally, in another example from a 1933 take of the opening of "The Burial of the Dead"—a take that was not finally integrated into the 1946 Library of Congress version—we have an example of a technique that is essentially the opposite of excessive intonational phrasing (fig. 17), where, instead, the sentence is broken up into smaller phrases that have their own discrete intonational curves, slowing down the movement of the phrase as one would generally expect it to be delivered, and drawing peculiar attention to individual words as sonic entities unto themselves. In this technique of reading, a word can constitute an entire phrase with an intonation curve of its own, rather than form part of a larger multi-word semantic phrase (which is what one normally hears in semantically oriented speech.) This technique of intoning in small phrases that do not represent semantic divisions is what I am calling truncated intonation curves.

Both the excessive and truncated intonational phrasing that I have just illustrated involve a dominant, pervading technique in Eliot's readings of *The Waste Land*, namely, the drone. Droning is what makes Eliot's voice sound robotic, at times as he works to deliver his poem. The drone as a vocal

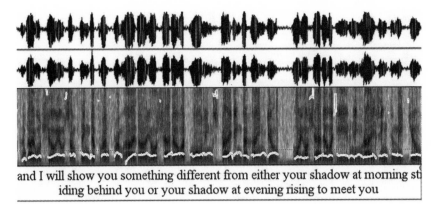

and I will show you something different from either your shadow at morning st
iding behind you or your shadow at evening rising to meet you

Figure 16. Praat annotated visualization of T. S. Eliot reading "The Burial of the Dead" from *The Waste Land* depicting "excessive intonation curves"

technique is another important point of focus in Eliot's explorations of artistic intonation. The drone effect has also been identified by sound sociologists with "urban and industrial soundscapes," that is, with the soundscape of industrial modernity.[63] Simply put, a drone occurs when a speaker holds a single tone without variation for an extended period of time. Usually it is used as a harmonic effect in musical composition. As a monovalent effect in verse speaking, it works formally and musically in combination with changes in amplitude, phrasing and, in a counterintuitive way, intonational movements within and across phrases. Its effect is counterintuitive because the drone deployed as extensively as it is in Eliot's reading of *The Waste Land* leads a listener to think about the relationship between the monophonic effect of a solid state drone—the sounding of a single tone continuously—and intonational variation. It introduces the interesting question: How does the drone intonate?[64] In other words, how does one move from word to word, from phrase to phrase, while emitting a solid-state drone? A first answer to this question would note that the sound signal is divisible into multiple pitches within the pitch spectrum. Any sound we (as humans) hear can have elements between 20h and 20,000kh. While a vocally emitted drone represents a single region in that spectrum, there are other possibilities for variation within that tonal region. For example, the shape of the oral cavity of the speaker (or singer) can render variation in the drone, audible as subtones within the primary tone of the drone. Variation in subtones allows us

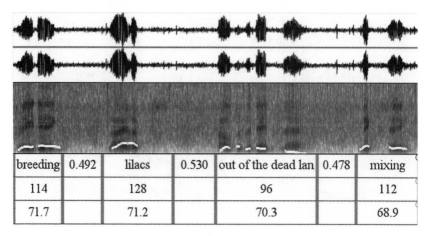

breeding	0.492	lilacs	0.530	out of the dead lan	0.478	mixing
114		128		96		112
71.7		71.2		70.3		68.9

Figure 17. Praat annotated visualization of T. S. Eliot reading "The Burial of the Dead" from *The Waste Land* depicting "truncated intonation curves"

to hear change within the dominant tone of the drone. Beyond this first kind of answer, which focuses on the speaker's technical capacity, it is equally important to recognize that our developed linguistic competence, that is to say, our predisposal to cues for discrete units when we are listening to speech, make us hear different kinds of meaning in subtones, which are in effect constituent pitches of the complex signal.

To introduce a demand in the listener to perceive variation in the drone, in effect, a demand that she or he listen for changes in amplitude and subtones, is to demand a perception of vocal timbre that is at once subtle and intimate, and yet discrete from more typical associations between timbre and affective, social, semantic communication. While benefitting from the frequency range that the carbon granules, the magnets, and the wires of electrical recording afford, Eliot's pursuit of formal vocal techniques specific to a performance of *The Waste Land* seems in many ways antithetical to the singing of a microphone-recorded crooner employing electrical recording technologies to produce a soft and intimate emotional timbre in his delivery of a popular song. The droning technique, so prevalent across Eliot's multiple takes and the compiled sections of the 1946 recording of *The Waste Land*, and especially prevalent in the section that Eliot identified to Ford Madox Ford as the most important part of the poem—"the 29 lines of the water-dripping song in the last part" (these being lines 331–58 near the beginning of "The Fire Sermon")—captures the overarching challenge that Eliot faced in rendering his poem with voice using an electrical recording media technology. Attentive in its own way to the diverse cacophony of human and nonhuman sounds that *The Waste Land* as a poem works to incorporate into a formal unity that is heard as sonic continuity, Eliot's performance of the poem in the voice of an oracular machine was his solution, his way of capturing, without leveling, the sundry sonic curves of modernity in rich yet formally solid monotonic frequencies.

CONCLUSION

Analog, Digital, Conceptual

THIS BOOK HAS told several stories about how some of the earliest sound-recording technologies adapted or mobilized literary works in such a way as to form new literary artifacts. I have argued for a methodology of audiotextual criticism that does its utmost in the first instance to account for the relationship between media format and modified conceptions of genre or form as applied to the audiotext. And I have demonstrated a variety of ways in which one may proceed to historicize early spoken recordings in the context of the literary, while speculating on the value for literary studies, and cultural studies in a broader sense, of the critical historicization and formal analysis of spoken sound recordings. An important aim throughout has also been to provide a framework for understanding the early literary history of spoken recordings, to develop a prehistory to the massive corpus of literary sound that has been developed (on magnetic tape to begin with) since the 1950s, which has been the primary area of interest for literature scholars until now. Telling the longer history of literary recordings provides new contexts for thinking about the rich and diverse archive of post–World War II literary sound, while articulating and modeling new methodological approaches that will be of use in the analysis of literary recordings and to the pursuit of phonopoetics as a critical project in all literary historical periods.

Something else readers may have sensed, if not explicitly noticed, while reading this book is that the essential nature of the artifact at the core of this study—the status of the literary recording, the audiotext as a cultural object, a *thing*—has become increasingly complicated, difficult, less substantial, and more conceptual in its ontological contours. The Introduction began with explicit details about the nature of early sound-recording technologies and media formats in relation to particular examples of literary recordings. As digital reproduction of the recordings under consideration became part of the literary analysis, our understanding of the object of study grew deeper and more ethereal at the same time, as if we were traveling further into a cloud to find its source. The very idea that there can be a material record of a sonic event is called into question again. This is exactly where we want to be at this point in *Phonopoetics*.

This conclusion reflects further on the nature and status of the sound recording as an object of critical study at the present time by considering the materiality of the audible artifact and the event-oriented scenario of its use. In the process, it offers new points of departure for historically motivated theorizations of the voice recording and the voice archive. Neither "artifact" nor "event" is a simple term to define in relation to sound phenomena. R. Murray Schafer distinguishes between the sound object and the sound event by identifying the former with the acoustician Pierre Scheaffer's clinical definition of *l'objet sonore,* a specimen of recorded sound considered "in physical or psychophysical terms . . . without their semantic or referential aspects," and the latter as "something that occurs in a certain place during a particular interval of time" for which questions of "context" apply. The "soundscape" by extension, "is a field of interactions" consisting of component sound events.[1] Don Ihde, in his explorations of sound phenomenology observes that, "insofar as all sounds are also 'events,' all the sounds are within the first approximation, likely to be considered as 'moving.'" Ihde, in this instance, imagines sounds as divorced from visible objects, existing as auditory presences within the horizons of silence that surround them.[2] In both cases, one might say that the sound object is identified with some primitive version of the audio signal, itself, rather than with a material artifact that either produces or preserves it. Historical sound seems to present itself as a unique kind of artifact to the critic in that its nonvisual presence may make it seem more ephemeral than other kinds of visible, material artifacts, like manuscripts, for example, and because its presence depends on controlled temporal movement.

This last point is at the heart of Friedrich Kittler's insistence that sound-recording technology has had a transformative impact on our relationship to the past. Stressing first the importance of the nineteenth century's break with notational systems of transcription (for music, harmony, etc.) through its introduction of the concept of frequency—by which "the measure of length is replaced by time as an independent variable"—Kittler goes on to say that this transition from transposition to what he calls time axis manipulation (enabled by the concept of frequency) results in the real taking the place of the symbolic.[3] This is because technological media capture, preserve, and (re)produce aspects of the temporal event that the alphabet cannot, delivering the past without "the bottleneck of syntactical regimentation" associated with symbolic language.[4] As it captures and produces "the real" in its capacity to record a temporal event, the artifact that arises from technological media is mathematically and materially intertwined with the event it preserves. That time itself becomes a variable to be manipulated with technological media (you can speed up, slow down, or reverse the direction of the record) suggests that our capacity to manipulate the media artifact, not only enables us to process historical "real time" so that it is experienced as a temporal event in the present, but to transform historical "real time" into events of alternate temporal orders as well. When we are talking about sound recording, the intervolved relationship of artifact to event suggests the possibilities of replaying history and of making history.

In using the term "artifact," I am, to begin with, aware of its primary meaning referring to "an object made or modified by human workmanship, as opposed to one formed by natural processes."[5] The early spoken recording sits oddly at the crossroads of art and nature as both a crafted speech and a sound wave, an empirical phenomenon mechanically captured. The implications of this crossroads position has preoccupied me in many of the readings I have pursued in this book, from my consideration of early ways of framing the meaning of the voice of the phonograph, to my discussion of T. S. Eliot's experiments in voicing multiple perspectives with a practiced kind oracular-mechanical intonation. Just what, in fact, is the artifact of the sound archive, and how has it shaped our ideas and expectations of what the contents of such a repository are? Where the early Edisonian idea of an archive of voices was selective and specific in its imagined motivations of use, contemporary capacities for digitization and media aggregation raise the possibility of expanding our own idea of a historical archive of voices from including "the best that has been said" to "everything said that has ever been recorded." My exploration, in this Conclusion, of the questions posed above will proceed with an awareness of the digitally mediated reception of our regular experience of the archival signal, the audio that emanates, post–media migration, as if from some notion of an ever-expanding archive of voices.

Theorizing the implications of the digital reproduction of sound is crucial to the development of phonopoetics as a historicist critical practice. When I began research for this book, many years ago, I was required to visit sound archives in buildings made of bricks and mortar to listen to the recordings I wished to study. I was installed in a listening booth with a bench, a table, a loudspeaker, and an intercom system that allowed me to communicate with the technician who would play a record for me once, twice at most, lest the replay result in detrimental deterioration of the material sound media artifact whose contents I wished to hear. I listened carefully, desperately, one might say, knowing that every passing moment represented unique and fleeting access to the object—the audiotext—I wished to think about. I took notes, jotted down "time-stamps" of particular sonic features that interested me, did my best to capture for critical discussion what I was hearing. In some instances, the sounds that I listened to were already affected by earlier reproduction processes. The T. S. Eliot instantaneous disc recordings, for example, had been transferred to magnetic tape in the 1970s, and it is from these tapes held at the Library of Congress, and not the acetate and aluminum discs held at the Columbia University Archives, that I first heard Eliot's experiments in modernist verse speaking. This means that the signal I was hearing through the loudspeaker in the Library of Congress listening booth had already been through a degree of transformative processing. It had been sent across wires to a pre-amplifier, possibly boosted, compressed, equalized according to particular frequency curves, and those transformations were then captured in the reorientations of the magnetic domains of the oxide particles embedded in the tape that would come to preserve the remediated signals for decades to come. Eventually, with the aid of some research funds, I was able to pay to have the Eliot readings I wished to study transferred to digital WAV files and given to me to take home on archival quality compact discs. In a sense, that was the key, transformative moment, as far as *Phonopoetics* research was concerned. Digital media technologies seemed to have liberated the sound artifact from its traditional preservation archive. I could now take the archive home with me and do what I pleased with the digital files they gave me, with one important exception: I was not permitted to disseminate them publicly. But I could run them through digital filters, edit them, line them up in multitracking software for comparison to other Eliot recordings, run them through spectral analysis software to help me think about Eliot's reading techniques, use them in teaching, and even integrate them into multimedia scenarios of literary performance.

WAV files on a compact disc may now seem as archaic as engraved signals on wax a cylinder. The scenario of alleged archival liberation that I have just described has expanded exponentially with the compression of digital audio media formats, the expanded capacities of digital storage (on hard drives and servers), and the related possibility of streaming and disseminating these files via online digital environments. Recordings that I had at one time only read about in rare record catalogues found at national libraries and archives in London, Washington, and Ottawa can now often be found with a simple Google search, sometimes in the YouTube videos of audiophiles and record collectors eager to share their new discoveries, and, increasingly, in online archives like the UCSB Cylinder Audio Archive, designed to digitally preserve, document, and disseminate (with free downloads) as many examples of early audio recordings as possible.[6] Our experience of historical audio recordings is now increasingly (if not decidedly) a digital experience.[7] Consequently, we must proceed in our work with an awareness of its implications for our practice as cultural historians. Proceeding with an awareness of the digital does not imply a circumvention of the original material artifacts in question; nor does it erase a critical motivation to locate historically the voices in this expansive archive—but it qualifies both the artifacts and our historicist motivations in significant ways. Conceptual and computational manipulation of the audio signal as divorced from the original material artifact allows us to engage in new kinds of contextualization and expands our capacity for philological engagement.

A list of historical media artifacts used for sound capture over the years—phonautograph sheet, cylinder, record disc, tape, compact disc, mp3 file, to name some of them—presents a variety of physical substances ranging from paper, metal, paraffin and plastic, and ends in the ironic fact of the mp3 as a new kind of entity, one that is less substantial than representational (one cannot hold an mp3 file, but one can handle it—select it, "click" it—as a digital representation presented through software, a graphic user interface and the specific hardware, computer, iPod, etc.) that delivers the GUI. Each one of these media artifacts, whether it is substantial, or not—and its audible content—invites the critic to engage in self-conscious scrutiny of the possible status of that artifact within the context of digital rendering. Increasingly, audio artifacts demand the use of digital tools that enable new possibilities for navigation, manipulation, visualization, and examination of the audio signal, and, in some cases, the sonification of visualizations derived from the original material media formats, themselves. It is the digital side of historical audiography that I will focus on in this conclusion as I meditate on the status for historical research of the artifacts that comprise the archive of voices at the present time.

I will return to the work of Jerome McGann one last time to help expand my previous arguments about audiography to the digital sphere. In his recent discussions of digital media in relation to research in the humanities, McGann argues that "what digital technology has exposed is not that we need a new program of humanities study, a Digital Humanities, but a recovery of philological method for our changed circumstances. Philology in a New Key."[8] By philology McGann means, a discipline of skills designed to "preserve, monitor, investigate, and augment our cultural inheritance, including the various material means by which it has been realized and transmitted."[9] Noting how the migration of our cultural heritage into digital formats has exposed "the serious limitations" of our critical methods for capturing the "vast network of agents and agencies" through which the material objects that compose the historical record have passed, McGann argues that "only a sociology of the textual condition can offer an interpretive method adequate to the study of this field and its materials."[10] McGann's call for a philology in a new key entails a renewed application of practical skills, procedural and interpretive tools that include descriptive bibliography, scholarly editing, theory of texts, book history, and, I would add, media history and theory, to the new kinds of databases and interfaces we are creating. This is the big work in the growing field known as the digital humanities that has begun, the kind of work that has motivated initiatives like NINES (Nineteenth-century Scholarship Online),[11] and many of the individual web projects that have been aggregated into that consortium. Rigorous engagement with the physical materials—volumes of *The Yellow Book*,[12] artworks, ceramics, and realia on display in John Ruskin's St George's Museum in Sheffield, England,[13] multiple copies of William Blake's illuminated books,[14] Emily Dickinson's manuscripts,[15] Walt Whitman's notebooks[16]—that populate sites designed for their digital presentation results in well-researched glosses adjacent to the digital images of the materials, just as the audiophiles delivered for playback and download in the UCSB Cylinder Audio Archive are accompanied by extensive metadata on each audio file that can be heard. Indeed, beyond the informative gloss, rigorous historical engagement with digitized historical artifacts, under the best of circumstances, results in thorough metadata, and, consequently, expands the ways in which we may remodel and investigate our understanding of historical cultural artifacts. Online, we do not touch paper, canvas, clay, or wax. We organize richly prepared simulacra of the artifacts we imagine to be a part of our rational archive in an environment that exposes them to transformative imagination.

In this sense, the digital "archive" is not to be understood as a preservation medium, but as a circulation and transformation medium that opens texts and material artifacts to new contexts, new interpretations, and new uses, including transformations of our conception of historical research itself. This work is not a replacement for more empirical methods of writing history, but makes us aware of the significance of media contexts for the kinds of history we wish to pursue, and the kinds of assumptions about the status of the artifacts we wish to contextualize. It also allows us to discover aspects of our objects of inquiry that might not have been discoverable had they remained in a single media format.

To approach texts and objects in the digital environment is to encounter the destabilizing material element inherent in all cultural artifacts, which encourages an approach to research materials as "*differential* texts," a term introduced by Marjorie Perloff to mean "texts that exist in different material forms, with no single version being the definitive one."[17] Following the media theorist Darren Wershler, I transmute Perloff's term and support a claim for the concept of "differential media" as one that demands our awareness of the transformative impact of media contexts as an object of interpretation migrates across, or exists multifariously within, different media platforms.[18] In the natural sciences, a differential medium refers to a growth ("culturing") medium containing compounds that work to visually distinguish microorganisms by the way the colony either appears or contrasts with the surrounding medium.[19] This idea of the differentiation of content by a medium is relevant to the present discussion insofar as the media through which a signal may migrate will distinguish certain of its characteristics, and erase others. The idea of differential media seems particularly well suited to a consideration of a historical sound recording that can be said to exist, uniformly ("*that* Tennyson recording") yet differentially, on cylinder, LP, audio-cassette tape, and as an mp3 file (not to mention as a textual transcription or visual representation).

There are other concepts with currency that might be considered for our purposes, but they don't work as well for sound. Katherine Hayles speaks of "media specificity" to delineate the characteristics of media environments in relation to the development of digital texts—the movement "from the language of 'text' to a more precise vocabulary of screen and page, digital program and analogue interface, code and ink, mutable image and durably inscribed mark, texton and scripton, computer and book"[20]—but the concept is too visual in its orientation to serve the present meditation on the archive of voices; Jay David Bolter and Richard Grusin's elaboration of "remediation"—while extremely useful for, among other things, its observation that "no medium . . . can now function independently and establish its own separate and purified space of cultural meaning"—seems similarly biased toward the visual arts and visual media.[21]

The idea of differential media in relation to sound media technologies and formats can better accommodate Kittler's sense of the continuity between technological media and digital media as differential (yet continuous) forms of data processing, so that the wax cylinder and the mp3, the phonograph and the digital audio workstation (DAW) can be conceptualized, at one level, as engaging in the same processes of temporal manipulation, but through different media formats and interfaces, and with significantly variable degrees of transformative impact on the audible temporal event. "Differential media" is also a useful concept for considering the possibilities and implications of migrating our own digital interventions, our digital "archive" projects, maps, databases, and visualizations back into print or other media formats—perhaps even audible formats—and for imagining new forms of scholarly production that are not exclusively concerned with designing web sites.

As I hope I have shown throughout this book, much significant work that can help us understand the import of how we search, write, think, and hear has emerged from media historians who have developed concepts of comparative "new" media, "format studies," "platform studies," and media archeology, respectively.[22] Such cultural theorists and historians are working to articulate the presuppositions we bring to our new media environments, to have us see the historical underpinnings of what we suppose. This is part of the work that needs to be done, and it functions in line with McGann's call for a "philology in a new key." And then there is a more ludic, experimental kind of digital engagement that I would argue also has an important role to play in the present recalibration of our understanding of what we, as literary and cultural historians, can do in relation to our changing media environments. These more experimentally transformative kinds of digital engagement can function as useful and revealing methods of experimental critical play. As Jussi Parikka has argued, play and tinkering can be an important way of revealing the subphenomenal ways in which technical media function. When understood as part of didactics, "such a manner of tinkering with media-technological effects" can form a productive "circuit with theoretical work."[23]

Two dominant branches of digital work in the humanities have been those pertaining to "humanities computing" (tool building, text analysis and encoding), on the one hand, and "new media studies and design" (often pursued by theorist-practitioners interested in exploring the nature and implications of new media), on the other. Alan Liu has framed an analysis of the value and potential of both branches just mentioned by considering their relative degrees of critical awareness. Observing, first, that the expanding domain of digital humanities must "in some manner, for better or for worse, . . . serve the postindustrial state," Liu decides that "the digital humanities are not ready to take up their full responsibility [within the discipline] because the field does not yet possess an adequate critical awareness of the larger social, economic, and cultural issues at stake."[24] Historicist audiography and the broader field of phonopoetics is concerned with the historical recontextualization of an analogue signal and its related media so that we can gather the aesthetic, social, and material relations that informed their use and meaning.

Strange new things can be done to sound media artifacts using digital processes. Scraps of tinfoil once used to capture the voices of speakers and destroyed to prevent possible use on a tinfoil phonograph machine can be made to sound again. Something happens when the analogue artifact is approached with a digital process. A fragment of phonographic tinfoil captured by the University of Southampton's Sound Archive Project researchers as a high-resolution 3D digital scan, performed for preservation purposes and for digitally generated replay by a virtual stylus, is transformed by a precise coordinate mapping (including the calculation of depth) of the cylinder scrap's surface, from which a quantitative analysis of signal reproduction can be generated.[25] Such processes offer a new answer to the question that asks what a dumb and static sound memento, like a cutting from a tinfoil phonograph sheet, might mean and *be* as a historical artifact in the present. As Ihde has speculated, sound—with its intrinsic movement, and its affirmation of the verb over predicate, represents a challenge to the "realm of mute objects" that has functioned as "the implicit standard of a visualist metaphysics."[26] The digital process works to render the material fragment eventful and potentially whole again. Assuming the possibility of artifacts as abstract, immaterial entities—for example, the way a thesis exists as a necessary, universalizing artifact for philosophical discourse and the production of certain kinds and movements of knowledge—I would suggest that the analogue sound recording, when approached through digital processes, mutates from a delimited, manifest material thing into an eventful performance of the abstract ideal of that material thing.

A binary conception of silence as static and sound as kinetic is reversed when we move from analogue models of sonification to digital ones. This is most dramatically apparent in the recent sonification through digital scanning of Édouard-Léon Scott de Martinville's phonautograph transcripts. Scott de Martinville's phonautograph was introduced circa 1860 as a way of writing sound, rendering it visible and (ideally) legible. It was not designed for sound reproduction. Thus, from Scott de Martinville's perspective, a phonautogram was not a sound recording in the way we understand that category today. It was a graphically captured sound inscription; a machine-generated audio fossil—a static artifact materially bearing the trace of a once living sound event. The First Sounds researchers[27] have reanimated these artifacts into actual sound events again by playing back high-resolution digital scans of the phonautograms (with a lot of adjustment and preconception) via digital sonification.[28] One example of this work is the sonification of Scott de Martinville's voice singing the folk song "**Au clair de la lune.**"[29]

In their first attempt at sonification of the phonautogram sheet (the March 2008 release), prior to their discovery of documentation suggesting that it was recorded by Scot de Martinville himself, the pitch of the voice and sonic quality of the recording rendered resembled that of an otherworldly, angelic young woman, as if the voice of La Svengali as described in extensive, elaborate passages from George du Maurier's fin-de-siècle novel *Trilby* itself had finally been allowed to sound again as it did in the Paris of du Maurier's imaginary.[30] "The romantic image of a woman singing to us through the veiled curtain of time was at the heart of Scott's allure as we introduced his work in 2008," the First Sounds researchers observe.[31] With the new information, adjustments were made to approximate the pitch of voice that might have emanated from Scott himself. Such flights of fancy aside, the process used to generate such a recording represents an audible rendering, through new media, of a visual script of voice that was never intended to be heard and is, in effect, a digital reversal of Scott de Martinville's intention. He sought to turn sound into visual data, but the First Sounds researchers have reconverted his visual data back into sound. And thus, where once there were only silent sheets of smoke-blackened paper, the potential for a new historical sound archive of phonautograms emerges.

The process that allows for such a creation is an innovative form of digital processing that the folklorist and First Sounds researcher Patrick Feaster calls "paleospectrophony." The goal is to use digital tools to convert wave-form images of different kinds into playable frequency and amplitude values, enabling us to hear them, in a form of Friedrich Kittler's "time axis manipulation."[32] While originating from a material visual object, the audio artifacts generated from this technique are born digital and thus represent a digital realization of the abstract idea of the phonautogram as an audible artifact. When we listen to such a sonified recording, one might say, we are listening to the sound of a conceptual artifact.

What we have with such examples are signals that may, or may not have existed in relation to their corresponding material artifacts, and the ability to speculate about the status of this signal as an actual archival artifact that has been simultaneously generated and divorced from its original, material medium. Digital processes of visualization and sonification of audible frequencies paint a picture of our desire to substantiate the fugitive signal as materially artifactual and historically authentic. The deeper we immerse ourselves in such highly mediated representations of the signal of historical voices, the more familiar we become with the elaborate conceptual properties of the artifacts of the historical voice archive. In a paradoxical way, the further we move from the material artifact itself, the closer we come to touching its seemingly intangible, historically entrenched features. This, I must admit, is an optimistic formulation of the implications of the digital for the kind of grounded philological research methodologies McGann calls for.

The discourse of liberation that I have used above to describe what happens to a material audio artifact when it is digitized and freed from its bricks-and-mortar archive can be subject to caution and critique as well. In a recent essay translated with the title *Why Hasn't Everything Already Disappeared?* Jean Baudrillard speaks to the inherent dangers of our movement from analog to digital in useful, if apocalyptic terms. Reflecting on reality-capture media and the traces they leave behind, Baudrillard speculates that it is not "the real and the reality principle" that we worship in them, but "its disappearance."[33] As Baudrillard goes on to argue, this state of "disappearance" arises from computer systems operating and replacing "any thought-sensitive surface of confrontation" with limitless proliferation and flow. The 0/1 binary construct of software programs, he says, removes "any suspension of thought between illusion and reality" and replaces it with "a single integrated circuit."[34] Secrets and pleasures, and the possibility of critical knowledge become lost in the flow of the massive digital stream as we come to confuse thought and imagination with boundless proliferation. Analogue media, in the process of disappearing, represent a last point of possible resistance according to this argument. The analogue medium allows for our sense and understanding of such disappearance. As an indexical medium, as a trace of the real, the analogue artifact already communicates the significant loss in what it provides. So, according to this logic, the recording of a speaking voice communicates the disappearance of the event of speech that it attempts to preserve in another form. The analogue artifact functions as the anchor for our conceptual distinction between the real and its mediated capture, which signifies a loss. While the real does not exist (for real) in the mediated capture of the event (e.g., in the wax cylinder), the idea of the real, our sense of the real, and our sense of our loss of the real, does exist in our experience of it. According to Baudrillard, analogue media preserve this sense of the real—and hence awareness of its absence—which paradoxically reinforces our conceptual faith in its existence.

The proximity of digital literary recordings to printed texts allows us to imagine other possible modes of engagement with the historical corpus of literary readings, digitally sampled from all prior sound media—for example, allowing new media technology to practice what is known as "unsupervised learning" and discover things for itself. Unsupervised learning seeks to find hidden structures in data (in our case, digitized audio) that has *not* been marked up for the detection of particular properties (in the manner that I have annotated my tiny data set of Victorian elocutionary recordings, or T. S. Eliot recordings, for specific manifestations of pitch, duration, and amplitude). This alternate conception of critical "listening" (in quotation marks) in the form of unsupervised learning moves away from discursive contextualization, historical narrative, and even traditional metadata, into an algorithmic reading of the sound signal as numerical data. It proceeds without any concern for the real, or its disappearance, or other such dialectical fits that Baudrillard attributes to an analogue medium. Unsupervised learning does not think and learn against or in relation to a conception of or longing for the real. Instead we have a vision that has been articulated elegantly by the media theorist Wolfgang Ernst who argues that the archive "is no longer simply a passive storage space but becomes generative itself in algorithmically ruled processuality."[35]

The archive of voices according to this idea, already disengaged from its original media formats, can evolve and propagate in infinite iterations and directions and generate new variations on an ever-growing data set of digitized sound. This vision of an ever-increasing archive of digital voices differs significantly from the vision of archival futurity characterized by augmented capacities in deciphering previously undetected but *real* traces of events, articulated by Charles Sanders Peirce when he wrote: "Give science only a hundred more centuries of increase in geometrical progression, and she may be expected to find that the sound waves of Aristotle's voice have somehow recorded themselves."[36] Rather than *find* that those sound waves have been recorded somehow, somewhere in the real world, the archive that lives and "becomes generative itself in algorithmically ruled processuality" may *discover* Aristotle's voice by other, synthetic means, instead, just as the First Sounds researchers discovered (according to their fantasy), a woman's voice through the veil of time in a phonautograph sheet. Would there be a discernible difference between Aristotle's voice in the two kinds of archives? Would we care about any such difference, or even understand its significance in "a hundred more centuries"? Baudrillard would answer in the negative to this last question.

My own answer to the question, on the other hand, resists the binary to end all binaries that Baudrillard seems to set up by pitting the analogue against the digital in the way he does. It resists by adding that third term, conceptual, into the formula. In listening to the sound of a conceptual artifact (as I have described the digitally sonified phonautogram) we are impelled into confrontation again, in this case, into a critically productive confrontation with the tangible techniques, effects and meaning of digital mediation as a historicist practice. In pursuing a critical and historical understanding of literary audio, it is, as I have argued throughout this book, important to locate the history of specific voice recordings within the discursive frames and protocols of production and use that informed those media-documented, historical voices. Going forward, it will become increasingly and equally important and illuminating to explore the resemblances, connections and reorganizations of the "media inherent" elements of the audible archive that digital media enable.[37] By engaging in both narrative and discursive as well as "media inherent" methods of engagement, and by articulating the parallels and conflicts we, as historical scholars, perceive between them, we can benefit significantly from the differential media structures that continue to inform and will increasingly shape our attempts to understand the archive of historical voices, and, our attempts to sound the wider world around us.

NOTES

Introduction

1. Jeffrey Sconce, *Haunted Media: Electronic Presence from Telegraphy to Television* (Durham, NC: Duke University Press, 2000), 8–10. Sconce treats such "disembodiment" and "teleportation" as "electronic fictions," but they figure in acoustic-era recordings as well, and even more so when those recordings are delivered (often via digital media players) through loudspeakers that transduce electrical signals into sound waves.

2. Bennett Maxwell, "The Incunabula of Recorded Sound: A Guide to Early Edison Non-Commercial Recordings" (MS, 1990), 10.

3. Wolfgang Ernst, *Digital Memory and the Archive*, ed. Jussi Parikka (Minnesota: University of Minnesota Press, 2013), 182–83.

4. Christian Metz, "Aural Objects." *Yale French Studies* 60 (1980): 25–26.

5. Christopher Ricks, *Tennyson* (New York: Macmillan, 1972), 244.

6. Patrick Feaster cites several examples in which listeners at early phonograph exhibitions "associated the strange noises educed from damaged cylinders with such familiar sounds as the 'roar' of locomotives and the 'snap' of torpedoes" and provides an account of an exhibitor who convinced his audience that one such sound was a violinist tapping his foot in time with the music. Patrick Feaster, "'The Following Record': Making Sense of Phonographic Performance, 1877–1908" (diss., Indiana University, 2007), 187.

7. Thomas Edison announced in 1877 that, with the introduction of the tin-foil phonograph, "the captivity of all manner of sound-waves heretofore designated as 'fugitive' and their permanent retention" was already a fait accompli. Edison, "Phonograph and Its Future," *North American Review* 126 (1878): 530.

8. James Lastra, *Sound Technology and the American Cinema: Perception, Representation, Modernity* (New York: Columbia University Press, 2000), 46.

9. Wolfgang Ernst, "Temporalizing the Present and Archiving Presence: The Impact of Time-Critical Media Technologies," public lecture at Concordia University, Montréal, September 26, 2014.

10. Early cylinder recordings intended for dictation were made at 80–100 rpm and were of low sound quality but could run at that speed for up to five minutes. Feaster, "'Following Record,'" 203. Commercial cylinder recordings of the 1890s turned at 120 rpm and then at 160 rpm in the early twentieth century, and held about three minutes of sound. David L. Morton Jr., *Sound Recording: The Life Story of a Technology* (Baltimore: Johns Hopkins University Press, 2004), 40. Labels on cylinder cases or stickers on the

back of flat-disc records would sometimes bear notes indicating recommended speeds for the best results in playback of a particular record format. See, e.g., the reverse sticker appearing on Victor "De Luxe" 14" records (ca. 1903–4), which read: "By adjusting governor to permit but 60 revolutions per minute, you will obtain the best results from this record." Reproduced in Michael W. Sherman, *The Collector's Guide to Victor Records* (Tustin, CA: Monarch Record Enterprises, 2010), 49.

11. George Bernard Shaw, *Spoken English and Broken English*, Linguaphone, SH 1 E, 78 rpm disc (1927).

12. Raymond Williams, *Writing in Society* (New York: Verso, 1991), 194.

13. D. F. McKenzie, *Bibliography and the Sociology of Texts* (Cambridge: Cambridge University Press, 1999), 4.

14. Jerome McGann, *A Critique of Modern Textual Criticism* (Chicago: University of Chicago Press, 1982; reprint, Charlottesville: University Press of Virginia, 1992); Donald F. McKenzie, *Bibliography and the Sociology of Texts*, The Panizzi Lectures, 1985 (London: British Library, 1986).

15. McKenzie, *Bibliography and The Sociology of Texts*, 4, 15.

16. Francis Rumsey and Tim McCormick, *Sound and Recording*, 6th ed. (Burlington, MA: Focal Press, 2009), 1–4.

17. Jonathan Sterne, *The Audible Past: Cultural Origins of Sound Reproduction* (Durham, NC: Duke University Press, 2003), 34.

18. Rumsey and McCormick, *Sound and Recording*, 29–36.

19. Lisa Gitelman, *Scripts, Grooves and Writing Machines: Representing Technology in the Edison Era* (Stanford: Stanford University Press, 1999).

20. Jay Hodgson, *Understanding Records: A Field Guide to Recording Practice* (New York: Continuum, 2010), 2.

21. Stefan Helmreich, "Transduction," in *Keywords in Sound*, ed. David Novak and Matt Sakakeeny (Durham, NC: Duke University Press, 2015), 223.

22. Hermann von Helmholtz, *On the Sensations of Tone as a Physiological Basis for the Theory of Music*, trans. Alexander J. Ellis (1885; New York: Dover, 1954), 10.

23. C. E. Seashore, "A Voice Tonoscope," *University of Iowa Studies in Psychology* 3 (1902): 19.

24. Ibid., 27.

25. For examples of tonoscopic analysis from each disciplinary field, psychology, music, and speech education, respectively, see Evelyn Gough and Genevieve Robison, "The Tonoscope as a Means for Registering Combination Tones," *American Journal of Psychology* 31, no. 1 (January 1920): 91–93; Max Schoen, "Pitch and Vibrato in Artistic Singing: An Experimental Study," *Musical Quarterly* 12, no. 2 (April 1926): 275–90; Giles Wilkeson Gray, "A Stroboscopic Disc for the Study of Vocal Pitch," *Quarterly Journal of Speech* 3, no.13 (1927): 236–43.

26. Robin Gareus and Chris Goddard, "Audio Signal Visualization and Measurement," *Proceedings ICMC/SMC* (2014): 1348.

27. Alexander Lerch, *An Introduction to Audio Content Analysis: Applications in Signal Processing and Music Informatics* (Hoboken, NJ: Wiley, 2012), 2.

28. Roland Barthes, "From Work to Text," trans. Richard Howard, *The Rustle of Language* (New York: Farrar, Straus & Giroux, 1986), 57.

29. Tanya Clement, "Towards a Rationale of Audio-Text," *digital humanities quarterly (dhq)* 10.2 (2016), www.digitalhumanities.org/dhq/vol/10/3/000254/000254.html.

30. The longer passage in which this idea is articulated runs as follows:

> Poetry [in its C18 sense] had been the high skills of writing and speaking in the special context of high imagination; the word could be moved in either direction. Literature, in its C19 sense, repeated this, though excluding speaking. But it is then problematic, not only because of the further specialization to *imaginative* and *creative* subject-matter (as distinct from *imaginative* and *creative* writing) but also because of the new importance of many forms of writing for speech (*broadcasting* as well as *drama*) which the specialization to books seemed by definition to exclude.

Raymond Williams, *Keywords: A Vocabulary of Culture and Society* (New York: Oxford University Press, 1983), 187.

31. Edison, "Phonograph and Its Future," 534.

32. Jonathan Sterne, *MP3: The Meaning of a Format* (Durham, NC: Duke University Press, 2012), 9.

33. Charles Bernstein, "Introduction," in *Close Listening: Poetry and The Performed Word*, ed. Bernstein (New York: Oxford University Press, 1998), 10, 13–21.

34. Ibid., 12.

35. Ibid., 10.

36. The historical process in question is similar to that deployed by Jerome McGann in his critical redress of the historical neglect of the "poetical styles of sensibility and the sentimental" in his book *The Poetics of Sensibility: A Revolution in Literary Style* (New York: Oxford University Press, 1998), 6.

37. *The Phonograph and How to Use It . . . Including also a Reprint of the Openeer Papers,* a series of short narratives concerning Mr. and Mrs. Openeer and their domestic adventures in the use of the phonograph. (London: National Phonograph Company, 1900), 152–58.

38. "In making talking records, speak naturally, but with energy. Do not force the voice too much. Articulate plainly, sounding the s's and c's with particular distinctness. In using the speaking tube, the lips should just about touch the mouth piece. With the 14-inch horn, or the 26-inch Japanned tin horn, the speaker should be from two to four inches away. Experiments will prove the proper position for each speaker. In making tests, announce upon the record each change you try, so that the effect of each experiment may be traced when the record is reproduced" (ibid., 156–57).

39. Morton, *Sound Recording,*26. For a more detailed account of the expertise required by a recordist of commercial cylinder records, see Susan Schmidt Horning, *Chasing Sound: Technology, Culture, and the Art of Studio Recording from Edison to the LP* (Baltimore: Johns Hopkins University Press, 2013), 22–29.

40. Horning, *Chasing Sound*, 21.

41. Walter L. Welch and Leah Broadbeck Stenzel Burt, *From Tinfoil to Stereo: The*

Acoustic Years of the Recording Industry, 1877–1929 (Gainsville: University Press of Florida, 1994), 107–8; Horning, *Chasing Sound*, 18.

42. Alan Williams, "Is Sound Recording Like a Language?" *Yale French Studies* 60 (1980): 53–54, 65.

43. Richard Bauman, *A World of Others' Words: Cross-Cultural Perspectives on Intertextuality* (Malden, MA: Blackwell, 2004), 4–10.

44. Elements informing the generic features of an early audio text include the various speech formulae that preceded the performance on record, such as announcements, and any other para-audiotextual features that might have been recorded before or after a reading; the acts of framing, compression and adaptation that were often applied to the texts prepared for recording thus altering significantly the form of the source text as it had been published, originally, and the enactment of elocutionary or performative protocols in relation to the text or partially improvised sketch that was being recorded.

45. S. S. Curry, *Foundations of Expression: Studies and Problems for Developing the Voice, Body, and Mind in Reading and Speaking* (Boston: Expression Company, 1907), 299–300.

46. Mikhail Bakhtin, "The Problem of Speech Genres," in *Speech Genres and Other Late Essays*, trans. Vern W. McGee (Austin: University of Texas Press, 1992), 92.

47. Erving Goffman, *Forms of Talk* (Philadelphia: University of Pennsylvania Press, 1981), 128.

48. Patrick Feaster, "Framing the Mechanical Voice: Generic Conventions of early Phonograph Recording," *Folklore Forum* 32, nos. 1–2 (2001): 59.

49. Marjorie Garber, " " " (Quotation Marks)," *Critical Inquiry* 25, no. 4 (1999): 657.

50. Heather Dubrow, *Genre* (New York: Methuen, 1982), 3–4.

51. Feaster, "Framing the Mechanical Voice," 78–91.

52. Edison-Bell, *List of Records* (London: Edison-Bell Consolidated Phonograph Company, 1898), 19–21, http://sounds.bl.uk/related-content/TEXTS/029I-ED-IGX1898XXX-0000A0.pdf.

53. The Edison-Bell Consolidated Phonograph Co. Ltd. (1898–1901) was the fourth in a series of short-lived business ventures organized to develop a commercial market for the phonograph in the United Kingdom and beyond, and the first successfully to consolidate the rights to sell commercially viable phonograph machines (with spring motors to turn the cylinders) in England as devices for entertainment. Catalogues of entertainment records had been developed in the United States since the early 1890s, but analogous lists did not appear in the United Kingdom until a few years later due to an array of legal disputes and restrictions around the sale of the phonograph in England and the rights to sell American records abroad. Frank Andrews, *The Edison Phonograph: The British Connection* (Rugby, England: City of London Phonograph and Gramophone Society, 1986), 1–33, 8.

54. Edison-Bell, *List of Records*, 19–20.

55. Williams, *Keywords*, 187.

56. Most of these categories identify the dominant instrument of the recording and

can be understood in one sense as frequency-based categories: the frequencies produced by brass instruments were well within what acoustic recording technology then allowed.

57. Reprinted in Sherman, *Collector's Guide*, 16.

58. Ibid., 17.

59. Catherine Robson, *Heart Beats: Everyday Life and the Memorized Poem* (Princeton, NJ: Princeton University Press, 2012), 56.

60. The use of a high elocutionary delivery for such recordings spoken in the voice of the phonograph or gramophone was a common tactic of record companies that will be discussed in chapter 1. "On the Gramophone," David C. Bangs, performer, Emile Berliner Record 619Z, 1895–6. *Discography of American Historical Recordings*, s.v. "David C. Bangs (speaker)," http://adp.library.ucsb.edu/index.php/talent/detail/97449/Bangs_David_C._speaker.

61. *Discography of American Historical Recordings*, s.v. "Berliner matrix 618[a]. The Lord's Prayer / David C. Bangs," http://adp.library.ucsb.edu/index.php/matrix/detail/2000148132/618a-The_Lords_Prayer.

62. Joan Shelley Rubin, *Songs of Ourselves: The Uses of Poetry in America* (Cambridge, MA: Harvard University Press, 2007), 116.

63. The persistence of a kind of liturgical gravity in contemporary poetry performance has been discussed by Marit J. MacArthur in "Monotony, the Churches of Poetry Reading, and Sound Studies," *PMLA* 131, no. 1 (2016): 38–63.

Chapter 1

1. Edison, "Phonograph and Its Future," 53.

2. Thomas A. Edison, "The Perfected Phonograph," *North American Review* 379 (June 1888): 645.

3. "Julian Hawthorne in 'America,'" *The Phonograph and Phonograph-Graphophone* (New York: Russell Bros., 1888; reprint, London: London Phonograph and Gramophone Society, 1973), 24; J. Mount Bleyer, "Living Autograms," *Phonogram* 1 (1893): 16.

4. "Voices of the Dead," *Phonoscope* 1 (November 1896): 1.

5. Bleyer, "Living Autograms," 16.

6. Sir Joshua Steele, *Prosodia Rationalis: Or, An Essay Towards Establishing the Melody and Measure of Speech, to Be Expressed and Perpetuated by Peculiar Symbols* (London: J. Nichols, 1779), 14, 13.

7. Edison, "Phonograph and Its Future," 533–34.

8. Steele, *Prosodia Rationalis*, 14.

9. Samantha Matthews, "Psychological Crystal Palace? Late Victorian Confession Albums," *Book History* 3 (2000): 127.

10. Seem e.g., T. C. Mendenhall, "The Characteristic Curves of Composition," *Science* 9 (1887): 238; Lucius Sherman, "Some Observations upon the Sentence-Length in English Prose," *University Studies* 1 (1888): 119, 127. This kind of computational stylistic analysis that followed "style" patterns (regardless of semantic content) for the purpose of tracing authorial character, aimed to be a scientific means of identifying an author irrespective of the semantic, expressive content of the writing.

11. Gitelman, *Scripts*, 59.

12. John G. M'Kendrick, *Waves of Sound and Speech* (London: Macmillan, 1897), 12–15.

13. Ivan Kreilkamp, *Voice and the Victorian Storyteller* (New York: Cambridge University Press, 2005), 86. For an extended discussion of the historical confluences between shorthand and the Edison phonograph, see Gitelman, *Scripts*, 21–96.

14. Friedrich A. Kittler, *Gramophone, Film, Typewriter*, trans. Geoffrey Winthrop-Young and Michael Wutz (Stanford: Stanford University Press, 1999), 14.

15. Roland Gelatt, *The Fabulous Phonograph: From Tin Foil to High Fidelity* (New York: Lippincott, 1955), 31.

16. Sterne, *Audible Past*, 236.

17. Gitelman, *Scripts*, 86.

18. McKenzie, *Bibliography and the Sociology of Texts*, 62.

19. Gitelman, *Scripts*, 152.

20. Theodor W. Adorno, "The Form of the Phonograph Record," trans. Thomas Y. Levin, *October* 55 (1990): 57.

21. Thomas Y. Levin, "For the Record: Adorno on Music," *October* 55 (1990): 31–32.

22. Adorno, "Form of the Phonograph Record," 60.

23. Edison, "Perfected Phonograph," 645.

24. Edison, "Phonograph and Its Future," 534.

25. The phonograph, "in its power to record and replay, promised . . . to build communal bridges" across time, John Picker suggests in "The Victorian Aura of the Recorded Voice," *New Literary History* 32 (2001): 770.

26. Bennett Maxwell, "The Steytler Recordings of Alfred, Lord Tennyson—A History," *Tennyson Research Bulletin* 3 (1980): 153–55.

27. A digital version of this recording, dubbed from a tape copy of Gouraud's cylinder, is available at the British Library National Sound Archive,
http://sounds.bl.uk/Accents-and-dialects/Early-spoken-word-recordings/024M-1CD0239287XX-0214V0.

28. Cited in Frank Andrews, *Edison Phonograph*, xiv.

29. Ibid., xv.

30. John Keats, "Ode to a Nightingale," in *John Keats: Complete Poems*, ed. Jack Stillinger (Cambridge, MA: Harvard University Press, 1982), 281.

31. William Wordsworth, "To the Cuckoo," in *William Wordsworth: Selected Poems and Prefaces*, ed. Jack Stillinger (Boston: Houghton Mifflin, 1965), 159.

32. As Mary Jacobus has remarked on "the oral fallacy of Romantic theories of language—the pervasive notion that 'the voice / Of mountain torrents' (*The Prelude*, V, 408–9) speaks a language more profound than that of books, and is carried further into the heart." Jacobus, "The Art of Managing Books: Romantic Prose and the Writing of the Past," in *Romanticism and Language*, ed. Arden Reed (Ithaca, NY: Cornell University Press, 1984), 217.

33. Will Carleton, *The Festival of Praise; or, Thanksgiving Day* (New York: Harper & Bros., 1881), 58.

34. W. H. Preece, *The Phonograph; or, Speaking Machine* (London: London Stereoscopic Co., 1878), 54.

35. Timothy C. Fabrizio and George F. Paul, eds., *Antique Phonograph Advertising: An Illustrated History* (Atglen, PA: Schiffer Publishing, 2002), 12.

36. Ibid., 44, 52.

37. For a detailed account of the use of "Mary Had a Little Lamb" in tinfoil phonograph demonstrations, see Feaster, "'Following Record,'" 91–98.

38. Sterne, *Audible Past*, 251, 255.

39. "Editorial Grams," *Phonogram* 1 (1893): 10.

40. "Improved Gram-o-phone as a Christmas Present" (advertisement, 1898), in James N. Weber, ed., *Talking Machine: The Advertising History of the Berliner Gramophone and Victor Talking Machine* (Midland, Ontario: Adio Inc., 1997), 14.

41. "Flat, Signed, Indestructible" (advertisement, 1898), Weber, ed., *Talking Machine*, 13.

42. Brian Kane, *Sound Unseen: Acousmatic Sound in Theory and Practice* (Oxford: Oxford University Press, 2014), 184.

43. Horatio Nelson Powers, "The First Phonogramic Poem," Thomas A. Edison Papers, Edison National Historic Site, D-88–50; 124:705. This Edison archive document is available for viewing in digital format at http://edison.rutgers.edu.

44. Horatio Nelson Powers's "The Phonograph's Salutation" was later published in his *Lyrics of the Hudson* (Boston: D. Lothrop, 1891). In this chapter I continue to work from the text of the poem as it appears in the slip prepared to accompany the sound recording: Powers, "First Phonogramic Poem."

45. The dedication slip that was printed and sent with the accompanying phonogram notes that the poem was "spoken into the phonograph by the author / . . . Dedicated to Mr. Edison. / Addressed to Col. Gouraud. / Communicated to the Latter in the Author's own voice / By the Phonograph itself." Powers, "First Phonogramic Poem."

46. "The Reginaphone Speaks for Itself" (advertisement), *The Cosmopolitan* (April 1904): back matter, n.p.

47. Morton, *Sound Recording*, 16.

48. Record catalogue stock list, November 16, 1898, Catalogue Collection of the Music Division, Library and Archives Canada, R13984 183.

49. *Davenport Democrat*, May 19, 1857, cited in Maxwell, *Incunabula of Recorded Sound*, 5.

50. Len Spencer, "I Am the Edison Phonograph" (advertising record), preserved on a 1906 two-minute Edison black wax cylinder, but possibly recorded prior to that year, https://archive.org/details/iamed1906.

51. My transcription from the promotional audio recording recorded by Len Spencer, West Orange, New Jersey, 1906. This two-minute wax cylinder was distributed to dealers for the purpose of demonstrating the Edison phonograph, but was not sold commercially.

52. Steve J. Wurtzler, *Electric Sounds: Technological Change and the Rise of Corporate Mass Media* (New York: Columbia University Press, 2007), 76.

53. Spencer, "I Am the Edison Phonograph."

54. The purchase of a phonograph offered the promise of an analogous cultural ascendancy for the consumer.

55. David Appelbaum, *Voice* (Albany: State University of New York Press, 1990), xi, 3, 5.

56. Ibid., 4.

57. George Bernard Shaw, *Pygmalion* (1916; New York: Dover, 1994), 67.

58. Appelbaum, *Voice*, 6.

59. These accounts in the *New York Sun*, 94 (February 22, 1878): 115; *Philadelphia Weekly Times*, 25 (April 27, 1878):189; and *Philadelphia Press*, 94 (March 9, 1878): 121, from the *Thomas A. Edison Papers: A Selective Microfilm Edition*, ed. Thomas E. Jeffrey (Frederick, MD: University Publications of America, 1985), are cited in Feaster, "'Following Record,'" 125n153.

60. Jacob Smith, *Vocal Tracks: Performance and Sound Media* (Berkeley: University of California Press, 2008), 19, 22.

61. Examples of the laughing record genre included George Washington Johnson's enormously popular "Laughing Song" (1898) and its numerous iterations by other artists, Sally Stembler's "The Laughing Girl" (1918), the "The OKeh Laughing Record" (1922), and Cal Stewart's Uncle Josh recordings, which feature spoken sketches punctuated by his "trademark laugh." Smith, *Vocal Tracks*, 29, 28.

62. Sally Stembler and Edward Meeker, "Laughing Record (Henry's Music Lesson)" Edison 51063-R (1923), https://memory.loc.gov/ammem/vshtml/vssnde.html.)

63. Appelbaum, *Voice*, 17, 20, 21.

64. Ibid., 24, 25.

65. Terence E. Hanley, "Robert J. Wildhack (1881–1940)" (blog), *Indiana Illustrators and Hoosier Cartoonists* (January 16, 2011), http://indianaillustrators.blogspot.ca/2011/01/robert-j-wildhack-1881–1940.html.

66. Robert J. Wildhack, "Snores," Victor 35590-A, shellac twelve-inch disc, 78 rpm (January 1917); Robert J. Wildhack, "Sneezes," Victor 35590-B, shellac twelve-inch disc, 78 rpm (January 1917). https://www.discogs.com/Robert-J-Wildhack-Snores-Sneezes/release/7460984;https://wfmu.org/playlists/shows/62753; www.loc.gov/jukebox/recordings/detail/id/5194/.

67. "Wildhack, Robert J.," *Victor Records 1917 Catalogue, with biographical sketches, opera plots, new portraits and special Red Seal section* (Camden, NJ: Victor Talking Machine Co., November 1917), Wi.

68. Ibid.

69. My full transcript of Robert J. Wildhack, "Snores," is as follows:

> In discussing the human snore or in scientific terms, soft palate calisthenics, I need scarcely point out that the basic snore or Type 1 is the Ordinary or Pullman Car form sounding as follows: [Two illustrative snores.] Now snores are produced by two movements of the breath, an inspirational movement and an expirational movement, and the types appearing under the heading Varied Expirational Form are all dependent upon Type 1 for their inspirational elements. So we have Type 2a, The Labial or Ah-Poo variety, like this: [Two illustrative snores.] And then Type 2b, the Non-Lubricated or Frictional variety, as fol-

lows: [Two illustrative snores.] And Type 2c, a further development of this variety, I have called The Fourth of July or Whistling Bomb type. [Two illustrative snores.] And the final form of this variety is Type 2d, The Westinghouse Air [unintelligible]. [Two illustrative snores.] We now come to Type 3a, The Sad or Melancholy form. [Two illustrative snores.] Which merges and extends itself into Type 3b The Conversational or Troubled Conscience Variety. [Two illustrative snores.] Now leaving the various expirational forms we find that under the general heading of varied inspirational, we have first Type 4a, The Light and Thin or Blond Type. [Two illustrative snores.] Then the Larger and Fuller or Brunette variety, Type 4b. [Two illustrative snores.] And then we have Type 4c, The Ascending Diapason. [One illustrative snore.] And 4d, The Descending Diapason. [One illustrative snore.] And then Type 4e, The Double Diapason, first ascending and then descending, or vice versa. [Two illustrative snores.] We may now consider under Type 5 a characteristic one of the sentry combinations or gymnastic variety, which are of course great in number, our selection being The Double Diapason on the inspiration and The Conversational or Troubled Conscience variety on the expiration. [Two illustrative snores.] We may well take note in passing of Type C which I have called The Bucksaw, it sounding much the same no matter which direction the breath travels. [Two illustrative snores.] And now we approach the evident sign of the experienced and accomplished snorer, Type 7, The Interrupted Inspiration or Static Lag. [Two illustrative snores.] Which, logically and almost inevitably develops into the [unintelligible] the last word in snoring, Type 8, The Auto-Resuscitation or Self-Awakening variety. [Two illustrative snores.] [Third half-snore leading to awakening . . .] What's the matter? Huh? I was not. I don't snore. Must have been somethin' else. Good night. [Snoring.]

70. Appelbaum, *Voice*, 39.

71. To explain this point further, consider for a moment a full transcript of Wildhack's "Sneezes" recording as an illustration of how we use transcription to rationalize and control the productions of the human voice:

I have just prepared myself for my little talk on sneezes by getting my feet wet. And if someone will open the window to my left (that one), and also the door on my right (thank you, Billy), I may perhaps be able to illustrate my lecture with appropriate [*sneeze*], with appropriate examples. [*Clearing throat*]. That one was The Feline or Pussycat Sneeze, Type 1. We're all so familiar with sneezes that it may be well to name them, list them, and become acquainted with the different forms and types so that we may learn to recognize our friend by his sneeze. Following Type 1, The Feline or Pussycat Sneeze which you have just heard, we have Type 1a, The Atomizer or Seltzer Siphon variety. [*Two illustrative sneezes.*] Type 2, The Trombone or Cataclysmic, is an interesting example resulting generally from an ineffectual attempt to impede the expulsion of the breath by compressing the superior and inferior labia or lip. [*Two illustrative sneezes.*] And another result of attempted silencing, more than [*unintelligible*], of course, is Type 3, The Ratchet or Clock

Winding type. [*Two illustrative sneezes.*] Perhaps after all it is just as well for one to attempt to control a sneeze, in as much as some of the results of the lack of stifling are quite extreme. Many of us have heard, I'm sure, heard the windows rattle when in some large building a man has seemed to suddenly shout an order to a boarding house kitchen, as in Type 4, The Mess Call. [*Two illustrative sneezes.*] There [clearing throat] there is strong, there is strong optimistic tone in Type 5 which may be called The Encouraging or Cowboy Yell sneeze, sounding as the ... [*Two illustrative sneezes,* "Aaah, Aaah-WHOOPIE! Aaah, Aaah-WHOOPIE!]. And, uh, for contrast there is Type 6 The Disappointing or Non-Eventuating Clever in which the inspiration plays a much greater part than the, shall we not say, anticipated climax? [Two illustrative sneezes]. [*Clearing throat.*] A rather ordinary and prevalent form is the Tickle or [*unintelligible*] Mandatory Type, Number 7: [*Two illustrative sneezes,* "Aaah-CHOO! Aaah-CHOO!"]. While a somewhat rare and individual sneeze may be called The Carburetor Backfire or Explosive Type 8. [*Three illustrative sneezes.*] But after all the commonest and most familiar form is Type 9, The Interrogatory or Scandal Monger's sneeze, a free and unfettered expression of the fundamental spirit of science, curiosity and inquiry: [*Two illustrative sneezes.*] Will somebody please close the window? I have change of shoes and socks in the next room. I thank you [*restrained sneeze*] for your kind [*restrained sneeze*] attENTION? [*Two involuntary sneezes,* "Aaah-CHOO! Aaah-CHOO!"].

72. Jennifer Lynn Stoever, *The Sonic Color Line: Race and the Cultural Politics of Listening* (New York: New York University Press, 2016), 7.

73. Gustavus Stadler, "Never Heard Such a Thing: Lynching and Phonographic Modernity," *Social Text* 28, no. 1 (2010): 98–99.

74. Ibid., 98–99.

75. Ibid., 100.

76. Samuel Burdett, *A Test of Lynch Law: An Exposé of Mob Violence and the Courts of Hell* (Seattle, 1901), 17. Cited in Stadler, "Never Heard Such a Thing," 89.

77. Elaine Scarry, *The Body in Pain: The Making and Unmaking of the World* (Oxford: Oxford University Press, 1985), 4.

78. Charles Bernstein, "Objectivist Blues: Scoring Speech in Second-Wave Modernist Poetry and Lyrics," *American Literary History* 20, nos. 1–2 (2008): 354.

79. A few examples of such titles include J. A. Ferguson's *The Star Reciter: A Collection of Prose and Poetical Gems, Grave and Gay, from British & American Authors* (London: J. Heywood, Simpkin, Marshall, and Co., 1873); *Wehman Bros. 100 Popular Comic, Dramatic and Dialect Recitations* (New York: Wehman Bros., 1900); and the periodical *Scrap-Book Recitation Series* published in Chicago by T. S. Denison between 1879 and 1916.

80. Alongside these broadly cast general recitation books, more specific collections were developed according to either genre (Vaudeville Sketches, Blackface Plays, Christmas Comedies) or niche audience (monologues aimed at children "or monologists who impersonate children"; monologues "particularly for women"). My focus will be on the general late Victorian anthology. For descriptions of some of these niche-market collec-

tions, see advertisements in Henry M. Soper's *Scrap-Book Recitation Series: A Miscellaneous Collection of Prose and Poetry for Recitation and Reading, Designed for Schools, Home and Literary Circles* 5 (1887): 142, and back flap and cover.

81. E.g., "The Light from Over the Range" is cited as having come "From Scrap Collection of Miss Julia A. Richardson." Soper, *Scrap-Book Recitation Series* 5 (1887): 115.

82. Soper, *Scrap-Book Recitation Series* 5 (1887): 2.

83. *Prescott's Drawing Room Recitations* (New York: De Witt, 1881), 2.

84. Henry James, *The Question of Our Speech. The Lesson of Balzac: Two Lectures* (Boston: Houghton, Mifflin, 1905), 11.

85. Ibid., 25, 31, 44–45. Bernstein articulates this idea most effectively when he observes that "American mass culture is founded (and founders) on a streamlining, not to say mainstreaming, of vernaculars in order to forge a synthetic mass slang that is the antithesis of dialect, which remains marked by the local and unassimilated. Mass culture entails the absorption of dialect by refinement, assimilation, and ultimately standardization." Bernstein, "Objectivist Blues," 350.

86. J. E. Frobisher, *Good Selections, No. 2: Selected Readings, Serious and Humorous, in Prose and Poetry, with an Appendix on Elocution* (New York: J. Schermerhorn, 1875), 149.

87. Soper, *Scrap-Book Recitation Series* 3 (1882): 16.

88. Edgar Allan Poe, "The Bells" (1849). Stanza 1, here quoted from Soper, *Scrap Book Recitation Series* 3 (1882): 16.

89. Stanza 1 of Frobisher's parody of "The Bells," as found in Frobisher, *Good Selections*, 103. It runs as follows:

Hear the hotels with their bells,—
Morning bells!
What a thundering sound of Bells!
How they twang-ee-tee-bang!
Tee-bang, tee-bang!
Up the stairs and halls around;
Twang-ee-tee-bang, tee-bang,
What a bustling, hurrying sound!
Now the lodgers cease from snoring,
Now the morning cock is crowing,
Now the meadow lark is soaring,
And the cattle they are lowing,
While the bells are clanging,
Whanging,
Clang-ee-tee-bang, tee-bang, tee-bang, tee-bang,
Clang-ee-tee-bang, tee-bang—
Oh! such a clanging never was heard,
Even in the lurid lower world.

90. "Medley: Mary's Little Lamb—*New*," in Soper, *Scrap-Book Recitation Series* 1 (1879): 55.

91. Feaster, "'Following Record,'" 93.

92. Francis P. Richardson, *Werner's Readings and Recitations No. 13* (New York: Edgar S. Werner, 1894), front cover inner-flap advertisement for *Emma Dunning Banks's Original Recitations with Lesson Talks* (New York: Edgar S. Werner, 1890).

93. Frobisher gives this advice to his readers who might practice on the selections he provides, whether it be Dante Gabriel Rossetti's poem "Sister Helen," a Dutch dialect piece entitled "The Dutchman's Shmall Pox," or the parody of "The Bells" mentioned above: "Go into you room and read to the chairs without the effort of trying to read *well*, but simply *naturally*. Think how you would tell it to the family circle. The perfection of such reading would be so to read that the eyes only of your audience, and not their ears, could tell them that you *are* reading. The practice may be slow but sure. Have no other care than how to read *naturally*." Frobisher, *Good Selections*, 149.

94. Ibid., 149, 158.

95. Susan A. Glenn, "'Give an Imitation of Me': Vaudeville Mimics and the Play of the Self," *American Quarterly* 50, no. 1 (1998): 54.

96. Ibid., 55.

97. J. Arthur Bleackley, *The Art of Mimicry* (New York: Samuel French, 1911), 35–44.

98. As Bleackley elaborates: "You may yourself imitate the gesticulations of a master, but it will be mechanical as the movements of a working model without the master's spirit too. You may mimic the movements of form and limb, and the modulation of tone and voice, but not the vital force that makes the dead limb live, and fills the voice with inspiration." Ibid., 12, 74. Glenn cites another interesting example of this kind of comparison in a theatre critic's statement from an 1899 newspaper review that the imitative work of mimic Cossie Loftus was "better than a Phonograph" because it was "finished and artistic." Cited in Glenn, "'Give an Imitation of Me,'" 56.

99. Bleackley, *Art of Mimicry*, 12.

100. As Bleackley puts it, "The stronger your imagination, the more original will be your powers of mimicry." Ibid., 68.

101. Ibid., 73.

102. Ibid., 15–16. The original passage is from Philip Gibbs, *Knowledge is Power: A Guide to Personal Culture* (London: E. Arnold, 1903), 242.

103. Justus Nieland, *Feeling Modern: the Eccentricities of Public Life* (Urbana: University of Illinois Press, 2008), 48–49.

104. Glenn, "'Give an Imitation of Me,'" 61–65.

105. Patrick Feaster, "Cal Stewart and the Phonographic Text" (MS, 1999). As Feaster remarks in this paper: "Edison Blue Amberol cylinder 1583 is a four-minute celluloid cylinder recording of Cal Stewart's 'Uncle Josh Buys an Automobile,' released in November, 1912. When the original cylinder was released, it was accompanied by a printed slip of paper prepared by the manufacturer, containing a transcription of the recording . . . for purposes of 'reading along'" (5). Cited with permission.

106. Mark Morrison, "Performing the Pure Voice: Elocution, Verse Recitation, and Modernist Poetry in Prewar London," *Modernism/Modernity* 3 (1996): 30.

107. Gavin Jones, *Strange Talk: The Politics of Dialect Literature in Gilded Age America* (Berkeley: University of California Press, 1999), 167.

108. A context of private listening (as opposed that of a public, theatre audience) might have eliminated some of the pressures of a conformist social response.

109. "Cohen on His Honeymoon," Monroe Silver, performer, Edison Diamond Disc record 7154 (1920).

110. Harold D. Smith, "The Thing Talked: Some Memories of Days Spent inside and outside the Phonograph Business" (MS), 142. Harold D. Smith fonds, MUS 113, box 7, folder 119. Tim Brooks, ed., *Columbia Repertoire History: Popular Recordings, 1901–1925, Volume I* (1999), http://adp.library.ucsb.edu/index.php/resources/detail/118.

111. "Cohen on the Telephone," Joe Hayman, performer, Columbia, A1516 (1913).

112. Homi Bhabha and Sander L. Gilman, "Tête-à-Tête," in *Talk Talk Talk: The Cultural Life of Everyday Conversation*, ed. S. I. Salamensky (New York: Routledge, 2001), 4.

113. Marlis Schweitzer and Daniel Guadagnolo, "Feeling Scottish: Affect, Mimicry, and Vaudeville's 'Inimitable' Harry Lauder," *Journal of Dramatic Theory and Criticism* 26, no. 2 (2012): 151–52.

114. This observation of Armond Fields (grand-nephew of Lew Fields) is cited in John Koegel, *Music in German Immigrant Theater: New York City, 1840–1940* (Rochester, NY: University of Rochester Press, 2009), 189.

115. "What I Heard at the Vaudeville," Len Spencer, performer. Edison Gold Moulded Record 8693 (1904/5), www.library.ucsb.edu/OBJID/Cylinder2745. The text of the entry for this recording in a 1907 catalogue appears—in the category of "Talking Records by Len Spencer" is as follows: "8693 What I Heard at the Vaudeville (*Introducing Gus Williams' German dialect recitation, "Only a Lock of hair," with Orchestral Embellishment*)," *Edison Gold Moulded Records, British-American List* (London: National Phonograph Co., 1907), 64.

116. The cover copy of these recitation anthologies advertised the selections as "especially adapted for reading and speaking by the members of refined, select home circles," and also as having "been delivered by the compiler, with every mark of popular appreciation, before large intellectual audiences throughout the United States." Gus Williams, *Gus Williams' Fireside Recitations: Being a Choice Collection of Instructive, Emotional, and Humorous Pieces in Prose and Poetry. Especially Adapted for Reading and Speaking by the Members of Refined, Select Home Circles* (New York: De Witt, 1881); Gus Williams, *Gus Williams' Standard Recitations: Containing a Great Number of Pathetic, Powerful, Instructive and Humorous Articles, by the Best Authors of the Times* (New York: De Witt, 1882).

117. Tim Gracyk, *Popular American Recording Pioneers, 1895–1925* (New York: Routledge, 2008), 180–83.

118. "Pathé Jobbers' Convention Proved Most Successful," *Talking Machine World* 13 (October 1917): 129. Also cited in Gracyk, *Popular American Recording Pioneers*, 182.

119. Gracyk, *Popular American Recording Pioneers*, 314–19. Information for the recordings mentioned: "Lincoln's Speech at Gettysburg," Len Spencer, performer, Edison Standard 8154 (1902); "Uncle Tom's Cabin (Flogging Scene)," Len Spencer, performer, Edison Standard 865 (1904); "Dr. Jekyll and Mr. Hyde," Len Spencer, performer, Edison Standard 8879 (1905).

120. "A Few Words in Regard to Drinking," John Terrell, performer, Berliner 6484 (n.d.); "Casey's Address to the G.A.R.," John Terrell, performer, Berliner 608 (n.d.).

121. "Coloured Preacher/Auctioneer," George Graham, performer, Berliner 626W (1900).

122. "Drama in One Act," George Graham, performer, Berliner 627Z (1896).

123. Raymond Wile, "Record Makers in 1891." *ARSC Journal* 3 (1971):10–12.

124. "A Study in Mimicry—Vaudeville," introduced by Len Spencer. John Orren and Lillian Drew, Performers, Edison 50485-R (1918).

www.americaslibrary.gov/assets/sh/humor/sh_humor_imitat_1.wav.

125. The discerning consumer of mimetic performance was called upon to compare phonographic reproductions with live performance, as in the staged Edison tone tests of 1915–20 in which live singers were compared in blind presentation with the records they had made, or when mimic Cissie Loftus played an Enrico Caruso record on stage and then proceeded to imitate the voice before a live audience. Glenn, "'Give an Imitation of Me,'" 56, Wurtzler identifies the Edison tone tests as "one of the most pervasive and important methods used to construct an identity for the phonograph." Wurtzler, *Electric Sounds,* 80.

126. Mladen Dolar, *A Voice and Nothing More* (Cambridge, MA: MIT Press, 2006), 75.

127. See, e.g., Rand Richards Cooper, "Can We Really Read with Our Ears?" *New York Times Book Review,* June 6, 1993, 49; and Sarah Kozloff, "Audio Books in a Visual Culture," *Journal of American Culture* 18 (1995): 89.

128. Matthew Rubery, "Introduction: Talking Books," in *Audiobooks, Literature and Sound Studies,* ed. Rubery (New York: Routledge, 2011), 12–15.

129. "The Flogging Scene from Uncle Tom's Cabin," Len Spencer, Performer, Victor 2674 (1904); "Talking Uncle Tom's Cabin," Len Spencer, Performer, Edison Cylinder 8656 (1904); "Svengali Mesmerizes Trilby," Herbert Beerbohm Tree, performer, Gramophone Company, ten-inch disc, 1313 (1906).

130. Cooper, "Can We Really Read?" 15, 49. As Cooper puts it: "The process of constructing a writer's voice, far from being a burdensome chore that can be simplified for us, as washing dishes is simplified by a dishwasher, is rather more like the main event of literature itself" (49).

131. Denis Donoghue, *The Practice of Reading* (New Haven, CT: Yale University Press, 1998), 56.

132. Andrew Miller, *The Burdens of Perfection: On Ethics and Reading in Nineteenth-Century British Literature* (Ithaca, NY: Cornell University Press, 2008), xii.

133. Books "are not . . . simply 'dead things' carrying performed information from authors to readers. They are crucial agents in the cycle of production, distribution, and consumption," Paul Duguid observes in "Material Matters: The Past and Futurology of the Book," in *The Future of the Book,* ed. Geoffrey Nunberg (Berkeley: University of California Press, 1996), 79.

Chapter 2

1. For a history of the modern full-length audio book, which begins in earnest with an account of the Library of Congress Books for the Blind project, see Matthew Rubery, *The Untold Story of the Talking Book* (Cambridge, MA: Harvard University Press, 2016).

2. Edison, "Phonograph and Its Future," 534.

3. "It is very likely that when the human voice has taken its place in literature, companies of persons will exist whose calling will be to personate characters in stories and speak their dialogues. They must be persons of ability and culture, and marked histrionic ability. They must be, in fact, a higher class of actors. The novelist—who, in this case, would be a kind of stage manager and dramatist in one—would assign to each his part, explaining its nature and limitations, and the general purport of the situations and conversations. Then the actors must rehearse their parts together until, in the judgment of the manager, they were approximately perfect in them; after that the graphophones must come into play, and the story, in its final form, be talked into them by the dramatis personae. The narrative and descriptive parts could be given to a special elocutionist, trained for that especial function." Julian Hawthorne, "The Human Voice in Literature," *America: A Journal of Today* 1, no. 8 (May 26, 1888): 12.

4. "Edison estimates that *Nicholas Nickleby* can be transcribed upon six cylinders, six inches in diameter by twelve inches in length," Philip G. Hubert Jr. reported in "The New Talking Machines," *Atlantic Monthly* 63 (1889): 259.

5. John Cookson et al., *Digital Talking Books: Planning for the Future* (Washington, DC: Library of Congress, 1998), 3–4; Leroy Hughbanks, *Talking Wax* (n.p.: Hobson, 1945), 106. As Sterne notes, long-playing format records were first introduced in 1926 by Western Electric for the synchronization of sound with eleven-minute film reels. They were not used for the purpose of recording entire novels until over a decade later. Sterne, *MP3*, 14.

6. Jay David Bolter and Richard Grusin, *Remediation: Understanding New Media* (Cambridge, MA: MIT Press, 2000), 6, 14.

7. Ibid., 19.

8. "Julian Hawthorne in 'America,'" 24; Bleyer, 16.

9. See, e.g., Deborah Vlock, *Dickens, Novel Reading, and the Victorian Popular Theatre* (Cambridge: Cambridge University Press, 1998), and Kreilkamp, *Voice and the Victorian Storyteller*.

10. Kreilkamp, *Voice and the Victorian Storyteller*, 91.

11. John Guillory, "Genesis of the Media Concept," *Critical Inquiry* 36 (Winter 2010): 321.

12. Bauman, *World*, 10.

13. "Transformation Scene from Dr. Jekyll and Mr. Hyde," Len Spencer, performer, Columbia Phonograph Company 32604 (1905); "Svengali Mesmerizes Trilby," Herbert Beerbohm Tree, performer, Gramophone Company, ten-inch disc, 1313 (1906); "The Awakening of Scrooge," Bransby Williams, performer, Edison Company 13353 (1905).

14. *Discography of American Historical Recordings*, s.v. "Columbia matrix 1908. The transformation scene / Len Spencer," http://adp.library.ucsb.edu/index.php/matrix/detail/2000138428/1908-The_transformation_scene.

15. As the recording was described in the 1906 *Columbia Phonograph Company Catalogue*: "This tragic scene from the last act of the play depicts the final transformation of Dr. Jekyll into the demon Hyde, and his subsequent death by his own hand. The ringing

of the chimes and pealing of the organ lend realism to the intensely thrilling climax."
Cited in Wurtzler, *Electric Sounds,* 350.

16. "Svengali Mesmerizes Trilby," Herbert Beerbohm Tree, performer.

17. "The Art of a Past Generation," *His Master's Voice: Records of Unique and Histori-cal Interest* (London: Gramophone Company, 1910), 2.

18. George du Maurier, *Trilby* (1895; Broadview Encore Edition, Peterborough, ON: Broadview Press, 2003), 28.

19. Alex Woloch, *The One vs. The Many: Minor Characters and the Space of the Pro-tagonist in the Novel* (Princeton, NJ: Princeton University Press, 2004), 14.

20. For example, an early education-oriented cluster at the back of a 1912 Victor catalogue states that the selections have "been made to help in the uplift of the ideas and tastes" of students. Given that many of the pieces were very short, some of them were "grouped several on one record with small spaces between, enabling the teacher to present any one she may choose without the unpleasantness of guessing where it begins and getting a part of another song." This improvement in disc navigation seems to have been developed with the classroom in mind. *Victor Record Catalogue* (Camden, NJ: November 1912): n.p.

21. The Victor Talking Machine Company at Camden, New Jersey, was the first to found an education department when in 1911 it appointed Mrs. Frances Elliott Clark as its inaugural Educational Department director. Smith, *The Thing Talked,* 123. Colum-bia followed a few years later with publications like *Literature and Music: A Manual for Teachers and Students in School and Home* (New York: Columbia Gramophone Co., Educational Department, 1918).

22. Recall that the common generic categories for spoken recordings used in early record catalogues included "Descriptive Specialties," "Recitations," "Novelties," or the general "Talking Records." See *Victor Record Catalogue* (Camden, NJ: Educational De-partment of the Victor Talking Machine Co., May 1906), 104–11, and *Columbia Records* (New York: Columbia Phonograph Co., June 1897), 12.

23. The first published Library of Congress inventory of items it identified explicitly as literary sound recordings appeared in 1961 under the title, *Archive of Recorded Po-etry and Literature: A Checklist* and was followed five years later by *Literary Recordings: A Checklist of the Archive of Recorded Poetry and Literature in the Library of Congress* (1966). The "Preface" to a later expanded version of *Literary Recordings* explains the origin and content of the collection that appears under this rubric: "The collection was begun in 1943 when Allen Tate was Consultant in Poetry to the Library. Developing under the general direction of past Consultants in Poetry, this archive now contains recordings of nearly a thousand poets reading their own work. It includes recordings of poetry readings and other literary events held in the Library's Coolidge Auditorium or the Whittall Pavilion, tapes of poets reading their poems in the Recording Laboratory or elsewhere for the archive, and recordings received through occasional gifts, exchanges, or purchases." "Preface," *Literary Recordings,* Jennifer Whittington, compiler (Washing-ton, DC: Library of Congress, 1981), iii.

24. Guillory, 346–48.

25. Jeffrey Scott Maxwell, "Timeline: The Tulsa Chautauqua Assembly, 1905 to 1908," *The Complete Chautauquan: The Tulsa Chautauqua Assembly,* article posted 10/08/2000, www.crackerjackcollectors.com/Jeffrey_Maxwell/alphachautauquan/tulshist.html.

26. "Life Portrayals: A Masterpiece of Interpretive Impersonation" (pamphlet, n.d.), Library and Archives Canada, Harold D. Smith fonds, MUS 113, vol. 1, folder 4.

27. "Daniel Peggoty," *The Platform* (Dickensian Number), n.d., n.p., Library and Archives Canada, Harold D. Smith fonds, MUS 113, vol. 1, folder 4.

28. "Two Immortal Characters," *The Platform* (Dickensian Number), n.d., n.p., Library and Archives Canada, Harold D. Smith fonds, MUS 113, vol. 1, folder 4.

29. "William Sterling Battis: Interpreter of Dickens," *The Lyceumite,* Scorer Lyceum Bureau, Philadelphia (pamphlet, n.d.), Library and Archives Canada, Harold D. Smith fonds, MUS 113, vol. 1, folder 12.

30. "William Sterling Battis," *The Platform* (Dickensian Number), n.d., n.p., Library and Archives Canada, Harold D. Smith fonds, MUS 113, vol. 1, folder 4.

31. Edwin M. Eigner, *The Dickens Pantomime* (Berkeley: University of California Press, 1989), 4, 157.

32. Malcolm Andrews, *Charles Dickens and His Performing Selves: Dickens and the Public Readings* (Oxford: Oxford University Press, 2006), 114–15.

33. Ibid., 109–25.

34. Collins, "Introduction," in *Charles Dickens: The Public Readings,* ed. Philip Collins (Oxford: Clarendon Press, 1975), li.

35. Ibid., xlvi.

36. Ibid., xxii.

37. George Gissing, *Charles Dickens* (London: Blackie and Son, 1898), 83.

38. "As everywhere else in [Victorian fiction], and never more openly, the 'you to whom I write,' the reader, is only a code name, only a figure, for sentiment itself in circulation." Garrett Stewart, *Dear Reader: The Conscripted Audience in Nineteenth-Century British Fiction* (Baltimore: Johns Hopkins University Press, 1996), 49.

39. "Narrative reading is made possible by an extroversion of the fictional inner life: a mimesis of emotion as well as milieu whose only point of occlusion is the scene of reading itself when set off within plot." Stewart, *Dear Reader,* 75.

40. Kreilkamp, *Voice and the Victorian Storyteller,* 76.

41. Ibid., 78.

42. Robert Giddings, "The Mystery of Ackroyd and Callow," *Dickens on the Web,* http://charlesdickenspage.com/ackroyd_callow_dickens-giddings.html..

43. "The Birthday Dinner in London," *The Dickensian,* June 1955, 113, cited in Fred Guida, *"A Christmas Carol" and Its Adaptations* (Jefferson, NC: McFarland, 2000): 46.

44. Bransby Williams, *An Actor's Story* (London: Chapman & Hall, 1909), 61–63. Williams's account suggests that the novels themselves, and not Dickens's reading copies (published editions of which were limited), served as his primary source material. On the publication history of Dickens's reading copies, see Collins, "Introduction," in *Charles Dickens: The Public Readings,* xlii–xlv.

45. Williams, *Actor's Story,* 62–63.

46. The cover of Bransby Williams's 1913 anthology *My Sketches from Dickens* (London: Chapman & Hall, 1913), depicts a motley crew of unmistakable Dickens personages emerging from a splayed A-frame volume of his *Works* as if liberated to reenact their characters.

47. "Pickwick Papers (Charles Dickens): Wardle's Christmas Party (w Carol Singers [male quartet])," Bransby Williams, performer, Edison 13352 (1905); "A Christmas Carol in Prose (Charles Dickens): Scrooge's awakening (w Carol Singers [male quartet])," Bransby Williams, performer, Edison 13353 (1905).

48. For this information I am indebted in the first instance to Damian's 78s, "Bransby Williams—Discography," http://discog.damians78s.co.uk/performers/u-z/bransby-williams.

49. This being "SCROOGE. A Monologue Adapted from the 'Christmas Carol,'" in Williams, *My Sketches from Dickens*, 9–12.

50. Jim Walsh, "Russell Hunting, Sr.," *Hobbies,* November 1944, 27–28. Cited in Feaster, "Framing the Mechanical Voice," 85.

51. "The Awakening of Scrooge," Bransby Williams, performer, Edison Amberol 12378 (1911). www.library.ucsb.edu/OBJID/Cylinder4551.

52. "A Christmas Carol—Scrooge—After the Dream," Bransby Williams, performer, Columbia 6277 (1912/1924).

53. "SCROOGE," in Williams, *My Sketches from Dickens*, 11.

54. Williams, *My Sketches from Dickens*, 3.

55. "A Christmas Carol—Scrooge—The Dream," performed by Bransby Williams, Columbia twelve-inch disc, 6276–2 (1912–24).

56. My transcript of "A Christmas Carol—Bob Cratchit Telling of Scrooge (Dickens)," Bransby Williams, performer, HMV 2632f 01012 (1912).

57. Charles Dickens, *A Christmas Carol in Prose, Being A Ghost Story of Christmas*, with illustrations by John Leech (Boston: Little, Brown, 1920), 164.

58. Ibid., 164. See John Leech, "Scrooge and Bob Cratchit" or "The Christmas Bowl," Wood-Block Engraving from the last page of *A Christmas Carol* (1843). Image scanned by Philip V. Allingham, www.victorianweb.org/victorian/art/illustration/carol/8.html.

59. "David Copperfield (Charles Dickens)—Wilkins Micawber's Advice," Bransby Williams, performer, Edison cylinder 13508 (March 1906).

Williams recorded eight versions of the Micawber monologue during his career, for Edison, Columbia, Pathé, and Decca.

60. Williams, *Actor's Story*, 75–76.

61. Ibid., 83.

62. According to the advertisement, Speaight was embarking upon his fourth American-Canadian tour in the fall of 1909. His "Dickens Recitals" season ran from 1 October to 28 January. Advertisement, *The Dickensian: A Magazine for Dickens Lovers and Monthly Record of the Dickens Fellowship* 4, no. 8 (August 1908):198, Library and Archives Canada, Harold D. Smith fonds, MUS 113, vol. 1, folder 4.

63. "Walter J. Lowenhaupt Presents Mr. Mortimer Kaphan: Realistic Portrayals of Charles Dickens Characters" (pamphlet, 1–2), Library and Archives Canada, Harold D. Smith fonds, MUS 113, vol. 1, folder 11.

64. W. B. Matz, *The Dickensian Magazine*, Library and Archives Canada, Harold D. Smith fonds, MUS 113, vol. 1, folder 12.

65. John Dewey and Evelyn Dewey, *Schools of Tomorrow* (1915; New York: Dutton, 1962), 53.

66. Smith, *New Correlation*, 3.

67. Dewey and Dewey, *Schools of Tomorrow*, 47.

68. Smith oversaw the production of several education catalogue guidebooks for Victor, including a revised edition of Ann Shaw Faulkner's popular music appreciation book *What We Hear in Music* (Camden, NJ: Victor Talking Machine Co., 1913) of which 305,000 copies were printed by the Victor education department in 1916, and a revised edition of his own *A New Correlation*, of which 83,000 copies were produced for sale (at a dollar apiece) and distribution in the same year. Smith, *The Thing Talked*, 167.

69. Smith, *New Correlation*, 4.

70. John Dewey, "My Pedagogic Creed," *School Journal* 54 (January 1897): 77–80.

71. Elmer W. Smith, "The Advance Movement in English," *English Journal* 6, no. 1 (January 1917): 15.

72. Ibid., 15.

73. Ibid., 16.

74. *English Journal* 6, no. 1 (January 1917), back matter.

75. "The Victrola and Victor Records" (advertisement), *Journal of Education* 86 (December 6, 1917): 588. The description of Battis's recorded monologues arranged from *A Christmas Carol* runs as follows: "Scrooge—Part 1—Marley's Ghost," "Scrooge—Part 2—The Ghost of Christmas Past," "Scrooge—Part 3—The Ghost of Christmas Present," and "Scrooge—Part 4—The Ghost of Christmas to Come."

76. See, e.g., *English Journal* 14, no. 7 (September 1925), back matter full-page ad run by Victor's educational department depicting Battis costumed and posed as the characters he recorded.

77. *The Victrola in the Schools* (1918), n.p., Library and Archives Canada, Harold D. Smith fonds, MUS 113, vol. 3, file 85.

78. Brochure, Hepworth Co., back page, Library and Archives Canada, Harold D. Smith fonds, MUS 113, vol. 1, folder 12.

79. Joss Marsh, "Dickens and Film," in *The Cambridge Companion to Charles Dickens*, ed. John O. Jordan (Cambridge: Cambridge University Press, 2001), 207.

80. S. S. Curry, *Imagination and Dramatic Instinct: Some Practical Steps for Their Development* (Boston: Expression Company, 1896), 235.

81. "William Sterling Battis," *The Platform* (Dickensian Number), n.d., n.p., Library and Archives Canada, Harold D. Smith fonds, MUS 113, vol. 1, folder 4.

82. Curry, *Imagination and Dramatic Instinct*, 236. See also S. S. Curry, *Browning and the Dramatic Monologue* (New York: Haskell House, 1965), 30.

83. Woloch, *The One vs. The Many*, 149.

84. See ibid., 125–76, on the "over-significance" of Dickens's minor characters.

85. Collins, "David Copperfield," in *Charles Dickens: The Public Readings*, ed. Philip Collins (Oxford: Clarendon Press, 1975), 214.

86. W. S. Battis to Harold D. Smith (February 15, 1915), Library and Archives Canada, Harold D. Smith fonds, MUS 113, vol. 1, folder 4.

87. J. Hillis Miller, *Charles Dickens: The World of His Novels* (Cambridge, MA: Harvard University Press, 1958), 151.

88. Schweitzer and Guadagnolo note a similar combination of typicality and particularity in the reception of Scottish mimicry performances and recordings made by Harry Lauder. See Schweitzer and Guadagnolo, "Feeling Scottish," 146.

89. "Micawber (from 'David Copperfield')," William Sterling Battis, performer, Victor 35556-B twelve-inch disc (1916), www.loc.gov/jukebox/recordings/detail/id/4471/autoplay/true.

90. Woloch, *The One vs. The Many*, 14, 129.

91. Jonathan Sterne, "The MP3 as Cultural Artifact," *New Media & Society* 18 (2006): 828.

Chapter 3

1. Jerome McGann, *The Beauty of Inflections* (Oxford: Oxford University Press, 1985), 190–91.

2. Cited in Ricks, *Tennyson*, 244.

3. Ray Porter, "The Charge of the Lightning Judge," in *Scrap-Book Recitation Series*, no. 3, ed. Henry M. Soper (1882), 92.

4. J. Timothy Lovelace, *The Artistry and Tradition of Tennyson's Battle Poetry* (New York: Routledge, 2003), 105.

5. McGann, *Beauty of Inflections*, 202.

6. Lovelace, *Artistry and Tradition*, 107.

7. "The force of the poem is in its own envious yearning, its knowledge that it was 'their's,' but not Tennyson's, 'not to make reply,' and 'not to reason why,' and 'but to do and die'" (Ricks, *Tennyson*, 244).

8. See Don Geiger, *The Dramatic Impulse in Modern Poetics* (Baton Rouge: Louisiana State University, 1967) and Wallace Bacon, *The Art of Interpretation* (New York: Holt, Rinehart & Winston, 1966).

9. Don Geiger, *The Sound, Sense, and Performance of Literature* (Glensview, IL: Scott, Foresman, 1963), 2–5.

10. The title of Geiger's *The Dramatic Impulse of Modern Poetics* is no doubt indebted to Curry's *Imagination and Dramatic Instinct*.

11. Cleanth Brooks and Robert Penn Warren, *Understanding Poetry* (New York: Holt, 1938), cited in Geiger, *Dramatic Impulse*, 7.

12. Curry, *Imagination and Dramatic Instinct*, 235.

13. Natalie M. Houston, "Reading the Victorian Souvenir: Sonnets and Photographs of the Crimean War," *Yale Journal of Criticism* 14 (2001): 358.

14. McGann, *Beauty of Inflections*, 192.

15. Houston, "Reading the Victorian Souvenir," 359.

16. Tennyson, "The Charge of the Light Brigade," in *Tennyson: A Selected Edition*, ed. Christopher Ricks (Berkeley: University of California Press, 1989), 508–11.

17. McGann, *Beauty of Inflections*, 173–203.

18. Ibid., 188.

19. James Fleming, *The Art of Reading and Speaking* (1896; London: Edwin Arnold, 1908), 204.

20. F. R. Leavis, *New Bearings in English Poetry* (London: Chatto & Windus, 1932), 95; Cleanth Brooks Jr., "*The Waste Land*: An Analysis," in T. S. Eliot, *The Waste Land*, ed. Michael North (New York: Norton, 2001), 175.

21. For a range of recent discussions about this reading style see Lisa Marie Basile, "Poet Voice and Flock Mentality: Why Poets Need to Think for Themselves," *Huffington Post*, November 16, 2014, www.huffingtonpost.com/lisa-marie-basile/poet-voice-flock-mentality_b_5830452.html; Rich Smith, "Stop Using 'Poet Voice,'" *CityArts*, July 15, 2014: www.cityartsonline.com/articles/stop-using-poet-voice; "The Linguistics behind the Insufferably Annoying 'Poet Voice,'" *Mashable*, February 7, 2015, http://mashable.com/2015/02/07/poet-voice/#_MtfıDCifkq6.

22. MacArthur, "Monotony," 44.

23. Ibid., 41–42, 59–60.

24. Bernstein, "Introduction," in *Close Listening*, 10.

25. MacArthur, "Monotony," 60.

26. John Rice, *An Introduction to the Art of Reading* (1765), cited in Jacqueline George, "Public Reading and Lyric Pleasure: Eighteenth Century Elocutionary Debates and Poetic Practices," *ELH* 76 (2009): 375.

27. George, "Public Reading and Lyric Pleasure," 374.

28. Ibid., 384.

29. Ben McCorkle, "Harbingers of the Printed Page: Nineteenth-Century Theories of Delivery as Remediation." *Rhetoric Society Quarterly* 34 (Fall 2005): 27.

30. Matthew Rubery, "Canned Literature: The Book after Edison," *Book History* 16 (2013): 224.

31. This said, digital platforms for the circulation of poetry recordings and videos of readings have been useful for the efforts of organizations such as Poetry Out Loud (USA), Poetry In Voice (Canada), and Poetry By Heart (UK). Over the past decade these organizations have used a combination of recitation competitions, online repositories of recorded readings, and pedagogical exercises to reintegrate the oral performance of poetry into elementary and high school literature curricula.

32. Mary Margaret Robb, *Oral Interpretation of Literature in American Colleges and Universities: A Historical Study of Teaching Methods* (New York: H. W. Wilson, 1941), 22.

33. The terms "elocution" and "pronunciation" came to be used interchangeably by about 1750 "The right Management of the Voice in reading or speaking . . . is indifferently called by us, *Elocution* and *Pronunciation*," John Mason says in *An Essay on Elocution, or, Pronunciation, Intended Chiefly for the Assistance of Those Who Instruct Others in the Art of Reading and of Those who are Often called to Speak in Publick*, 4th ed. (London: J. Buckland, J. Waugh, 1757), 5.

34. Eugene Bahn and Margaret L. Bahn, *A History of Oral Interpretation* (Minneapolis: Burgess, 1970), 121.

35. Thomas Sheridan, *Lectures on the Art of Reading* (London: Dodsley, Wilkie, Dilly,1775), 3.

36. Ibid., 76.

37. Walker acknowledges that "the art of speaking, though founded on grammar, has principles of its own: principles that arise from the nature of the living voice, from the perception of harmony in the ear, and from a certain superaddition to the sense of language, of which grammar takes no account." But the overarching nature of his approach is to proceed to develop rules for reading from more abstractly described rules of grammar and rhetoric. John Walker, *A Rhetorical Grammar* (1785; London: Longman, 1823), 40. Other examples of what can be called mechanical approaches from the period include James Burgh's *The Art of Speaking* (1762), which identifies set rules for reading the punctuated elements of a sentence (such as reading parenthetical material rapidly) and catalogues "the ability of the body to express ninety-eight different moods and emotions" (Robb, *Oral Interpretation of Literature*, 38), and William Scott's *Lessons in Elocution* (1779) which builds upon Walker and Burgh to teach such things as "the attitude in which a boy should always place himself when he begins to speak" and how best to "*accompany the Emotions and Passions which your words express, by correspondent tones, looks and gestures.*" William Scott, *Lessons in Elocution* (1779; Boston: Isaiah Thomas, 1814), 10, 54.

38. Thomas Sheridan, *A Course of Lectures on Elocution* (London, W. Strahan, 1762), 54.

39. Scott, *Lessons in Elocution*, 20.

40. Bernstein, "Introduction," in *Close Listening*, 10.

41. Carrie Preston, *Modernism's Mythic Pose: Gender, Genre, Solo Performance* (Oxford: Oxford University Press, 2011), 64.

42. Ibid., 60–61.

43. Ibid., 65. As Preston has shown, Delsarte's influence was substantial and wide-ranging, but his greatest positive and lasting legacy lies in its impact on the development of modern dance, as, e.g. in Isadora Duncan's solo dance performances.

44. Roberta E. Pearson, *Eloquent Gestures: The Transformation of Performance Style in the Griffiths Biograph Films* (Berkeley: University of California Press, 1992), 24.

45. James Naremore, *Acting in the Cinema* (Berkeley: University of California Press, 1988), 46.

46. Ibid., 40–41.

47. Ibid., 46.

48. For an extended discussion of the differences between melodramatic and modern vocal performance styles in relation to the advent of electronic sound media, see Smith, *Vocal Tracks*, 81–162.

49. Preston, *Modernism's Mythic Pose*, 144–90.

50. Delsarteanism was brought to America by Steele Mackaye who had studied with Delsarte in Paris and first lectured on his teacher in Boston in 1871. Paul Edwards, "Unstoried: Teaching Literature in the Age of Performance Studies," *Theatre*, annual 52 (1999): 64–65.

51. "Art is at once the knowledge, the possession, and the free direction of the agents,

by virtue of which are revealed the life, soul, and mind. It is the appropriation of the sign to the thing. It is the relation of the beauties scattered through nature to a superior type. It is not, therefore, the mere imitation of nature." Genevieve Stebbins, *Delsarte System of Expression* (New York: Edgar S. Werner, 1885), 91.

52. Other reading and speech theorists of the period claimed the concept of natural expression in their own ways, and sketched them out within their own specific theories of performance. Identifying the intonation patterns of natural speech as heard in private conversation as the desired goal for public speaking and reading, James Fleming called on readers to learn to read as they speak:

> There are few of us who, when speaking to a friend in private, do not utter our words naturally and earnestly. Why, then, should we, as soon as we speak in public, become unnatural, unreal, and monotonous? And yet, if the words of some simple, earnest conversation spoken by friend to friend were written down, and given to the man to read, it should be found that he changed his whole manner. Tone, expression, emphasis, would be altogether different. The words read would become dull, flat, and unreal, wholly opposite to the words spoken just before. This fault must arise either from some natural or artificial cause. But there are no natural impediments in the way, for just now the friend spoke quite naturally to his friend. Therefore it must be artificial. In other words, our faults in reading are artificial, through bad methods of teaching, bad habits contracted, and what we really need is to go back to nature. Fleming, *Art of Reading and Speaking*, 5.

Fleming was calling for the cultivation of an art of reading with conversational intonations that disguised the printed nature of the textual source. His method entailed the subtle use and implementation of expressive vocal techniques such as rising and falling intonation, emphasis and tremor, for which he did still provide a minimal diacritical notation system for the reader's reference. Thus, Fleming's aim "to make none artificial or stilted, but to help all to be natural and real" is yet another iteration of the longer elocutionary goal to improve the reader as an effective medium for text, in this case, by making that text sound like normal talk. Another aspect of Fleming's idea of reading naturally entailed a recognition in performance of the distinction between the voice of the narrator, and the voice of the speaker within the poem.

53. Curry, *Imagination and Dramatic Instinct*, 235.

54. Ibid., 236.

55. Ibid., 193.

56. Ibid., 244.

57. Curry, *Browning and the Dramatic Monologue*.

58. S. S. Curry, *The Province of Expression* (Boston: School of Expression, 1891), 29.

59. Goffman, *Forms of Talk*, 128.

60. "Above all we must throw away the horrible false tradition of 'recitation,' . . . which destroyed all true faculty of poetic interpretation," Fogerty insisted. "The greater part of the elaborate directions, 'rules' and 'methods' devised by teachers of 'elocution' to help speakers of verse, are nothing but attempts to find a substitute for true understand-

ing and love of poetry." Elsie Fogerty, *The Speaking of English Verse* (London: Dent; New York: Dutton, 1923), x, 106.

61. Margaret Prendergast McLean, *Oral Interpretation of Forms of Literature* (New York: Dutton, 1936), 12.

62. Cornelius Carman Cunningham, *Literature as a Fine Art, Analysis and Interpretation* (New York: Nelson, 1941), 262.

63. The Central School of Speech Training and Dramatic Art, now the University of London's Royal Central School of Speech and Drama, was founded by Elsie Fogerty at the Royal Albert Hall in 1906. See: www.cssd.ac.uk/content/centrals-history.

64. René Wellek and Austin Warren, *Theory of Literature* (New York: Harcourt Brace, 1949), 158. Cited in Andrew Elfenbein, *Romanticism and the Rise of English* (Stanford: Stanford University Press, 2009), 202.

65. Elfenbein, *Romanticism*, 202.

66. Ibid., 202.

67. Harold D. Smith, *A New Correlation* (Camden, NJ: Educational Department of the Victor Talking Machine Co., 1915), 5.

68. Marian Wilson Kimber, *The Elocutionists: Women, Music, and the Spoken Word* (Urbana: University of Illinois Press, 2017), 29, 31.

69. "Musically Accompanied Recitations," *Werner's Magazine* 19, no. 3 (March 1897): 226.

70. Milnor Dorey and Louis Mohler, eds., *Literature and Music: A Manual for Teachers and Students in School and Home* (New York: Educational Department, Columbia Gramophone Co., 1920).

71. S. Dana Townsend, *The Victrola in Correlation with English and American Literature* (Camden, NJ: Educational Department, Victor Talking Machine Co., 1921).

72. Ibid., 4.

73. Smith, *New Correlation*, 7–8.

74. Dorey and Mohler, eds., *Literature and Music*, 17.

75. Townsend, *Victrola*, 9.

76. As Feaster, "Framing the Mechanical Voice," 84, notes, used of this genre of sound recording, the term "descriptive" seems to have been borrowed from music, where it designates compositions that seek to imitate natural sounds with musical instruments.

77. While the means by which a sense of spatial location and immersion could be evoked was limited with acoustic recording methods, elements of these early dramatic recitations with musical accompaniment can certainly be understood as prescient of the more sophisticated techniques of blocking, microphone placement, reverberation, etc., used to craft a sense of "place" for auditors in radio drama productions of the late 1930s. For discussion of some of these techniques in producing sonic perspective and atmosphere in American radio drama, see Neil Verma, *Theater of the Mind: Imagination, Aesthetics and American Radio Drama* (Chicago: University of Chicago Press, 2012), 35–56.

78. "The Charge of the Light Brigade," Rose Coghlan, performer, Victor twelve-inch

disc, 31728 (January 30, 1909), www.loc.gov/jukebox/recordings/detail/id/1584/autoplay/true.

79. Cf. the Edison recordings of Edgar L. Davenport reciting the cowboy poem "Lasca," set in Texas Rio Grande country, with those he recorded for the Victor label. The latter deploy Mexican/Spanish-sounding music to evoke setting and use castanets and kettledrums to depict a stampede in the poem, whereas the Edison versions include musical accompaniment only at the most dramatic moments; over 60 percent of the recitation is backed by music in the Victor recordings versus 15 percent or less in the Edison versions. Davenport's recordings of "Lasca" include a 1905 Edison Gold Moulded Record (Cylinder) 9087; a 1906 Victor twelve-inch C-3283; a 1908 Victor twelve-inch 31529 (apparently a reissue of the 1906 one); a 1909 Edison Amberol Cylinder 296; a 1909 Victor twelve-inch C-3283/4; a 1910 Columbia twelve-inch A-5218; a 1910 U.S. Everlasting Cylinder 1381; a 1911 Indestructible Phonograph Co. Cylinder 3143; a 1913 Edison Blue Amberol Cylinder 1868; and a 1920 Edison Diamond Disc 50575L. Tim Brooks, "One Hit Wonders of the Acoustic Era (and a few beyond . . .)," *Antique Phonograph Monthly* 9, no. 2 (March 1990): 8; Brian Rust, *The Complete Entertainment Discography: From mid-1890s to 1942* (New Rochelle, NY: Arlington House, 1973), 208–9; and the Library of Congress online catalogue.

80. Tennyson, "Charge of the Light Brigade," in *Tennyson*, ed. Ricks, 508–11.

81. Coghlan's recording introduced a genre of audiotext paralleling the celebrity opera recordings of the Victor Light Opera Co., created around 1909 (the same year Coghlan recorded "Charge") to produce excerpts from operas, operettas, and Broadway musicals. *Encyclopedia of Recorded Sound*, ed. Frank Hoffmann, 2nd ed. (New York: Routledge, 2005), 2255.

82. "The Charge of the Light Brigade," Edgar L. Davenport, performer, United Talking Machine Co. ten-inch disc, A1371 (1913).

83. "The Charge of the Light Brigade," performer unknown, Emerson Phonograph Co. seven-inch disc, No. 755 (ca. 1917).

84. Between 1917 and 1918, after the United States declared war on Germany in April 1917, "recording artists gave special attention to our own [American] patriotic airs and those of our allies; and to any war-song of sentiment," Harold Smith notes in *The Thing Talked*, 183.

85. Emerson Records ad, *New York Times*, June 8, 1917, 7.

86. "The Charge of the Light Brigade," Canon Fleming, performer, HMV ten-inch shellac disc E-160 (1910). www.historicalvoices.org/amvoices/view_audio.php?kid=63–246–1D7.

87. "The Charge of the Light Brigade," Lewis Waller, performer, HMV E164 (c1907).

88. "The Charge of the Light Brigade," Henry Ainley, performer, Gramophone Co. ten-inch disc, B393 (1912). Ainley made acoustic recordings for the Gramophone Company, and later also electric recordings for it (as HMV).

89. John R. Bennett, *Voices of the Past: A Catalogue of Vocal Recordings from the English Catalogues* (Jedburgh, Scotland, 1955), 16, 142.

90. Ibid., 6–7, 142. See Henry Chappell, "The Day," in *The Day and Other Poems* (London: John Lane, Bodley Head, 1918), 13–14.

91. "Foresters' Palace of Varieties," *Lloyd's Weekly London Newspaper*, November 9, 1890, 7

92. "Theatrical Gossip," *The Era*, June 14, 1890, 8.

93. "Radway," *Warwick and Warwickshire Gazette*, January 18, 1908, 3.

94. "The Brixton," *The Stage*, December 14, 1899, 18; "The Britannia," *The Stage*, November 9, 1889, 15.

95. "The Alhambra," *The Era*, May 5, 1900, 19.

96. "The 'Punch' Matinee," *Morning Post*, May 4, 1900, 3.

97. "Chit Chat," *The Stage*, November 2, 1899, 13; "For the War Funds," *The Stage*, December 7, 1899, 11; "The Profession and the War," *The Era*, December 9, 1899, 14.

98. "Grand Gramophone Concert," *North Eastern Daily Gazette*, July 6, 1915, 2.

99. "March Gramophone Records," *The Sketch*, March 13, 1907, 264.

100. S. R. Littlewood, "Ainley, Henry Hinchliffe (1879–1945)," rev. K. D. Reynolds, in the *Oxford Dictionary of National Biography* (Oxford University Press, 2004), www.oxforddnb.com/view/article/30353.

101. Discus [pseud.], "Gramophone Notes," *Belfast News-Letter*, March 19, 1931, 13.

102. "Rev. Canon Fleming," *The Sunday at Home: Family Magazine for Sabbath Reading* (London: Religious Tract Society, 1881), 581–83.

103. The existence of the "wired" electrophone was one reason why radio was called "the wireless" in the United Kingdom. See J. Wright, "The Electrophone," *Electrical Engineer*, September 10, 1897, 343–44.

104. "Canon Fleming on Tennyson," *York Herald*, October 26, 1878, 2.

105. Ibid.

106. A. F. Munden, "Fleming, James (1830–1908)," in the *Oxford Dictionary of National Biography* (Oxford University Press, 2004), www.oxforddnb.com/view/article/33169.

107. See www.fon.hum.uva.nl/praat.

108. In using Praat to think about historical recordings, I am using a tool from a discipline other than my own (a tool that embodies the assumptions and ideology of that discipline) against the grain of its own design. But I am also taking advantage of the descriptive vocabulary for speech prosody that the discipline of linguistics has developed. Linguistic information such as intonation, stress, phonemes, words, and phrases are not directly measurable in the acoustic signal. These are abstract concepts from linguistics that have to be found there. With such software we are looking for acoustic correlates (defined by an academic discipline) in a digital visual representation of the sound wave. These are abstract concepts from linguistics (imposed by the listener) that we use to annotate (mark up) the wave form representing the audio signal, and then attempt to compute and render it visually for the purpose of analysis. Speech-analysis software can tell us about the measurable acoustic properties of a speech signal, but can only give us clues about linguistic or expressive information conveyed by the representational signal.

109. Naremore, *Acting in the Cinema*, 47.

110. James Rush, *The Philosophy of the Human Voice* (Philadelphia: Lippincott, 1867), 447.

111. Tennyson, "Charge of the Light Brigade," in *Tennyson*, ed. Ricks, 511.

112. Robert I. Fulton and Thomas C. Trueblood, *Practical Elements of Elocution* (Boston: Ginn, 1893), 153.

113. Ibid., 153.

114. Ibid., 149.

115. Ibid., 149.

116. Ibid., 153–154.

117. Ibid., 124.

118. For other examples of this prescription, see S. S. Hamill, *New Science of Elocution* (New York: Philips & Hunt, 1886), and George Lansing Raymond, *The Orator's Manual* (London: Putnam's Sons, 1910).

119. Fleming, *Art of Reading and Speaking*, 53.

120. For a discussion of intonation in conversation within the context of the Spoken English Corpus (SEC) consisting of a range of speech styles, mostly scripted and/or read, see Anne Wichmann, *Intonation in Text and Discourse: Beginnings, Middles, Ends* (New York: Routledge, 2013), 123–47.

121. Bernstein, "Introduction," in *Close Listening*, 10.

Chapter 4

1. As traced in Ned Tobin's *The Presence of the Past: T. S. Eliot's Victorian Inheritance* (Ann Arbor, MI: UMI Research Press, 1983).

2. T. S. Eliot, "The Three Voices of Poetry," in id., *On Poetry and Poets* (1953; London: Faber & Faber, 1957), 89.

3. John Stuart Mill, "What Is Poetry?" in *Literary Essays*, ed. Edward Alexander (1833; Indianapolis: Bobbs-Merrill, 1967), 56.

4. Eliot, "Three Voices," 98, 100.

5. Ibid., 96.

6. Ibid., 94.

7. Omri Moses, *Out of Character: Modernism, Vitalism, Psychic Life* (Stanford: Stanford University Press, 2014), 157.

8. Robert Speaight, *The Waste Land* (New Rochelle, N.Y.: Spoken Arts, 1956), LP record; *The Four Quartets* (New Rochelle, N.Y.: Spoken Arts, 1959), LP record; and *Speech from "Murder in the Cathedral"* (Hayes, England: HMV), 78 rpm record.

9. T. S. Eliot to Miss Mary Allen, February 12, 1942, Written Archives Centre, R CONT 1, T. S. Eliot Scriptwriter File, 1935–1968.

10. T. S. Eliot, *T. S. Eliot Reading His Own Poems*, 78 rpm mono twelve-inch records (1946; Washington, DC: Library of Congress Recording Laboratory, 1949). For brevity's sake, I refer to these Library of Congress records, said to have been produced and/or recorded in 1946, but released in 1949, as the 1946 recordings.

11. I concur with Richard Swigg's conclusion that *The Waste Land* recordings were most likely made in the same year as the other recordings Eliot made at Columbia (1933), and not in 1935 as the Columbia University card catalogue suggests. I would add

to Swigg's conclusion that some of the 1933 records may have been duplicated from acetate disc to solid aluminum disc in 1935, as the year 1935 is inscribed on several of the aluminum discs (but not the acetates). This may explain the ambiguous dating in the card catalogue. Richard Swigg, *Quick, Said the Bird: Williams, Eliot, Moore and the Spoken Word* (Iowa City: University of Iowa Press, 2012), 126–27n5.

12. "Thomas F. Kilfoil," obituary, *Hartford Courant*, August 23–24, 2005, www.legacy.com/obituaries/hartfordcourant/obituary.aspx?pid=14927122.

13. Thomas F. Kilfoil to Mrs. Elizabeth Mason, February 23, 1966, Columbia University Rare Book and Manuscript Library, Brander Matthews Dramatic Museum Records, 1910–1971, MS #0364, box 1.

14. William Cabell Greet, "Records of Poets," *American Speech* 9, no. 4 (1934): 312–13.

15. "Phonetic Transcription," *American Speech* 15, no. 1 (February 1940): 84–86.

16. Louise Pound, "Phonograph Records of Robert Frost," *American Speech* 11 no. 1 (1936): 98.

17. Selections from the Frost recordings (1933–34), along with recordings made by Vachel Lindsay in 1931 and Harriet Monroe in 1932, are now available at http://writing.upenn.edu/pennsound/x/authors.php. On the provenance of some of these recordings, and the integration of a selection of digitized tape dubs made form the original instantaneous discs, see Chris Mustazza, "Provenance Report: William Carlos Williams's 1942 Reading for the NCTE," *Jacket 2*, May 21, 2014, https://jacket2.org/article/provenance-report. A selection of Eliot's 1933 recordings can be heard at www.poetryarchive.org/explore/browsepoems?f[0]=sm_field_poet%3Anode%3A192462.

18. Swigg, *Quick, Said the Bird*, 38–39.

19. Wurtzler, *Electric Sounds*, 3.

20. Record sleeve holding aluminum instantaneous disc recording of "Sweeney Among the Nightingales," T. S. Eliot, performer, Columbia University Rare Book and Manuscript Library, Speech Lab Archives, box 4, 8, 9, 10.

21. I have digitized the 1946–49 Library of Congress recordings to WAV format myself from the original 78s using an Audio Technica LP120 Professional Stereo Turntable with an Audio-Technica Moving Coil Mono Cartridge.

22. In the context of professional digital recording and processing, the process of synching up the timing of audio tracks (in this case, tracks derived from different analogue sources) is known as "quantizing." See Steve Savage, *Bytes & Backbeats: Repurposing Music in the Digital Age* (Ann Arbor: University of Michigan Press, 2013), 28–30.

23. Text on front album cover of T. S. Eliot, *T.S. Eliot Reading His Own Poems*, 78 rpm mono twelve-inch records (1946; Washington, DC: Library of Congress Recording Laboratory, 1949).

24. William McGuire, *Poetry's Catbird Seat: The Consultantship in Poetry in the English Language at the Library of Congress, 1937-1987* (Washington, DC: Library of Congress, 1988), 94.

25. Other authoritative sources list the 1933 and 1946 recordings as two distinct entities. For example, the textual notes of *The Poems of T. S. Eliot*, edited by Christopher Ricks and Jim McCue, state that *The Waste Land* was first "Recorded in full, 1933, Co-

lumbia U. (often misdated)" and then "Second: 26 July 1946, NBC (NY) for the Library of Congress; released Feb. 1949." Christopher Ricks and Jim McCue, *The Poems of T. S. Eliot*, vol. 1: *Collected and Uncollected Poems* (London: Faber & Faber, 2015), 547.

26. T. S. Eliot to Robert Lowell, cited in McGuire, *Poetry's Catbird Seat*, 104.

27. For an extended discussion of T. S. Eliot's substantial role in the establishment of New Criticism as a dominant critical approach, see John Henry Raleigh, "The New Criticism as an Historical Phenomenon," *Comparative Literature* 11, no. 1 (1959): 21–28.

28. Michael North, *The Dialect of Modernism* (New York: Oxford University Press, 1994), 78.

29. The acetate and aluminum instantaneous disc records referenced in this paragraph are performed by T. S. Eliot and can be examined at the Columbia University Rare Book and Manuscript Library, Speech Lab Archives, boxes 4, 8, 9, 10.

30. Eliot did allow the BBC to produce a dramatized script of the poem (by Geoffrey Bridson) in 1938, but he disliked it so much that this was a primary reason Valerie Eliot refused Terence Tiller permission to produce a new dramatic adaptation in 1972. See letters to Eliot dated January 4 and 11, 1938; BBC circulating memo, (December 20, 1937; Terence Tiller, Drama (Radio) 6083 B.H. 3720 (January 11, 1972), BBC Written Archives Centre, R CONT 1/ T.S. Eliot/ Scriptwriter: 1935–1968.

31. Rayner Heppenstall, "T. S. Eliot," memo, January 25, 1951, BBC Written Archives Centre, T. S. Eliot File 3, 1944–1954.

32. Juan A. Suarez, "T. S. Eliot's *The Waste Land*, the Gramophone, and the Modernist Discourse Network," *New Literary History* 32 (2001): 756.

33. C. B. Cox and Arnold P. Hinchliffe, *T. S. Eliot, The Waste Land: A Casebook* (London: Macmillan, 1968), 30–31.

34. Suarez, "T. S. Eliot's *The Waste Land*," 757.

35. Steven Connor, *Dumbstruck: A Cultural History of Ventriloquism* (Oxford: Oxford University Press, 2000), 40.

36. Charles Sanders, " 'Beyond the Language of the Living': The Voice of T. S. Eliot," *Twentieth Century Literature* 27, no. 4 (1981): 378–79.

37. Moses, *Out of Character*, 156.

38. T. S. Eliot, "In Memoriam: Marie Lloyd." *The Criterion* 1 (October 1922–July 1923), 194–95.

39. Ibid., 192.

40. Barry J. Faulk, "Modernism and the Popular: Eliot's Music Halls." *Modernism/Modernity* 8, no. 4 (2001): 619.

41. Michael Coyle, "'This rather elusory broadcast technique'": T. S. Eliot and the Genre of the Radio Talk," *ANQ* 11, no. 4 (Fall 1998): 38.

42. Burton Paulu, *British Broadcasting: Radio and Television in the United Kingdom* (Minneapolis: University of Minnesota Press, 1956), 153; cited in Coyle, "'This rather elusory broadcast technique.'"

43. T. S. Eliot, "The Metaphysical Poets," in id., *Selected Essays, 1917–1932* (New York: Harcourt, Brace, 1932), 247.

44. Morrison, "Performing the Pure Voice," 40.

45. Ibid., 26.

46. T. S. Eliot, "Tradition and the Individual Talent," in id., *The Sacred Wood and Major Early Essays* (Mineola, NY: Dover, 1998), 32.

47. James Stephens, "How Should Poetry Be Read?" *The Listener*, May 22, 1941, 732.

48. T. S. Eliot to Christopher Salmon, May 25, 1941, BBC Written Archives Centre, R CONT 1, T. S. Eliot Talks, file 2, 1938–43.

49. T. S. Eliot, memo, December 16, 1958, copied onto Terrence Tiller, memo to A.H.D., January 25, 1972, BBC Written Archives Centre, R CONT 1, T. S. Eliot Scriptwriter File, 1935–1968.

50. Terence Tiller, memo to A.H.D., January 21, 1972, BBC Written Archives Centre, R CONT 1, T. S. Eliot Scriptwriter File, 1935–1968. Tiller was eventually granted permission to produce a multivoiced dramatic adaptation in 1972, but on the condition that it be approved (and not integrate any abandoned passages from *Waste Land* manuscripts that had recently been made available). A recent exception to this rule against multi-voiced adaptations of *The Waste Land* is a voice collage, consisting of a new recording by Lia Williams mixed with existing recordings of the poem as read by Ted Hughes and by Eliot himself, aired on BBC 4 in 2011. This episode is interesting for the way it foregrounds the sounds of different interpretive reading styles as well as the different media formats that captured them. "Poetry Please," BBC Radio 4, January 30, 2011, www.bbc.co.uk/programmes/b00y2156.

51. Eliot, "Three Voices," 89–102.

52. Ibid., 94.

53. James Stephens, "On Speaking Verse," *James, Seumas and Jacques: Unpublished Writings* (1937; New York: Macmillan, 1964), 179.

54. The phrase "a musical composition of ideas" is borrowed from Graham Good's description of Theodor Adorno's approach to the essay as a compositional form, which Good argues is analogous to the "spontaneous *aesthetic* design" based on "musical structures" used by Eliot in his poetry. Good, *The Observing Self: Rediscovering the Essay* (New York, NY: Routledge, 1988), 19.

55. T. S. Eliot, "Choruses from 'The Rock', IX. 'Soul of Man,'" in id., *Collected Poems 1909–1962* (London: Faber & Faber, 2002), 172.

56. Fleming, *Art of Reading and Speaking*, 204.

57. I. A. Richards, *Principles of Literary Criticism* (1926; New York: Routledge, 2001), 276; F. R. Leavis, "The Significance of the Modern Waste Land," from *New Bearings in English Poetry* (London: Chatto & Windus, 1932), 90–113, in T. S. Eliot, *The Waste Land*, ed. Michael North (New York: Norton, 2001), 175, 179.

58. Richards, *Principles*, 276.

59. Such phrasal annotation for use in the automated analysis of recorded literary speech has begun to be explored by Tanya Clement and collaborating researchers with the aim of performing different kinds of "distant listening" across large corpora of digitized literary audio. See, e.g.: Tanya Clement, "Distant Listening or Playing Visualisations Pleasantly with the Eyes and Ears," *Digital Studies / Le champ numérique* 3, no. 2 (2013), http://doi.org/10.16995/dscn.236.

60. The approach taken to reading digital visualizations of Eliot's sound signals (combined with intensive listening) is as follows: The first step in an analysis with Praat is to annotate the phrases that I have identified as of interest from the perspective of Eliot's performative method using an interval tier in Praat's text grid. Each phrase and the spaces between phrases constitute an interval. The interval tier, having been appropriately divided into phrases, is then duplicated for other annotation purposes. The original interval tier displays the text of the poem—the intervals corresponding to phrases are annotated with the textual content of that phrase, while the intervening pause intervals are annotated with the length of the pause in milliseconds. The first duplicated interval tier is created to be annotated with pitch information. Each phrase interval contains the average, minimum and maximum pitch values for the entire phrase. The third interval tier is similarly annotated with average, minimum, and maximum intensity values. Finally, a more fine-grained annotation of the pitch and intensity values is performed using Praat's point tiers, one for pitch and one for intensity. Under each phrase interval, a point is inserted at the beginning and ending of each pitch curve within the phrase. And significant variation in the curve is also marked with a point. Each point is annotated with the pitch or intensity value at the corresponding time.

61. Asemic Phrasing is distinct from what is called asemic writing, a tradition of art practice—from Henri Michaux's *Narration* (1927) to the works of Mirtha Dermisache and Michal Jacobson—exploring forms of writing that evoke, yet elude, semantic content. Asemic speech phrasing takes semantically recognizable speech sounds and alienates their semantic resonance with aesthetically motivated prosodic patterns. For discussion of asemic writing, see Peter Schwenger, "Asemic Writing: Backwards into the Future," in Marshall McLuhan and Vilém Flisser's *Communication and Aesthetic Theories Revisited,* ed. Tom Kohut and Melanie Padilovski (Winnipeg: Video Pool Media Arts Centre, 2014), 184–202; and Patrick Durgin, "Witness Mirta Dermisache: Being Recognized by a Stranger," *Jacket 2,* September 8, 2014, https://jacket2.org/commentary/witness-mirtha-dermisache.

62. Robert Speaight, *Poems of T. S. Eliot,* LP record (New Rochelle, NY: Spoken Arts, 1956).

63. Jean-François Augoyard and Henry Torgue, eds., *Sonic Experience: A Guide to Everyday Sounds,* trans. Andra McCartney and David Paquette (Montréal and Kingston: McGill-Queens University Press, 2005), 40.

64. A thematic version of the technical question would be: How does one individuate characteristically even with the homogenizing and flattening forces of modernity?

Conclusion

1. R. Murray Schafer, *The Soundscape: Our Sonic Environment and the Tuning of the World* (1977; Rochester, VT: Destiny Books, 1993), 129–31.

2. Don Ihde, *Listening and Voice: A Phenomenology of Sound* (Athens: Ohio University Press, 1974), 53.

3. Kittler, *Gramophone-Film-Typewriter,* 24

4. Sybille Krämer, "The Cultural Techniques of Time Axis Manipulation: On Friedrich Kittler's Conception of Media," *Theory, Culture & Society* 23, nos. 7–8 (2006): 94.

5. *Oxford English Dictionary*, www.oed.com, 1.a.

6. UCSB Cylinder Audio Archive: cylinders.library.ucsb.edu/index.php. Further, many of those same rare catalogues, and rarer ones, are now discoverable online via sites such the Internet Archive, https://archive.org.

7. I say "not decidedly" because one of the parallel consequences for research on early sound recordings that has resulted from the expansion of the web is renewed accessibility to original material audio media artifacts via commercial auction and e-commerce sites such as eBay. The new possibility of discovering and purchasing archaic media artifacts online has no doubt had a heretofore undocumented influence upon contemporary cultural historians, media historians, and media archeologists.

8. Jerome McGann, "Towards Philology in a New Key," interview by Scott Pound, *Amodern* 1 (2013): http://amodern.net/article/interview-with-jerome-mcgann.

9. Jerome McGann, *A New Republic of Letters: Memory and Scholarship in the Age of Digital Reproduction* (Cambridge, MA: Harvard University Press, 2014), 37.

10. Ibid., 22.

11. See www.nines.org.

12. See www.1890s.ca/Default.aspx.

13. See www.ruskinatwalkley.org/index.php?hotspots=off.

14. See www.blakearchive.org/blake.

15. See www.edickinson.org.

16. See http://whitmanarchive.org.

17. Marjorie Perloff, "Screening the Page/Paging the Screen: Digital Poetics and the Differential Text," in *Contemporary Poetics,* ed. Louis Armand (Evanston, IL: Northwestern University Press, 2007), 379.

18. For an expanded theory of differential media as an assemblage of materials (and their circulation) that characterize a "single" cultural production, see Darren Wershler, *Guy Maddin's "My Winnipeg"* (Toronto: University of Toronto Press, 2010), 9–11.

19. Natural philosophers of the seventeenth and eighteenth centuries used the term "differential medium," Robert Morrison says, "to denote the material spaces that connected otherwise disconnected points," usually with reference to "the transmission of forces or particles" across distance. For romantic-era writers it meant, among other things, being in the middle of it, existing within a medium that sustains life activities, or, as Morrison has argued, media came to be understood "not just as vehicles of transmission but also as conditions of possibility for the life and growth of living beings," like a plant in soil, a fish in water, bacteria cultured in an agar medium. Morrison, *Experimental Life: Vitalism in Romantic Science and Literature* (Baltimore: Johns Hopkins University Press, 2013), 145–47.

20. N. Katherine Hayles, "Flickering Connectivities in Shelley Jackson's Patchwork Girl: The Importance of Media-Specific Analysis," *Postmodern Culture* 10, no. 2 (2000), http://pmc.iath.virginia.edu/text-only/issue.100/10.2hayles.txt.

21. Bolter and Grusin, *Remediation,* 55.

22. As examples of such research, within the order of categories I have used to summarize it, I include Lisa Gitelman, *Always Already New: Media, History and The Data of Culture* (Cambridge, MA: MIT Press, 2008); Sterne, *MP3*; Ian Bogost and Nick Montfort, *Racing the Beam: The Atari Video Computer System* (Cambridge, MA: MIT Press, 2009); Matthew Kirschenbaum, *Mechanisms: New Media and the Forensic Imagination* (Cambridge, MA: MIT Press, 2008) and *Track Changes: A Literary History of Word Processing* (Cambridge, MA: Belknap Press of Harvard University Press, 2016); Jussi Parikka, *What Is Media Archeology?* (Cambridge: Polity Press, 2012); Ernst, *Digital Memory*.

23. Jussi Parikka, "Archival Media Theory," in Ernst, *Digital Memory*, 14.

24. Alan Liu, "The State of the Digital Humanities: A Report and a Critique Arts and Humanities in Higher Education," *Arts and Humanities in Higher Education* 11, nos. 1–2 (2012): 11.

25. See www.sesnet.soton.ac.uk/archivesound.

26. Ihde, *Listening and Voice*, 50.

27. The First Sound researchers include David Giovannoni, Patrick Feaster, Richard Martin, and Meagan Hennessey. Their work focuses on identifying, understanding, and playing very early sound recordings.

28. Jody Rosen, "Researchers Play Tune Recorded before Edison," *New York Times*, March 27, 2008, www.nytimes.com/2008/03/27/arts/27soun.html?hp. See also: www.firstsounds.org.

29. See: www.firstsounds.org/sounds/Scott-Feaster-No-44.mp3.

30. See, especially, du Maurier, *Trilby*, 306–18.

31. See: www.firstsounds.org/sounds/earlier-playback.php#auclair.

32. For a useful description of Scott de Martinville's phonautograph, and a "discocraphy" of the phonautograms he produced, see Patrick Feaster, "Édouard-Léon Scott de Martinville: An Annotated Discography," *ARSC Journal* 41 (2010): 43–81.

33. Jean Baudrillard, *Why Hasn't Everything Already Disappeared*, trans. Chris Turner (New York: Seagull Books, 2016), 32.

34. Ibid., 40.

35. Ernst, *Digital Memory*, 29

36. *The Collected Papers of Charles Sanders Peirce*, ed. Charles Hartshorne and Paul Weiss (Cambridge, MA: Harvard University Press, 1965), 5: 542. Cited in John Durham Peters, *Speaking into the Air: A History of the Idea of Communication* (Chicago: University of Chicago Press, 1999), 162.

37. Ernst, *Digital Memory*, 29.

INDEX

acoustic recording process, 14, 15, 113, 125, 142, 208n77

Adorno, Theodor, 214n54; on the phonograph record disc, 31–32, 35

advertisements, 35, 37, 39–44, 61, 65, 93, 203nn75,76

Ainley, Henry, 139; recordings of Tennyson's "Charge of the Light Brigade", 123, 124, 125, 128–29, 132, 134, 209n88

Allison, Raphael: on New Criticism, 117

American Dialect Society, 55–56

amplitude, 8–9, 56, 74, 112, 125, 127, 130; and electrical recording, 142–43; in Eliot's recordings of *The Waste Land*, 142–43, 147, 158, 159–60, 165–66, 181

analogue artifacts: digital processing of, 25, 144, 170, 172–73, 175, 178–79, 212n22, 215n60, 216n6; relationship to reality, 180–81

Andrews, Malcolm, 81

anti-theatricality, 12, 13, 110–11, 114, 135–36

Appelbaum, David: on human voice and speech, 44; on non-speech productions, 44, 47, 51; on tongue twisters, 47

Arnold, Matthew, 42–43

artifact riddles, 38

asemic phrasing: vs. asemic writing, 215n61; of Eliot, 25, 161–62, 163–67

Auden, W. H., 141

audible strangeness, 1–5

audiobooks, 67–69, 71–72, 78, 199n5

audiotextual criticism, 4, 5–11, 14, 15–16, 53–54, 169; role of sound signal in, 7, 8–11; vs. textual criticism, 6, 23. *See also* historical context

Bacon, Wallace, 103

Baird, Dorothea, 76

Bakhtin, Mikhail: on utterances as responses, 17

Bangs, David C.: as elocutionist, 21–22

Barnaby, Bertram, 157

Barthes, Roland: on "The Text" as methodological field, 11

Battis, William Sterling, 139; as Dickens impersonator, 24, 79, 80–81, 91, 95; "Dickens Man" recordings, 96; Dickens recordings of, 24, 74, 77–79, 93, 94–99, 118, 203nn75,76; recording of "Character impersonation from Dickens: Micawber (from 'David Copperfield')", 97–98; relationship with Harold D. Smith, 79, 91, 94, 96–97, 99, 118

Baudrillard, Jean: on digital vs. analogue media, 180–81, 182; on reality, 180–81, 182; *Why Hasn't Everything Already Disappeared?*, 180–81

Bauman, Richard: on entextualization, 16, 73; on recontextualization, 16, 73–74

BBC: productions of *The Waste Land*, 156–57, 213n30, 214n50; Third Programme, 152; *Well Versed* series, 155–56; Written Archives Centre, 148–49

Beerbohm, Max, 58

Bell, Melville: on visible speech, 29

Bentley, Thomas: *David Copperfield* (1913), 94

Bergson, Henri: on character-oriented comedy, 60

Berliner, Emile: flat disc gramophone of, 7, 149; United States Gramophone Co.'s

"List of Plates in Stock" (1894), 20–21, 188n56

Berliner, Herbert Samuel: recording of "Cohen on the Telephone", 63

Bernhardt, Sarah, 76

Bernstein, Charles: on American mass culture, 195n85; on audiotexts, 13; *Close Listening*, 13; on literary/poetry reading, 13, 107, 111; on speech transcription by modernist poets, 53

Blackton, J. Stuart: *A Modern Oliver Twist*, 80

Blake, William: illuminated books of, 175

Bleackley, J. Arthur: *The Art of Mimicry*, 58–59, 60, 196nn98,100; on imagination, 58–59, 196n100; on nature, 59

bodily gestures, postures and facial expressions, 109, 112–14

Bogan, Louise, 145–46

Bogost, Ian: *Racing the Beam*, 217n22

Bolter, Jay David: on immediacy vs. hypermediacy, 72, 73; on remediation, 73, 176

Brander Matthews Dramatic Museum Collection, 140–41

Bridson, Geoffrey, 156–57, 213n30

Brooks, Cleanth: on Eliot's *The Waste Land*, 106; *Understanding Poetry*, 103–4; *Well Wrought Urn*, 100

Browning, Robert, 137; dramatic monologues of, 103, 115, 138; Eliot on, 138

Bryan, William Jennings: "The Old World and Its Ways", 80

Burgh, James: *The Art of Speaking*, 206n37

Carleton, Will: "The Festival of Praise; or, Thanksgiving Day", 35; on God's soul vs. a phonograph, 35

Caruso, Enrico, 76, 124, 198n125

Casey the Irishman recordings, 19, 60, 65, 66

Chaplin, Charlie: on Bransby Williams, 83

Chappell, Henry: "The Day", 123

Clement, Tanya, 214n59

Coghlan, Rose, 139; recording of Tennyson's "Charge of the Light Brigade", 120–22, 123, 128, 134, 209n81

"Cohen on the Telephone" recordings, 60, 61, 63–64

Collins, Philip, 81–82

Columbia Phonograph Company Catalogue, 199n15

Columbia Records, 7, 63, 74, 86, 87

Columbia University Libraries, 140, 141, 172, 211n11, 213n29

conceptual artifacts, 170, 173–74, 180, 182–83

Connor, Stephen: *Dumstruck*, 150–51; on technologies of voice, 150–51

Cooper, Rand Richards, 198n130

Coyle, Michael: on Eliot as BBC broadcaster, 152

Crashaw, Richard, 155

critical sympathy, 102, 104

cultural artifacts: audiotexts as, 6–7, 13, 22–23, 67, 99, 170–71; as differential, 6–7, 175–76; study with digital media, 175

Cunningham, C. C.: on literary interpretation, 103; *Literature as a Fine Art*, 116; *Oral Interpretation of Forms of Literature*, 116

Curry, Samuel Silas: on Browning and dramatic monologues, 115; on dramatic instinct, 114, 115; on expression, 114, 115; on imagination, 104, 114; *Imagination and Dramatic Instinct*, 24–25, 94, 115, 133, 158; on literary interpretation, 94, 95, 103, 132, 133–34; on oral performance, 104, 105, 114–15, 133–34, 158

Davenport, Edgar L.: recording of Tennyson's "Charge of the Light Brigade", 122, 134–35; recordings of "Lasca", 209n79

Delsarte, François: on bodily gestures, 112–14; influence of, 206nn43,50

Dermisache, Mirtha, 215n61

Derrida, Jacques, 44

descriptive audiotextual format, 74–76, 85, 120, 208n76

Dewey, John: on learning by doing, 92; "My Pedagogic Creed", 92; *Schools of Tomorrow*, 92

dialect recordings, 5, 23, 48, 52, 54, 55–56, 57, 62–65, 74, 84, 197n108; Casey the Irishman recordings, 19, 60, 65, 66; "Cohen on His Honeymoon" recording, 62; "Cohen on the Telephone" recordings, 60, 61, 63–64

Dickens, Charles: Bill Sikes from *Oliver Twist*, 84; Captain Cuttle from *Dombey and Son*, 84; Bob Cratchit from *A Christmas Carol*, 88–90, 91; Dickens impersonators, 24, 79, 80–81, 83–84, 85–86, 87, 90–91, 95, 98, 202nn46,62; Betty Hidgen from *Our Mutual Friend*, 153; Wilkins Micawber from *David Copperfield*, 81, 84, 90, 91, 94, 96, 97–98; *Nicholas Nickleby*, 72, 199n4; public readings by, 81–83, 96, 201n44; and remediation, 81–83; Scrooge from *A Christmas Carol*, 84, 85–90, 91, 93, 112; sound recordings based on, 24, 74, 77–79, 84–90, 91, 92, 93–99, 112, 118, 203nn75,76; Uriah Heep from *David Copperfield*, 94, 97, 98
Dickinson, Emily: manuscripts of, 175
differential media, 176–77, 183, 216n18; in natural sciences, 176, 216n19
digital media, 2, 172–82, 205n31, 214n59, 216n7; vs. analogue media, 3, 7–8, 26, 32, 181; and differential texts, 175–76; digital processing of analogue artifacts, 25, 144, 170, 172–73, 175, 178–79, 212n22, 215n60, 216n6; digital signals, 10, 11; digital storage, 173; digital streaming, 146, 173; and humanities, 177–78; MP3 format, 99, 174; relationship to research in the humanities, 174–75; reproduction of analogue artifacts with, 170, 172–73, 175, 216n6; UCSB Cylinder Audio Archive, 173, 175, 216n6; and unsupervised learning, 181–82; voice archive as digital repository, 26, 171–72, 180, 181–82; WAV files, 142, 144, 173, 212n21. *See also* Praat
disruptive/disarticulate sounds, 44–51
Dolar, Mladen: on listening as obeying, 68
Donoghue, Denis: *The Practice of Reading*, 68; on reading and imagination, 68–69
Dorey, Milnor: *Literature and Music*, 119
Drew, Lillian: recording of "A Study in Mimicry–Vaudeville", 66–67
Dryden, John, 155
Duguid, Paul: on books, 198n133
Du Maurier, George: *Trilby*, 76–77, 179
duration of early recordings, 69–70, 87, 95–97, 142, 185n10

duration of sounds, 25, 56, 127, 158, 181

Edison, Thomas: on markings of a phonographic recording, 27, 35; "Perfected" cylinder phonograph of, 7, 27, 36; "The Perfected Phonograph", 27, 35; "The Phonograph and Its Future", 27, 185n7; on phonograph as time-capture device, 32; at phonograph demonstrations, 45; on "phonographic books", 12; phonograph invented by, 29; on recorded novels, 71–72, 73; on recorded speech vs. reading, 27, 28, 30–31; relationship with Gouraud, 32, 33; foil cylinder phonograph of, 7, 36, 39, 71, 185n7; wax cylinders of, 1–4, 7, 19, 27, 30–31, 72, 84, 85–86, 87, 90, 149, 191nn50,51, 196n105, 199n4
Edison-Bell Consolidated Phonograph Company, 188n53; recordings for, 19–20, 74, 120, 123, 202n59, 209n79; record list from 1898, 19–20
Edison tone tests, 198n125
education: educational technology, 24, 78–79; education catalogues of record companies, 78, 122, 203n68; use of literary recordings in, 24, 62, 78–79, 91–99, 118–19, 140–42, 200n20; Victor's Education Department, 79, 91, 200n21, 203nn68,76
Eigner, Edwin, 81
electrical recording, 166–67, 206n48, 209n88; vs. acoustic recording, 15, 113, 123, 125; immediate playback capability, 143–44, 149; instantaneous disc recording, 7, 141, 142–45, 172, 213n29; magnetic tape, 7, 8, 14, 140, 142, 144, 169, 172–73
electrophones, 125, 210n103
Elfenbein, Andrew: on New Criticism, 117
Eliot, T. S.: asemic phrasing of, 25, 161–62, 163–67; as BBC broadcaster, 152–53, 155; on Browning's monologues, 138; "Choruses from the Rock", 158; and conception of "voice" in New Critical discourse, 25; on dissociation of sensibility, 153; "The Dry Salvages", 139; "East Coker", 139; on epic poetry, 138; *The Four Quartets*, 139, 146; "In Memoriam:

Marie Lloyd", 152, 153, 154; *Murder in the Cathedral*, 139; and New Criticism, 25, 147, 213n27; *On Poetry and Poets*, 137; on reading poetry, 25, 156; recording of *Four Quartets*, 146; recording of "Landscapes: I. New Hampshire; II. Virginia", 146; recordings of "Ash Wednesday", 146, 148–49; relationship with Speaight, 139, 157; "Sweeny among the Nightingales" recordings, 144, 146; techniques in vocalization, 25, 140, 142–45, 146–52, 153–54, 155, 158, 159, 160–61, 162–67, 171; "The Three Voices of Poetry", 137–38, 157–58; "Tradition and the Individual Talent", 154; use of allusions by, 149; Victorian voices of, 137, 138–39

Eliot's *The Waste Land*: BBC productions of, 156–57, 213n30, 214n50; "The Burial of the Dead", 142, 143, 145, 163, 165, 166; "Death by Water", 142, 143, 148, 162, 163, 164; Eliot's 1933 recordings, 25, 138–39, 140–45, 147–48, 153–54, 157, 158–59, 160–61, 162–64, 165, 166, 171, 172–73, 181, 211n10, 212nn17,25, 213n29, 214n54; Eliot's 1946 Library of Congress recording, 140, 142, 144–47, 148–49, 150–52, 158, 163–64, 166, 181, 211n10, 212nn21,25; "The Fire Sermon", 142, 143, 163–64, 166–67; "A Game of Chess", 140, 142, 143, 147–48; Leavis and Brooks on, 106; multivoiced renditions, 156–57, 213n30, 214n50; Speaight's recording, 139, 157, 162–63; "What the Thunder Said", 142, 143, 148, 163–64

elocution: and classical rhetoric, 109; elocutionists, 21–22, 24, 56, 57, 65, 94, 106, 109–11, 124, 125, 126–27; manuals of, 17, 31, 50, 108–9, 110–11, 127, 128, 130–32; John Mason on, 205n33; as mechanical, 106, 109–10, 114, 139, 140, 148, 149, 150–52, 155, 159, 206n37; as natural, 58, 109–11, 114, 116, 124, 133, 135–36, 154–55, 159, 196n93, 207n52; techniques of, 22, 24, 25, 31, 42–43, 50–51, 56, 106–14, 121–22, 127–36, 138–39, 140, 142–45, 146–52, 153–54, 155, 156, 158, 159, 160–67, 171

Emerson Phonograph Co., 114, 122–23, 134–35, 209n83

emotion, 109, 131, 201n39, 206n37; James-Lange theory of, 112; relationship to musical accompaniment, 118, 119, 120

English Dialect Society, 55–56

English verse-speaking movement, 25

entextualization, 16, 73

Ernst, Wolfgang, 182; on the drama of time-critical media, 3–4

Erpi Picture Consultants, Inc., 141

Faulk, Barry J., 152

Faulkner, Ann Shaw: *What We Hear in Music*, 203n68

Feaster, Patrick, 185nn6,10, 196n105, 217n28; on descriptive sound recordings, 208n76; on macrogeneric audiotextual formatting, 18–19; on paleospectrophony, 179–80; on phonography and context, 18

Fields, Armond, 197n114

Fields, Lew, 64

First Sounds, 179–80, 182, 216n27

Fleming, Canon James, 139; *The Art of Reading and Speaking*, 126, 132–33, 207n52; on oral performance, 106, 207n52; on reading mechanically, 159; recording of Poe's "The Bells", 123; recording of Tennyson's "Charge of the Light Brigade", 123, 124, 125–26, 128–29, 132, 134

Fogerty, Elsie: Central School of Speech Training and Dramatic Art founded by, 208n63; influence of, 116–17, 155; on reading aloud as interpretation, 115, 207n60; *The Speaking of English Verse*, 115, 207n60

force, vocal, 56, 57, 130–32, 133

Ford, Ford Madox, 166

frequency of sounds, 8–9, 56, 167, 171, 180; and electrical recording, 143, 166; fundamental frequency (f0), 127; patterns in natural speech, 135, 162

Frobisher, J. E., 101; parody of Poe's "The Bells", 57, 195n89, 196n93; on reading naturally, 58, 196n93

Frost, Robert, 141–42, 212n17

Fulton, Robert: *Practical Elements of Elocution*, 130–32, 133; on vocal force, 130–32, 133

Gannon, Joseph, 65

Garber, Marjorie: on writing as displacement, 18

Geiger, Don: *The Dramatic Impulse of Modern Poetics*, 103–4; *The Sound, Sense, and Performance of Literature*, 103, 134

Gelatt, Roland, 29–30

George, Jacqueline: on elocution, 108

Gilman, Sander: on Yiddishization of English words, 63

Giovannoni, David, 217n27

Gissing, George, 82

Gitelman, Lisa: *Always Already New*, 217n22; on oral and inscriptive action, 30; *Scripts, Grooves and Writing Machines*, 9

Gladstone, William, 19, 21

Glenn, Susan, 58, 60

Goffman, Erving: on phonemic clause, 17–18; on speaker's footing, 17–18, 115

Good, Graham: on musical composition of ideas, 214n54

Gough, Evelyn, 186n25

Gouraud, George, 32–33, 190n27

Graham, George, 65; recording of "Auctioneer", 66; recording of "Colored Preacher", 66; recording of "Drama in One Act", 66

Gramophone Company/HMV, 74, 76, 77, 88, 123, 139, 146, 209n88

graphology, 28

Graphophone, 39, 71

Greet, William Cabell: American and English dialect series, 140–41

Grimaldi, Joseph, 81

Grossmith, Weedon, 124

Grusin, Richard: on immediacy vs. hypermediacy, 72, 73; on remediation, 73, 176

Guadagnolo, Daniel, 204n88

Guillory, John: on the media concept, 79

Gullan, Marjorie, 155

Haley, William, 152

handwriting analysis, 28

Hawthorne, Julian: on audible novels, 71, 199n3

Hayles, Katherine: on media specificity, 176

Hayman, Joe: recording of "Cohen on the Telephone", 63–64

hearing as tympanic transduction, 8–9

Helmholtz, Hermann von: on wave analogy and sound, 10

Helmreich, Stefan: on transduction, 9

Hennessey, Meagan, 217n28

Hepworth Company: *David Copperfield* (1913 film), 94

Herbert, George, 155

historical context: of early sound recordings, 9, 53, 126–27, 170–72, 173, 174–75, 178, 183–84; and manipulation of media artifacts, 171; media history, 5–6, 7–8, 12–14, 169, 175, 177, 216n7, 217n22; and temporal specificity, 5. *See also* acoustic recording process; digital media; electrical recording

HMV, 74, 76, 88, 139, 146, 209n88

Horning, Susan Schmidt, 15

Houston, Natalie: on Tennyson's "Charge of the Light Brigade", 104

Hubert, Philip G., , Jr., 199n4

Hughes, Ted, 214n50

Hugo, Victor: recording of *Les Misérables*, 72

humanities computing, 177–78

Hunt, Thomas, 155, 156

Hunting, Russell, 19, 60, 65, 66, 85

identity, personal, 31–32, 60, 64

Ihde, Don, 170, 178

imagination: Curry on, 104, 114; and digital media, 181; as empathic, 60, 68–69; and mimicry, 58–59, 196n100; and poetry, 20, 34, 187n30; and reading literature, 68–69; as transformative, 175

immediacy: of phonographs, 72–73; vs. hypermediacy, 72, 116

Internet Archive, 216n6

intonation, 17, 22, 56, 100; as asemic, 25, 161–62, 163–67; drone, 25, 158, 163–67; in Eliot's recordings of *The Waste Land*, 25, 139, 140, 147, 151, 154, 158, 159–67, 171; as excessive, 161, 162, 163–65; and fundamental frequency (f_0), 127; intonational drift, 161; as melodic, 162; as modulating, 161–62; of natural speech, 135, 160, 161, 162, 207n52; of poet voice, 106–7; as sematically informed, 161–62; as speech-melodic, 162–63; and Spoken English Corpus (SEC), 211n120; as truncated, 161, 163, 164, 166. *See also* pitch

Irving, Henry, 83, 84

Jacobson, Michal, 215n61

Jacobus, Mary, 190n32

James, Henry: "On the Question of Our Speech", 55, 56, 62

Jerrold, Douglas William, 19

Johnson, George Washington: "Laughing Song", 192n61

Jones, Gavin: on vaudeville audiences, 62

Kaiser, John, 65

Kaphan, Mortimer, 91

Keats, John: "Ode to a Nightingale", 34

Kennedy, Frank, 19

Kilfoil, Thomas F., 141

Kimber, Marian Wilson, 118

Kirschenbaum, Matthew: *Mechanisms*, 217n22

Kittler, Friedrich: on Edison's invention of the phonograph, 29; on sound-recording technology and the past, 171; on techno-logical media and digital media, 176–77; on time axis manipulation, 171, 180

Knowles, Antoinette: *Oral English*, 93

Knowles, R. G., 19

Kreilkamp, Ivan: on Dickens and remedia-tion, 81, 82, 98; on Victorian performa-tive, mass reading, 73

Lacey, Catherine, 155

Lanfried, Martin: recorded bugle call of, 33

Lastra, James: on preservation through phonographic methods, 3; on substance and accident, 3

Lauder, Harry, 64, 204n88

laughing records, 45–47, 48, 51, 192n61

Leaves, F. R., 159; on Eliot's *The Waste Land*, 106

lectures/talks, 19, 49–51

Leech, John: illustration in *A Christmas Carol*, 90

Lerch, Alexander, 11

Lewis, Cecil Day, 155, 156

Library of Congress: *Archive of Recorded Poetry and Literature*, 200n23; Books for the Adult Blind project, 72; listening to Eliot's recordings at, 172–73; *Literary Recordings*, 200n23

Light Brigade Relief Fund, 32–33

Lindsey, Vachel, 141, 212n17

literary works: concept of literature, 5; interpretation of, 12–13, 21, 23, 24–25, 69, 92, 94, 95, 100, 103, 111, 115–17, 132, 133–34, 139, 147; literary criticism, 69; literary studies, 7, 103, 117, 169; materiality of, 69, 198n133; reading vs. listening, 67–70; sound recordings as, 4, 7, 11–16, 22–23, 169; Raymond Williams on literature, 5. *See also* oral performance

Liu, Alan: on digital humanities, 177–78

Lloyd, Marie, 152, 153, 154

Loftus, Cissie, 196n98, 198n125

Longfellow, Henry Wadsworth: "Hiawatha", 119; "The Village Blacksmith", 21, 22, 119

Lovelace, J. Timothy: *The Artistry and Tradition of Tennyson's Battle Poetry*, 102; on Tennyson's *Charge of the Light Brigade*, 102

Lowell, Robert, 146

Macabe, Fred, 83

MacArthur, Marit J.: on contemporary poetry performance, 189n63; on oral per-formance of poetry, 107

Mackay, Steele, 206n50

macrogenres of audiotexts, 7, 200n22; dialect monologue, 23, 60–65; dia-logue, 19; lectures/talks, 27, 49–51; vs. microgenres, 16–17; recitation, 19–22, 23, 24, 120; speech, 19; testimonial, 23, 33

Mansfield, Richard, 66

Marsh, Josh, 94

Martin, Richard, 217n28

"Mary Had a Little Lamb", 57, 123

Mason, John: on elocution, 205n33

Masters, Edgar Lee, 141

material artifacts, 12, 117, 178; vs. sound, 2,

26, 27, 31–32, 144, 169–70, 171–72, 173–74, 175–76, 180
Matthews, Charles, 81, 98
Matz, W. B., 91
McCorkle, Ben: on elocution, 108
McCue, Jim: *The Poems of T. S. Eliot*, 212n25
McGann, Jerome: *The Beauty of Inflections*, 102, 104; on critical sympathy, 102, 104; on digital media and research in the humanities, 174–75; on philology in a new key, 174–75, 177, 180; *The Poetics of Sensibility*, 187n36; on Tennyson's "Charge of the Light Brigade", 100, 102, 104, 105; on textual criticism, 6
McGuire, William, 145–46
McKenzie, Donald F.: on forms of record and communication, 5; on printed texts, 30; on sociology of texts, 6; on textual criticism, 6
McLean, Margaret Prendergast: *Oral Interpretation of Forms of Literature*, 116
Mead, George Herbert: on social theory of imitation, 60
Meeker, Edward: "Laughing Record (Henry's Music Lesson)", 46–47, 51
Michaux, Henri: *Narration*, 215n61
microgenres of audiotexts, 16–18, 188n44
Mill, John Stuart: "What is Poetry?", 137–38
Miller, J. Hillis, 97
Milnes, R. M., 101
mimicry, 58–61, 123–24, 132, 154, 204n88; Bleackley's *Art of Mimicry*, 58–59, 60, 196nn98,100; Dickens impersonators, 24, 79, 80–81, 83–84, 85–86, 87, 90–91, 95, 98, 202nn46,62; and imagination, 58–59, 196n100; and nature, 110, 208n76; and the phonograph, 36–37, 39; on sound recordings, 64–65, 66–67, 70, 74, 120, 198n125; vs. reproduction, 36–37; J. Lewis Young on the phonograph and, 36–37
modernity, 149, 153, 215n64; and Eliot's recordings of *The Waste Land*, 147, 154, 165, 167
Mohler, Louis: *Literature and Music*, 119
Monfort, Nick: *Racing the Beam*, 217n22
monologue recordings, character-based, 19, 60–65

monopolylogueism, 66, 74, 81
Monroe, Harriet, 141, 212n17
Morrison, Mark: on natural delivery and impersonality, 154; on recitation anthologies, 61
Morrison, Robert: on term "differential medium", 216n19
Morton, David L., Jr., 185n10
Moses, Omri: on Eliot and poetic voice, 151
musical accompaniment, 117–23, 208n77, 209nn79,81; by Edison Carolers, 85, 86; orchestral accompaniment, 24, 64, 120, 121–22, 123; relationship to emotion, 118, 119, 120
music halls, 19, 151–52, 153

Naremore, James: on Delsarte, 113; on Waller, 128
National Council of Teachers of English, 141
National Gram-o-phone, 37
National Library of Canada's Harold D. Smith Collection, 79
naturalization in recitation, 58–59, 70
New Criticism: Allison on, 117; Elfenbein on, 117; and Eliot, 25, 147, 213n27; and oral performance, 25, 102–3, 106, 107, 116–17, 155, 158, 159
new media studies and design, 177–78
New Rhetoric, 108
Nichols, Robert, 155
Nightingale, Florence: recording by, 33, 190n27
NINES (Nineteenth-century Scholarship Online), 175
Nolan, Louis Edward, 105
North, Michael, 147
Norton, Fleming, 83
novelty records, 44–54

Openeer Papers, 187n37; "The Secret of Making Phonograph Records", 14
oral performance, 12, 13–14, 189n63, 205n31; anti-theatricality in, 13, 110–11, 114, 135; bodily gestures during, 109, 112–13; Curry on, 104, 105, 114–15, 133–34, 158; expression in, 114, 115; as interpretation, 100, 103, 109, 111, 113, 115–16; with musical

accompaniment, 85, 86, 117–23, 208n77, 209nn79,81; and New Criticism, 25, 102–3, 107, 116–17, 155, 158, 159

Orren, John: recording of "A Study in Mimicry–Vaudeville", 66–67

Parikka, Jussi: on play and tinkering, 177; *What is Media Archeology?*, 217n22

Pathé Records, 91

Peake, Richard Brinsley, 81

Pearson, Roberta E.: on Delsarte, 113

Peirce, Charles Sanders, 182

Perloff, Marjorie: on differential texts, 176

phonautographs: sonification of, 29, 179–80, 182

phonographs: advertisements for, 35, 37, 39–44, 61, 65, 93; Edison's invention of the phonograph, 29–30; first-person recitation recordings, 22, 38, 41–44, 189n60, 191nn50,51, 192n192; immediacy of, 72–73; and mimicry, 36–37, 39; as miniaturized theater, 61–62; natural fidelity of, 23, 29–31, 35–37, 43, 44, 66–67; neutrality of, 31, 38, 39–41, 66, 67, 98–99; phonograph as new kind of speaker, 23, 30–32, 35, 38–39, 44, 52; pure voice of, 31–39, 41, 44, 52, 66; use for teaching elocution, 23; as versatile, 35–36, 41, 66

phonography, 9, 29, 82–83, 98

Picker, John: on the phonograph and time, 190n25

pitch, 10, 17, 36, 46, 89, 108, 112, 157, 179; in Eliot's recordings of *The Waste Land*, 148, 149, 158, 159–66, 181, 215n60; in monotonous incantation, 107; and Poe's "The Bells", 56, 57; Praat visualizations of pitch, 127–30, 134–35, 163, 164, 165, 166, 215n60; relationship to frequency of sound waves, 8; rises in, 4, 127; tremor (vibrato), 127–30. *See also* intonation

Pitman, Sir Isaac, 29

playback speeds, 4, 144, 185n10

Playfair, Arthur, 124

Poe's "The Bells", 56–57, 100, 101, 123, 195n89, 196n93

Poole, John, 81

Porter, Ray: "The Charge of the Lightning Judge", 101–2

Potter, Paul, 76

Powers, Horatio Nelson: recording of "The Phonograph's Salutation", 38–39, 41–44, 191nn44,45

Praat: annotated visualizations of literary recordings, 126–30, 134, 163, 164, 166, 181, 210n108, 215n60

Prescott's Drawing Room Recitations, 55

Preston, Carrie: on bodily gestures, 112; on Delsarte, 206n43

printed texts, 111, 126; vs. audiotexts, 16–17, 24, 27–29, 45, 67–70, 72–73, 78–79, 87, 92, 149, 156, 160, 181; and literature, 5, 12; reading vs. listening, 27–29, 67–70, 156. *See also* audiobooks; recitation anthologies

prolongation, 127–28, 129–30

prosodic elements, 25, 126–36, 156, 158, 159–67, 210n108; and Eliot's asemic phrasing, 161; of natural vs. recorded speech, 160, 161, 163. *See also* amplitude; duration of sounds; pitch

Punch, 19

Raleigh, John Henry, 213n27

reading: vs. listening, 67–70; of poetry aloud, 25, 100–104, 105–8, 112, 114–15, 135–36, 139–40, 155–58, 189n63, 205n31, 207n60, 214n50; reader as figure for sentiment in circulation, 82, 201n38; vs. theatrical performance, 110–11; Victorian performative, mass reading, 72–73

recitation anthologies, 31, 54–64, 101, 194nn79,80, 197n116; vs. character-based monologue recordings, 61, 64; dialect pieces in, 54, 55–56, 57; Poe's "The Bells" in, 56–57

recontextualization, 16, 73–74

Records of Unique and Historical Interest, 76

Regina Music Box Company, 39, 40

remediation, 72, 73–74, 79, 108, 110, 172–74; Bolter and Grusin on, 73, 176; and Dickens, 81–83, 98

Rice, John: on elocution, 108; *An Introduction to the Art of Reading*, 108

Richard, I. A.: on music of ideas, 159

Ricks, Christopher: *The Poems of T. S. Eliot*,

212n25; on Tennyson's "Charge of the Light Brigade", 102–3, 104, 204n7

Robb, Mary Margaret, 206n37

Robison, Genevieve, 186n25

Robson, Catherine: on recitation, 21

romantic poetry, 34, 190n32

Rossetti, Dante Gabriel, 138; "Sister Helen", 196n93

Rubery, Matthew: on audiobooks, 68

Rubin, Joan Shelly: on recitation, 22

Ruskin, John: St George's Museum, 175

Russell, W. H., 105

Salmon, Christopher, 155, 156

Sanders, Charles: on Eliot, 151

Scarry, Elaine: on physical pain, 52–53

Schafer, R. Murray: on sound object vs. sound event, 170

Scheaffer, Pierre: on l'object sonore, 170

Schultz the German sketches, 19

Schweitzer, Marlis, 204n88

Sconce, Jeffrey: on disembodiment, 1, 185n1; on electronic presence in haunted media, 1, 185n1

Scott, William: Lessons in Elocution, 111, 206n37

Scott de Martinville, Édouard-Léon: phonautograph of, 29, 179–80, 182

screams, 52–53

Seaman, Frank: on the Zon-o-phone, 37

Seashore, Frank: on voice tonoscope, 10

Shakespeare, William, 20–21, 22, 76

Shapiro, Karl, 146

Shaw, George Bernard: Eliza Doolittle in Pygmalion, 44–45; Henry Higgins in Pygmalion, 29, 45; recording of "Spoken English and Broken English", 4

Sheridan, Richard Brinsley: The School for Scandal, 20

Sheridan, Thomas: A Course of Lectures on Elocution, 111; on elocution, 109–11

shorthand, 9, 29, 82–83, 98

Silver, Monroe: recording of "Cohen on His Honeymoon", 62; recording of "Cohen on the Telephone", 63

Smith, Elmer W.: "The Advance Movement in English", 93, 94

Smith, Harold D.: on American recording artists during WWI, 209n84; A New Correlation, 92, 118, 119, 203n58; relationship with Battis, 79, 91, 94, 96–97, 99, 118

Smith, Jacob: on records of disruptive articulation, 45–46

Snazelle, H. G., 19

snoring and sneezing records, 48–51, 192n69, 193n71

Soper, H. M.: Scrap-Book Recitation Series, 54, 57, 101, 195n81

sound effects, 66–67, 74, 112, 118, 120, 121, 122

sound signals, 7, 8–11, 165

Speaight, Frank, 91, 202n62

Speaight, Robert: Eliot's The Four Quartets, 139; on reading poetry, 156; recording of Eliot's The Waste Land, 139, 157, 162–63; relationship with Eliot, 139, 157; speech from Eliot's Murder in the Cathedral, 139; in Well Versed discussion, 155, 156

speech transcription, 51, 53

Spencer, Len, recordings by: "I am the Edison Phonograph", 43–44, 65, 191nn50,51, 192n54; "Lincoln's Speech at Gettysburg", 66; "A Study in Mimicry-Vaudeville", 66–67; "The Flogging Scene", 66, 74; "The Transformation Scene", 66, 74–76, 199n15; "What I Heard at the Vaudeville", 64–65, 197n115

Spoken Arts, 162

Spoken English Corpus (SEC), 211n120

Stadler, Gustavus: on recorded reenactments of torture and lynching of black men, 52

Steadman, Walter, 123

Stebbins, Geneviève: Delsarte System of Expression, 114, 206n51

Steele, Sir Joshua: Prosodia Rationalis, 28

Stein, Gertrude, 141–42

Stembler, Sally: "Laughing Record (Henry's Music Lesson)", 46–47, 51; "The Laughing Girl", 192n61

Stephens, James, 155; "On Speaking Verse", 157–58, 161–62; on rubato, 156

Sterne, Jonathan: The Audible Past, 9; on hearing as tympanic transduction, 9;

on long-playing records, 199n5; *MP3*, 217n22; on MP3 format, 99; on spoken recordings as literary, 12; on spontaneity, 30

Stevenson, Robert Louis: recordings based on *The Strange Case of Dr. Jekyll and Mr. Hyde*, 66, 74–76, 199n15

Stewart, Cal: Uncle Josh recordings, 19, 60–61, 192n61, 196n105

Stewart, Garrett, 82, 201nn38,39

Steytler, Charles, 33

Stoever, Jennifer: on the sonic color line, 52

Stowe, Harriet Beecher: recordings based on *Uncle Tom's Cabin*, 66, 74–75, 84

stylistics, 29, 189n10

Suarez, Juan A.: on Eliot's 1933 recordings of *The Waste Land*, 149, 150

Sweet, Henry, 29

Swigg, Richard, 142, 211n11

Tainter, Charles Sumner: Graphophone of, 39, 71

Tate, Allan, 146

Tennyson's "The Charge of the Light Brigade", 24–25; Ainley's recordings of, 123, 124, 125, 128–29, 132, 134, 209n88; Coghlan's 1909 recording, 120–22, 123, 128, 134; dactylic meter of, 17, 101; in elocution manuals, 17; *Examiner* version, 104–5; Fleming's recording of, 123, 124, 125–26, 128–29, 132, 134; *Maud and Other Poems* version, 104–5; McGann on, 100, 102, 104, 105; oral performance of, 105–6, 107; parodies of, 57, 101–2; vs. Poe's "The Bells", 100, 101; reception history of, 100–101; as recitation piece, 101, 123–24; repetition in, 100; Tennyson's recording (1890), 1–4, 24, 33, 102–3; Waller's recording, 123, 124, 125, 127–28; Williams recording, 84

Terrell, John: recording of "Casey's Address to the G.A.R.", 66; recording of "A Few Words in Regard to Drinking", 66

Thurburn, Gwynneth, 155

Tiller, Terence, 157, 213n30, 214n50

Tillman, J. N.: "Life and Personality of Jesus", 80

time, 3–4, 31–32, 33–34, 57, 190n25; duration of early recordings, 69–70, 87, 95–97, 142, 185n10; duration of sounds, 25, 56, 127, 158, 181; temporal specificity, 5

tinfoil cylinder phonographs, 7, 35, 36, 39, 71, 178, 185n7

Tolstoy, Leo, 76

Townsend, S. Dana: *The Victrola in Correlation with English and American Literature*, 119

Tree, Herbert Beerbohm, 83, 124; recording of "Svengali Mesmerizes Trilby", 74, 76–77

tremor (vibrato), 127–30

Trueblood, Thomas: *Practical Elements of Elocution*, 130–32, 133; on vocal force, 130–32, 133

UCSB Cylinder Audio Archive, 173, 175, 216n6

Uncle Josh recordings, 19, 60–61, 192n61, 196n105

Uncle Josh's Punkin' Center Stories, 61

United States Gramophone Co.'s "List of Plates in Stock" (1894), 20–21, 188n56

United Talking Machine Co., 122–23

University of Southhampton's Sound Archive Project, 178

unsupervised learning, 181–82

vaudeville, 62, 64–65, 151–52

Victor Light Opera Co., 209n81

Victor Talking Machine Co.: Education Department, 79, 200n21, 203nn68,76; flat discs of, 72, 96–97; recordings for, 7, 48–49, 72, 94, 95–97, 120, 121, 122–23, 209n79; Victor Education program, 91; *Victor Record Catalogue*, 200nn20,22; *Victor Records Suitable for Use in the Teaching of English Literature*, 95; *The Victrola in the Schools*, 94, 95. *See also* Smith, Harold D.

Vitagraph Company: *A Modern Oliver Twist*, 80

voice archive, 170, 174; as cultural memory, 23; as digital repository, 26, 171–72, 180, 181–82 voice tonoscope, 10, 186n25

Walker, John: on elocution, 109–10, 206n37
Waller, Lewis, 76, 131, 139; recording of
Tennyson's "Charge of the Light Brigade",
123, 124, 125, 127–28
Ward, Cornelia Carhart: *Manual for the
Use of Pictures in the Teaching of English,
Latin and Greek*, 93
Warren, Austin: *Theory of Literature*, 117
Warren, Robert Penn: *Understanding
Poetry*, 103–4
Watts, Cecil: disc recorder of, 7
wax cylinders: of Edison, 1–4, 7, 19, 27,
30–31, 72, 84, 85–86, 87, 90, 191nn50,51,
196n105, 199n4; vs. photographs, 32;
of Charles Sumner Tainter, 39, 71; vs.
WAVE files, 173; vs. written records, 27,
28, 30–31, 32
Weber, Joe, 64
Wellek, René: *Theory of Literature*, 117
Werner's Magazine, 118
Wershler, Darren: on differential media,
176, 216n18
Western Electric, 199n5
White, Jim, 65
Whiteman, Walt: notebooks of, 175
Wichmann, Anne: *Intonation in Text and
Discourse*, 211n120
Wildhack, Robert J.: "Sneezes", 48–51,
193n71; "Snores", 48–51, 192n69
Williams, Bransby, 94, 139, 154; as Dickens
impersonator, 83–84, 85–86, 87, 90–91,
201n44, 202n46; "How I Became a
Dickens Actor", 83; *My Sketches from
Dickens*, 86, 87, 202n46

Williams, Bransby, recordings by: "The
Charge of the Light Brigade (Alfred
Lord Tennyson)", 84; "A Christmas
Carol–Bob Cratchit Telling of Scrooge
(Dickens)", 88–90; "A Christmas Carol
in Prose (Charles Dickens)–Scrooge's
Awakening", 84, 85–88, 93; "Christmas
Eve in Old England–Descriptive", 84;
Dickens recordings, 24, 74, 77–78,
79, 84–90, 97; "The Dream Scene
from 'The Bells' (Leopold Lewis)", 84;
"The Green Eye of the Little Yellow
God (Milton Hayes)", 84; "How We
Saved the Barge (Arthur Helliar)", 84;
"'Is Pipe-Monologue", 84; "Pickwick
Papers (Wardle's Christmas Party)",
84, 85; "The Puss in Boots", 84;
"The Showman", 84; "The Stage
Doorkeeper", 84; "The Three Little
Pigs", 84; "Uncle Tom's Cabin–Death
of Uncle Tom (H. B. Stowe)", 84;
"Wilkins Micawber's Advice", 90–91,
97, 202n59
Williams, Gus, 64–65, 197n116
Williams, Lia, 214n50
Williams, Raymond: *Keywords*, 12, 187n30;
on literature, 5; on 19th century notion
of literature and speaking, 12, 187n30; on
poetry in 18th century, 20
Woolf, Virginia, 142
Wordsworth, William, 42; "To the Cuckoo",
33–34
Wurtzler, Steve J., 198n125
Wyndham, Charles, 124

Young, J. Lewis: on mimicry, 36–37